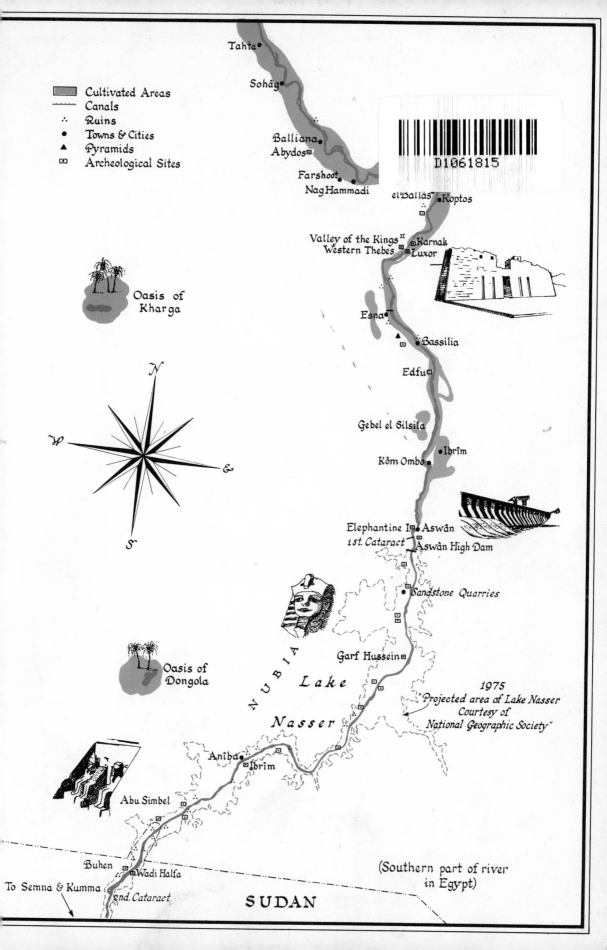

Cultivated Areas
Canals
Ruins
Towns & Cities
Pyramids
Archeological Sites

D1061815

Tahta
Sohâg
Balliana
Abydos
Farshoot
Nag Hammadi
el'Ballas • Koptos

Valley of the Kings • Karnak
Western Thebes • Luxor

Oasis of
Kharga

Esna
Bassilia
Edfu

Gebel el Silsila
Ibrîm
Kôm Ombo

N
W   E
S

Elephantine I. • Aswân
1st Cataract   Aswân High Dam

Sandstone Quarries

Garf Hussein

Oasis of
Dongola

Lake

Nasser

1975
"Projected area of Lake Nasser
Courtesy of
National Geographic Society"

NUBIA

Aniba
Ibrîm

Abu Simbel

Buhen
Wadi Halfa
To Semna & Kumma
2nd. Cataract

(Southern part of river
in Egypt)

SUDAN

Yankee
Sails
the
Nile

Books
by
the Same
Authors

Sailing to See
Yankee's People and Places
Yankee Sails Across Europe

Yankee Sails the Nile

*by Irving and
Electa Johnson*

NEW YORK

W · W · NORTON & COMPANY · INC.

Quotations from James Breasted's *History of Egypt* appear by
kind permission of the publishers, Charles Scribner's Sons.

Quotations from Jean and Simonne Lacouture's *Egypt in Transition*
appear by kind permission of the publishers, S. G. Phillips, Inc.

PRINTED IN THE UNITED STATES OF AMERICA

1 2 3 4 5 6 7 8 9 0

To

AHMED FAHMY

*Yankee's
Arabian Knight*

Contents

	A Chronology of Names and Dates	*xi*
I	*Alexandria*	*15*
II	*Alexandria to Cairo*	*27*
III	*Cairo*	*43*
IV	*Cairo Through Beni Suef*	*57*
V	*An Egyptian Village*	*71*
VI	*Beni Suef to Tell-El-Amarna*	*77*
VII	*Assiut and Balliana*	*87*
VIII	*Nag Hamadi to Luxor*	*99*
IX	*Luxor*	*111*
X	*Thebes West*	*119*
XI	*Luxor to Aswan*	*135*
XII	*Aswan*	*149*
XIII	*Nubia*	*163*
XIV	*Digs*	*173*
XV	*Abu Simbel*	*185*
XVI	*Wadi Halfa*	*197*

XVII   Ibrim   203

XVIII   The Begum Aga Khan   213

XIX   Aswan to Assuit   223

XX   New Valley   235

XXI   Cairo   241

XXII   Cairo to Rhodes   247

Illustrations:

Color plates between pages 128 and 129

Map: Asiatic Empire of the Pharaohs   94

Endpapers: The Nile from the Delta
    to the Second Cataract

≈ *A*
Chronology
of Names and
Dates

I AND II DYNASTIES
MENES UNITED EGYPT ABOUT 3300 B.C.

The Old Kingdom   2700-2280 B.C.
III THROUGH VI DYNASTY
CHEOPS, BUILDER OF THE GREAT PYRAMID AT GIZA

KHEPHREN, BUILDER OF 2ND PYRAMID AT GIZA. FACE OF THE GREAT SPHINX

MYCERINUS, BUILDER OF 3RD PYRAMID AT GIZA

The Middle Kingdom   2050-1786 B.C.
XII THROUGH XVI DYNASTY

AMENEMHET I	SESOSTRIS III
SESOSTRIS I	AMENEMHET III,
AMENEMHET II	BUILDER OF THE LABYRINTH
SESOSTRIS II	AMENEMHET IV

Hyksos—Foreign Rulers   1786-1580 B.C.

The New Kingdom or Empire   1580-1090 B.C.
XVIII THROUGH XX DYNASTY

AHMOSE, EXPELLED HYKSOS	AMENOPHIS III (CALLED MEMNON BY THE GREEKS)
AMENOPHIS I	AKHNATON (ORIGINALLY CALLED AMENOPHIS IV)
THUTMOSE I	TUTANKHAMON
QUEEN HATSHEPSUT	HOREMHEB
THUTMOSE II	RAMSES I
THUTMOSE III	SETI I—TEMPLE AT ABYDOS
AMENOPHIS II	RAMSES II—TEMPLE AT ABU SIMBEL
THUTMOSE IV	AND MANY OTHERS

≈

Foreign Domination and Late Egyptian Period 1090-525 B.C.
PIANKHI, XXV OR ETHIOPIAN DYNASTY, 8TH CENTURY B.C.

Persian Rule 525-332 B.C.
CAMBYSES, CONQUEROR OF EGYPT 525 B.C.

Greek Rule 332-30 B.C.
ALEXANDER THE GREAT 332–323 B.C.
PTOLEMY I 323–285 B.C.
CLEOPATRA 51-30 B.C.

Roman Rule 30 B.C. to 395 A.D.

Byzantine (Christian) Period 395-640

Arab Moslem Rule 640-1517
AMR, MOSLEM CONQUEROR OF EGYPT

Ottoman Rule 1517-1882
FRENCH OCCUPATION, NAPOLEON 1798–1803
MOHAMMED ALI FOUNDS LAST DYNASTY 1803
KHEDIVE ISMAIL 1863–79   OPENING OF SUEZ CANAL 1869

British Occupation 1882-1922
LORD CROMER, BRITISH DIPLOMATIC AGENT AND CONSUL-GENERAL

Modern Period 1922-
FAROUK 1936–1952
REVOLUTION 1952, GEN. NAGUIB, SUCCEEDED 1954 BY COL. NASSER
PRESIDENT NASSER 1956
SUEZ CRISIS 1956

*Yankee
Sails
the
Nile*

chapter I

≈

Alexandria

≈

The little American ketch was in unfamiliar waters. She had made her landfall on the Egyptian coast and was approaching the harbor of Alexandria. Irving and I strained more than just our eyes toward that shoreline. We could see the miles of tall waterfront buildings, the arrow-like minarets, the curve of the East Harbor, the structures of the commercial West Harbor. But what we wanted to know couldn't be seen. What would the next four months hold? Would we be able to take our ship 1000 miles up the Nile to the head of navigation at Wadi Halfa in the Sudan? Which shoals would be more difficult—officialdom or the sands and rocks of the Nile? Would those ruined, heavy-columned temples really appeal to us? Most important of all, would we get a real feeling for this unknown country so that the word "Egypt" would ever after turn on a light for us? As the answer to the last question proved to be *yes,* the answers to the others would take care of themselves.

For many years Irving had dreamed of taking the *Yankee* up the Nile. That dream had gone into her design by Olin Stephens and her building in the Dutch yard in 1959. With her two centerboards raised she was shallow enough for river navigation. Her large fuel capacity would take her all the way without replenishing, if necessary. Her interior circulation of cooling water meant that Nile silt would never reach our engine. With folding masts she would not be stopped by bridges that didn't open.

So far she had explored European rivers: the Rhine, Rhône, Saône, Seine, and lesser ones. Irving and I had accumulated valuable experience around bridges and locks, at putting our bowsprit over the river bank and setting the anchor in a field, at recognizing the vibrations that warned of shoaling water, and at getting the ship afloat when she went aground. Interesting as our inland European cruising had been, we sometimes thought of it as merely preparation for the Nile.

No other land shows itself so completely to the river traveler. Elsewhere one route across a country tells only part of its story; in Egypt it tells nearly all. Herodotus expressed it perfectly: "Egypt is the gift of the Nile." Swollen by the rains in the Ethiopian highlands, its flood rises regularly in August every year, reaches its peak in September, and subsides for the next month. It has then left a layer of silt on either bank, through the centuries a marvelously fertile deposit, in places a hundred feet deep. The habitable band of green running north and south on either bank sometimes narrows to a few feet. When its width reaches fifteen miles, that is a broad sweep for Egypt. But the fertile land stops more suddenly on the desert side than on the river side. The alluvial soil is cultivated to its farthest inch. Beyond that inch is sterile sand. North of Cairo, the Delta fans out in the richness and fertility of the mouths of the Nile. The river is the lifeline.

It had been extremely difficult to find out anything ahead of time about how a yacht would be treated in Egypt, just what navigational conditions were, or what kind of permissions were necessary. We had written letters months before to the U.A.R. Embassy in Washington, to our Consulate in Cairo, to any name suggested by anyone who might have some information we wanted. Many letters had gone unanswered, but no reply had stated that sailing the Nile was absolutely impossible or absolutely prohibited, so now we were here and would have to find out most things for ourselves.

We had received one letter from the Minister of Culture and National Guidance which sounded like an official, if rather vague welcome. Its tone was favorable, though generalized, and seemed to promise every assistance. At least it was on official paper and had a signature. We would soon see how it worked with Alexandria's harbor officials.

We understood that we must enter at the West or Commercial Harbor, though the Yacht Club was in the East Harbor, so we sailed past that entrance. The 15th-century Arab fort of Qait Bay on the point here looks like something out of a Foreign Legion story. Formerly this was the location of the great Lighthouse, Wonder of the Ancient World, 590 feet tall. With ramps instead of stairs to the top, donkeys could carry wood up daily for the open fire beacon that sent its rays over the Mediterranean. No lighthouse today is built so tall, though some stand on higher ground. Even in my rather apprehensive state of mind, I did cast a respectful look toward that historic point of land.

But there was nothing inspiring about the West Harbor with its dirty oil slick on the water, dust blowing off the ragged concrete docks, the assorted commercial ships of the Middle East, and a generally disorganized air. The sky was a wintry white, as it had been on the passage from Rhodes, but the air was warm. We tied up to a low dock with some heaps of scrap metal and a coating of sand. The first officials did not seem so bad. To various ones we showed our ship's papers, passports, and the letter from the Minister of Culture and National Guidance. We did not ask to go ashore, as we seemed to be far from the center of the city, but Irving did tell each one plainly that we were leaving next day for the East Harbor. We had no idea who had authority in that matter. They left a couple of armed guards on the dock and we spent our first night in Egypt.

In the morning we waited for permission to move, while more sand blew onto the ship and the harbor oil lapped and stuck onto *Yankee's* white hull. By eleven o'clock, when no officials had appeared, Irving decided to move. Telling the armed guards we were leaving, and choosing to interpret an answer from one of them as "Yes," he started the engine and we cast off. Then there was much shouting which we couldn't interpret, and as we made full speed for the entrance, the guards reached the point, waving guns and shouting.

"I'm sure we aren't supposed to go, Irving," I said, quite unnecessarily.

"Stay below the waterline till we're out of gunshot," he replied. He crouched behind the wheel, and the diesel at full throttle roared manfully but seemed to push us at a crawl.

"There's no reason for us to stay in that dirty harbor. We aren't running out on them, just moving to another berth. I told them I was going. This is a sort of test."

Testing Egyptian officials didn't appeal to me, but the test did prove to bring on shouting rather than bullets. When the *Yankee* felt the lift of the open sea, we were out of range and turned eastward. But she soon had to turn in again, into the arms of Customs. Their launch was anchored near the entrance of the East Harbor, and half a dozen barefoot, rough-looking characters boarded us. Their only uniform was a chevron partially tacked on the sleeve of unpressed, blue cotton jackets—no hats, shirts, ties, shoes, or socks. But anyway they pointed to a Yacht Club mooring for us. Others soon came out from shore, went off with our passports, and left two men with guns on board. But we felt we had made some progress. We weren't in a hurry to get ashore. They could sort out their requirements while I cleaned off the sand and Irving put in some hard work on that broad band of oil, a hundred feet of it to be scrubbed off.

Then we found we were beginning to enjoy ourselves as we watched the harbor activity. There were two or three sailing yachts at moorings and a couple of naval vessels farther out. A power craft had gone out fishing and returned. Lots of smaller boats were moving about under sail on various errands. None of these had motors, and oars were not needed as long as there was a bit of breeze, so the comings and goings of the East Harbor were almost always a matter of sail. How delightful! Rarely had we seen harbor activity carried on as it was a hundred years ago. The men in these lightly skimming craft moved people, goods, and messages with the hoist of a halliard, the handling of a sheet, and the pressure on a tiller. A motor here was a costly, imported non-essential.

An open pleasure craft came our way and an American voice called out, "Welcome to Alexandria! Can I do anything to help you?" Harlan Clark, the American Consul General, out for a Saturday afternoon sail, came aboard. We didn't think we needed any help; we expected some kind of permission to go ashore any time now, we hadn't minded waiting all day, and we told him of our independent move from the West Harbor. But of course he knew Eygpt better than we did, and without his help nothing might have happened for days. There is some sort of system—though that hardly seems the word for it—whereby it is impossible to find out who is in charge and just what is required—or more likely, how much. But thanks to Mr. Clark we got landing passes to go ashore for dinner. Immigration would keep our passports and the guards were still with us, but we were allowed to set foot in

Yankee has put her bow into a deserted Nubian village where the authors have found some interesting pots.

Egypt. It was a good thing we had arrived ten days ahead of schedule, because it was going to take every bit of that time to get the *Yankee* through the wondrous tangle of devious, formless, baffling, indefinite, high-priced obstructions raised up with a shrug, a smile, a difference in language, and a fiendish skill.

≈

The Alexandria we got acquainted with was a city fallen on bad days but her past had been colorful and glorious. Founded by Alexander the Great in 331 B.C., it became one of the great cities of the Ancient World. Here the traders of the Mediterranean and the West met the dhows of the Red Sea and the caravans of the East bringing merchandise from Damascus, Bagdad, and the far Orient. Merchants grew rich on the trading; the city grew rich on the duties. Scholars congregated and the greatest library of the ancients attracted more. When it was burned in Caesar's time it contained nearly a million scrolls. Christianity is believed to have come early to Alexandria through the missionary work of St. Mark, and for many years this was the great city of the Christian world in spite of sporadic persecutions. But after Christianity became the accepted religion of the Roman Empire, the Christians turned on the pagans and especially on some of the great monuments of the past, as we were to deplore later.

Then came the Moslems in the seventh century, only a few years after the death of their Prophet Mohammed, and the city took on a new character, with mosques and minarets supplanting the churches, and the buildings of Greek and Roman styles grafted onto pharaonic. The Crusaders never reached Alexandria. Their farthest west on this shore was at Damietta at the eastern extremity of the Delta. Some blue-eyed Egyptians today are said to be descendants of those Crusaders. The discovery of the sea route to the East by the Cape of Good Hope hastened the decline of the city, and under Ottoman rule it did not get much notice from Europe till Napoleon's campaign in Egypt.

Why did Napoleon choose to attack Egypt at all? The reasons were mixed. It was an indirect move against his primary enemy, England, on her trade with India and her merchants in Egypt. The country was a promising conquest for France, as its Turkish masters no longer had the earlier strength of the Ottoman Empire. And Napoleon's own ambition to rival Alexander the Great and his need for a spectacular success just then teamed with his imagination on the subject of Egypt's ancient glories, present riches, and future greatness under French rule. We should be grateful for that imagination, however, for it led Napoleon to bring along a contingent of scholars. Though the whole doubtful venture was a military failure, the scholars opened Egypt to the eyes of the West, and today's archaeologists are the direct descendants of Vivant Denon. Though bullets were flying and Mamelukes charging nearby, this enthusiastic artist kept at his drawing and recording of every bit of ancient Egypt he could put on paper. He eventually published the great two-volume masterpiece which is still the pride of any library that owns one. Where the General failed, the scientists, recorders, observers, and artists made conquests of knowledge. In the next era the great explorers passed through Alexandria, the men who searched for the source of the Nile and for the unknown interior of Africa. And after them came the British administrators, bringing the organization and control of the British Empire, of which Egypt was never a colony, but in some ways a victim. While the administrators kept the country orderly and at peace, the early English archeologists followed the French pioneers in that field. And on the side came the wealthy Victorian families to winter on the Nile. Sometimes their wealth had come from the cotton of this same country, produced at a human cost that Victorians didn't count. This generation saw the Nile in an ideal way, on their great floating houseboats, the dahabias, which moved either under sail or by what they called "tracking"—pulled by the crew on the bank, harnessed to long towlines. But the dahabias are no more and now the *Yankee* was about to venture in their wake, as different a craft as my shorts and slacks are from the bustles and petticoats of the dahabia era.

But when we went ashore that first night we got no impressions of these past glories. The only sight that lifted the city out of its dinginess was a glorious mosque, its huge dome as elaborately carved as an ivory jewel case, the minarets sharp-pointed beside it. Perhaps this large modern mosque, like an Oriental fantasy, serves one purpose in raising people's thoughts from the poverty and dinginess of their lives.

That night we met the Greek-Egyptian owner of the neighboring power yacht that went fishing. "I heard from an Aswan friend that they are closing the river to navigation in two weeks for some phase of the dam construction," he said casually. My heart sank. We had understood that the river would be not closed above Aswan until two months after the *Yankee* expected to be out of Egypt, so what was this preliminary shutoff? We have learned through the years not to let alarming pronouncements upset us too much. I have so often seen Irving do what we had been told was impossible. This was probably scuttlebutt and not worth a sleepless night. But I wasn't sure how to gauge Egyptian scuttlebutt.

Irving started right away to hunt up navigational information about the Nile. Preliminary letter writing had produced none, but one would expect to find some data on the river here in Alexandria. The best river charts, like those of the Rhine, still require every skipper to make allowances for high water and low water, unpredictable changes of channel, and the vagaries of the bottom. But there seemed to be no chart of any kind of the Nile. There wasn't even a good map with distances between towns and indications of islands.

To make a beginning, Irving wanted to find out the best route to Cairo, 200 miles inland. The Nile does not run in one good, deep stream to the sea, but breaks into multiple shallow channels. We knew that two entrances were used in modern times: the Damietta Mouth to the east and the Rosetta Mouth nearer Alexandria.

Then one day a man came alongside in a launch and called out, "I heard you were looking for some information on the river. I'm Stephanos Couvaris and I've had barges on the river for years. Can I come aboard?"

We almost pulled him over the side. He was a Greek in the barge business who had spent more time on the river than at his desk, out of love for the active side of the business. His information and advice were reliable —and given in English. No doubt the Nile had its great barge captains who could answer all Irving's questions, but in Arabic. Mr. Couvaris seemed heaven-sent. He became so interested in the *Yankee* and so understanding of Irving's needs and enthusiasm that he wrote out a sort of Nile "Pilot Book" for us in longhand, and for months we referred to it, most of all during our first days in the Delta before Cairo.

But if river information was hard to come by, getting official papers was even harder. Without some effective document in hand, how could we deal with the man in uniform who might show up at any bridge, at any turn, at any lock? We knew we must have some papers, but what were they and how did we get them?

We had that one cordial letter from the Minister of Culture and National Guidance. But now that we were in Egypt we needed something in Arabic as well as English. It took time to learn what difficulty was stalling us, but we finally discovered. The Minister who had signed our fine letter had been thrown out! We had been on the right track, but the wrong branch line.

While our paper work progressed so creakingly, we began to get our first taste of Egypt. The strangeness started with the costume. Though much of young, modern Egypt has taken to the Western clothes, the majority of

22

the men still wear the galabia and women the mylaya. The usual *galabia* (gal-uh-bee-uh) is an ankle-length nightshirt type of unbelted garment, most often in broad pajama stripes. It is not washed regularly or with good soap; water often has to be carried and soap is expensive. It may be cool in the hot season, but it is cold in chilly weather and awkward all the time. In their flowing *galabias* sailors clamber aloft on 100-foot spars to furl sail, cyclists pedal and stay free of the chain, old men ride on donkeys, riders mount camels, men operate machinery—in short do every sort of active job which seems to us much better done in trousers.

Mylayas (me-lie-uh) are as bad. They are light-weight black shrouds which cover a woman from the top of her head to the dust. If they trail, she is proving especially modest. Most no longer veil the face, but they can be pulled across to show either modesty or respect. Without hooks, buttons, or drawstrings, they are somehow held around a woman while she does her most active tasks, especially filling her heavy water jug at the river and raising it to her head again. This would be impossible for me even with a Spanish shawl, for example, and a chiffon-like *mylaya* is much more apt to float away than a heavy shawl.

There was more strangeness than the costumes in the Egyptian scene. The language was completely baffling, the signs like a decorative short-hand. Not only Arabic was heard on the streets, however. Greek sounded familiar by comparison. There was much French and quite a bit of English —all reflections of Alexandria's cosmopolitan character, which persisted even now when the large foreign colonies of the past had dwindled to a few thousand. The mixture of residents and visitors includes every national-ity of the Middle East and Europe, most of them difficult to identify in the variety of features, languages, shades of skin, or clothes. There is no Egyp-tian type of face any more than an American face. Almost the only general characteristic is the large and beautiful dark eyes.

Alexandria is now a shabby city, but we met people who could tell us how it used to be in the Bad Old Days. Then it was more fashionable than Cairo and the king spent more time here. Shops had beautiful clothes, stylish bags of fine leather made more cheaply in Egypt than elsewhere, Persian rugs, and every sort of imported article. Teas, dinners, races, servants made up the luxurious way of life. But now most of the foreigners have gone, though the street signs are still in French as well as Arabic. Today in Egypt imports from the Western world are almost non-existent, except for liq-uor, as Egypt cannot spend its hard currency on consumer goods. It is diffi-cult, if not impossible, to find such things as flashlight batteries, canned milk, plastic bags. Automobile traffic is light, but horse cabs are always available. Pavements are broken, buildings in disrepair.

But perhaps Alex (as they call it) looks better in its summer season. Its miles of Mediterranean beaches are magnificent and would be worth unimaginable sums on either our East or West Coast. In summer all that vast extent of waterfront apartments on one side of the marine drive, and the bathhouses on the other, must be full of people and activity. But this was October and we drove toward Farouk's old Montazah Palace past five or six miles of shuttered and uninhabited apartments. It was certainly the wrong time of year for Alexandria, but it was going to be the best time of year in Upper Egypt. Farouk's palace was like him—rich and repulsive. Its square turrets of yellow brick, its carpets in yellow and purple, its stained glass and orchid tile add up to a monstrosity, in a beautiful location looking over the bright blue Mediterranean. It is now open to the public as a museum of Farouk's extravagant, tasteless excesses.

For a long time I had been worried about my responsibility for feeding six people on board for four months in Egypt. During the last winter at home, I had asked questions about markets of everyone I could find who had been to Egypt. But, as most travelers have no need for this kind of information, I learned nothing definite or dependable. I queried a Cairo archeologist who was traveling around the United States with the Tutankhamon exhibit, but he had evidently never had to buy any groceries and knew more about what food was put into the tombs of the ancients than what was in today's markets.

So a big shipment of canned goods from S. S. Pierce had come to us in Amsterdam as it used to in Suva and Singapore when we were sailing our Brigantine *Yankee* on voyages around the world. In the months since Amsterdam I had opened every can thinking, "I may need this on the Nile." I had concluded that if only I could get eggs and bread, we could manage. That was my absolutely rock-bottom requirement, as any housewife can understand. I preferred not to think what the difficulties would be if I couldn't get those two items. As it turned out in the months ahead, most of my worries had been for naught. We got lots of fresh fruits and vegetables, plenty of eggs (pullet size), and even quite a lot of acceptable meat. So most of the S. S. Pierce tins are still in our lockers.

In Alexandria we knew that plenty of food was available, but I didn't have much confidence about getting it. Ashore on my own I felt much more helpless than in Greece or Italy, where I don't speak the language either. But here I couldn't even count to ten, the coins didn't seem to be uniform, and I didn't even have phrase-book facility at asking *how much?*, *where?*, *market, boat*. What was the matter with me? I had bought food all around the world. Why did Alexandria make me feel so feeble? Anyway it did.

Perhaps I should feel, or at least act, helpless more often, for just the right person came to my aid, Mimi Varotsis. How could this tall, energetic, forty-year-old Greek, with Mephistophelean beard, manager of the Windsor Hotel, have got the name of Mimi? He took me to the Souk Rathib with him, through its alleys and stalls, past barrels of olives, tons of fish both off-shore and Red Sea, crates of tiny, squeaking quail and pigeons, and tethered turkeys, to outlays of fresh fruits and vegetables and into back cold-rooms crowded with hanging meat caracasses—beef, lamb, buffalo, maybe camel? He would slap them knowingly and perhaps intentionally let one swing toward me occasionally. What advantage to trail along with the Big Buyer of the Windsor Hotel! Every vendor knew him and an understanding on prices had long since been reached, so there was only good will on this expedition. All the best was offered. If Mimi didn't buy certain offerings today, he might next time, so even his refusals were accepted with smiles. I loaded a week's supplies into his car while Mimi knowingly distributed the proper piastres to carriers, car watchers and incidental blind men. What a helpful Mephistopheles!

Now that I look back on those first ten days in Egypt, I see what an unsatisfactory, halting, discouraging start it was. If this sort of trouble had gone on for four months, we would not want to hear the word "Egypt," much less write a book about it. But the bad dream was to end—though not for another ten days—to be succeeded less by an awakening than by a changed and entrancing dream.

chapter II

≈

Alexandria
to Cairo

≈

At last we were ready to leave Alexandria. Our old friends from Detroit, Dr. Victor Nelson and his wife Mildred, whose two sons had sailed around the world with us in the Brigantine *Yankee*, had joined for the start of our Nile expedition, the six weeks we planned on from Alexandria to Luxor. We had talked about cruising the Nile together even before the Ketch *Yankee* was built. They were not tempted by our wanderings in European canals, the Mediterranean or the Baltic, but the Nile really attracted them.

Sheridan Fahnestock, just out of the Navy, whose family we had known for many years, had sailed from Rhodes with Irving and me and was going to stay with us to Cairo. A sailor from the Alexandria Yacht Club, Ibrahim, was also to go as far as Cairo, not only to give a hand, but to speak Arabic at the numerous bridges, locks, and unforeseeable obstacles. However, he said he could not make the 35-mile open sea passage to the Rosetta Mouth of the Nile with us. There was something about his having to paint the Yacht Club flagpole. Later we drew our own conclusions. We don't think he cared for an open sea passage.

In his place was our Rosetta pilot whose name we never knew. He spoke no English, but he looked very impressive, rather like a Bedouin chief, I thought. He wore the first good-looking *galabia* I had seen, tailored of pinstripe wool, and clean! Irving never likes to take a pilot, but here it seemed necessary. The bar of silt which the Nile builds up off Rosetta, or Raschid as it is called locally, is broad and shifting, so the entrance is not marked except in the head of a pilot.

We would be ready to leave at seven on Thursday morning, October 31st. But that early start had been deferred the night before to 10 A.M., as we still had to have the papers that would allow us to go. We also had to get our passports back. There was more finagling than we had ever met in any port in the world, and for the first time in our experience money under the table had to be passed out all along the line. The Consulate had provided their best expediter, an efficient, driving Nubian, Sayid Ibrahim Hamzer. The romantic-looking pilot was aboard and I had sandwiches made for lunch at sea.

It was six that night when we finally sailed. Paperwork went on and on. Various offices didn't see why another day wouldn't do just as well. At one point four Customs officers came aboard with Sayid to do their writing in our main cabin—possibly just to see the cabin? So we ate the sandwiches at anchor. Then various Yacht Club friends crowded aboard to wish us well, to say goodbye, to find out why we hadn't left. We certainly couldn't explain to them or to ourselves. I served them tea.

At last Sayid returned with a final delegation of six. We could leave. All we had gained was one small piece of paper on which Arabic writing said the *Yankee* was approved and permitted to travel from Alexandria to Cairo. The delegation had a ride with us to the Harbor Police boat near the entrance, and then we were rid of them all! Hooray! By this time it was dark and it might have been a good idea to get an early start next morning, but Sayid said we must go. Everything was dated October 31st and any change was unthinkable. Anyway the moon was up, nearly full, the wind was fair, we were eager to go, and the last word from Sayid to the pilot was that we should anchor in Aboukir Bay for dinner and go on from there in the morning. So leaving the curve of Alexandria's sparkling lights behind, the *Yankee* passed out the harbor entrance bound for the

Nile. The long-gowned pilot at the wheel looked more romantic than ever in the moonlight.

Romance did not hold up, however. Though the wind favored us, it had built up a sizable sea which threw us about. Irving set the main and mizzen to steady her, but kept the motor going for maximum progress. Mildred, not expecting the motion, took a neat, feet-first dive from the after deck into the cockpit, fortunately without hurting herself. I brought potatoes on deck to peel by moonlight. Anyway we would soon be at anchor. But the pilot seemed to be going right past Aboukir! We gathered that he had a better anchorage in mind just ahead. Should I have dinner ready in a half hour? In an hour? But no haven appeared. Powerless to protest in any common language, we finally concluded he intended us to go all the way to Rosetta. We thought he gestured that it would be smooth there.

Well, thirty-five miles with a fair wind would not take too long. We would have to have dinner on the way. Those lunch sandwiches eaten back in the harbor would have been just right now, but instead I was committed to a full-scale dinner with a tenderloin roast; it was served at a sort of seagoing gallop and no more appreciated by the guests than by the cook.

We shifted our hopes to a smooth anchorage for the night. Surely the pilot wouldn't try to go over the bar in the dark, but we now had no idea what to expect of him. His eyesight seemed to be poor and he had no understanding of steering by compass. Then, still in the open sea, he gestured for Irving to take down the sails. Without their steadying effect our gallop became wilder. Now he indicated that Irving should get the anchor ready. Anchor? Where? He wanted soundings. When Irving got five fathoms, he gave the sign. What an awful place! The current running out of the river mouth pushed against the incoming waves and tossed the *Yankee* unmercifully. But we had no choice. This was where he intended us to stay for the night. Would the Danforth hold in that bottom of silt? Irving got out the 110-pounder for good measure, but as it happened the 30-pound Danforth did the job, even through a screeching squall at two in the morning. If the night was disagreeable and mostly sleepless for us, what a horrible introduction to the *Yankee* this was for Mildred and Victor.

We were only too happy to get going at first light. We had heard a description of a large, white floating drum which marked the pass over the broad, amorphous bar, and we searched the tossing seas for this guide. It was not very encouraging to see the pilot also peering uncertainly through our binoculars. But we finally sighted a white float about the size of two lobster pots, and he indicated that Irving should head for that while he sounded with our long boathook. Though the whole procedure looked like blind groping, this one aid to navigation did suffice and *Yankee* galloped over the bar into deeper smooth water.

We were summoned alongside the rickety dock of an Army Post, and met by soldiers in long khaki great coats who didn't know how to take a line. There was nothing at all on the dock to tie to, but we were obviously required to stop, so in the end they tied our lines pretty much around the dock itself and they looked at our Arabic paper, ship's documents, and all the passports. These were finally returned to us. The pilot left and Ibrahim came aboard.

Though we were now in the waters of the Nile, our route to Cairo would be mostly by canal. Within the last week the river had dropped too low for navigation here, and an obstacle course of locks and bridges and unknown Egyptian problems lay ahead. Mr. Courvaris had said this was the "emotional route." I think "control-the-emotions" route would be more accurate. Cairo was only a few hours away by car or train, but we knew we must expect to use six or seven days. Sometimes during that week we wondered if we were going to spend four years rather than four months on the Nile. In retrospect, that was a passage unlike any we had ever made or ever hoped to. But its difficulties, delays, unreasonableness, and "emotion" made us appreciate the joys of the Nile which came after this severe initial test.

On this first day, as we left the Army Post astern, we forgot our troubles, for winging down toward us with fair wind and current came the thrilling sight of twenty or thirty feluccas, the marvelous sailing craft of the Nile, as fascinating to us four months later as they were on this first day when they seemed like an expression of welcome to the Dutch-built *Yankee*, so foreign and utterly different from them. The Nile is still in the Age of Sail and we appreciated its every aspect—the beauty of the birdlike craft, the special age-old techniques of its sailors, the particular difficulties and advantages of these vessels, and the evidence of a hard, spare life which must be rewarding to some of the felucca men, that small proportion of Egypt's enormous population who live the life of the river rather than of the land.

Before long we reached our first lock at Edfina. It would open at 2:30. Gradually feluccas of various sizes came up astern of us and moored to wait. Crowds by the lock stared down at the strange shining white yacht. When the lock opened, the *Yankee* and as many feluccas as possible

With the reliable northerly wind, this scene must have been repeated con-
tinuously down the centuries.

crowded in. We were glad of every bit of experience we had had in five years of Europe's inland waterways. The Delta canals would not be a good place to learn the problems of locks. But most of them were familiar, even though our companions were nothing like Rhine barges or old Dutch craft. Nylon mooring lines, boathooks, and fenders were our tools as usual. The older feluccas were of wood, but most of them are now of iron, with a particularly mean rubrail of channel iron. With building sand for Alexandria or other cargoes to go upstream, they were all loaded as deep as possible, leaving so little freeboard that they menaced us well below our protective rubrail. In the stream, they felt we menaced them with our bow wave because it didn't take much water over their sides to fill and sink them like stones. Actually our wake was never as fearsome as our bow-wave suggested, and they were never in danger from the *Yankee*.

Only a short distance beyond this lock was a bridge which would open at five. We rested. By five we were sufficiently revived to be intrigued by the preliminaries to opening. Large waterpipes cross the river at bridge level instead of underwater like ours, so when it must be opened, the pipes must be shut first. Several *galabia*-clad men work noisily with wrenches and crowbars, hanging over the middle of the bridge, and then it may swing open. Darkness was coming before six, so we tied up to the shore just beyond. The banks of the Nile are mostly about eight or ten feet above the water at this time of year, and here by the Edfina Bridge we had our first evening shadow play of the close of the Egyptian day. All the homing figures passing at that level were silhouetted for us against the sunset light. In the dusk the less attractive details of dirt and poverty and raggedness do not show, only the poetic silhouettes of two little boys on a donkey, an old man riding well astern on his little beast, a cow following a slow water buffalo, two children hand in hand, a woman of vague shrouded shape.

Night closed the passing scene and our attention was abruptly transferred to two uniformed men who tramped heavy mud aboard and loudly demanded passports, which they studied and made notes on at great length. Though we waved our official-blessing-paper at them, they still seemed to feel that duty demanded all thoroughness. We eventually got them out of the main cabin and into the cockpit, and after we were halfway through dinner they finally departed. Our first two days had been rather difficult, but we had advanced from Alexandria. We could probably have driven back into town in minutes, but we were far removed from its polyglot streets here at our riverbank in the farm country of the Delta.

Our third day began with a fine river sail for an hour and a half which gave us a pleasant, carefree start, just a little tonic before more of the "emotional route." Then we turned off from the Nile through a small, uncomplicated lock into the Mamoudia Canal. Right after the lock we settled down to wait until the bridge at Atf would be opened at three. Rather weakly, none of us went ashore to explore Atf. It was a crowded town of mud and plaster houses, not encouraging to those who do not speak Arabic. Besides, we had plenty to watch among the feluccas which were tied up thick all around us, waiting for the lock in one direction and the bridge in the other.

When three o'clock finally came and we thought there was some suggestion that the bridge might open, all of the ships got ready for a racing start. Bridge men appeared with cranks and levers. The jumble of traffic crowded to get across and seemed to intimidate the men who should be lowering the barriers. At last the barrier on the left came down. But up drove a squarish, vintage sedan full of people, the driver waving and shouting ferociously to get the pole raised. To our disgust, the cowardly bridge man put it up and the sedan raced onto the bridge, followed of course by every donkey, automobile, and oxcart that could squeeze behind him. Just as the sedan reached the other end and the bridge was full of vehicles, the right end barrier man boldly lowered his boom. To the felucca men and us it was worth the delay to watch the ensuing explosion. With all the emotion that had been generated, it is surprising the sedan didn't just crash through. Perhaps it was about to when the barrier surrendered and rose. After that the confusion, commotion, and competition shifted to the boats.

Before long a small country bridge barred our way, but here Ibrahim went up to talk to the keeper and for a certain contribution the latter agreed to open. A few feluccas profited by our generosity. We were glad to oblige. Baksheesh (literally, a gift) would not open many bridges on the way to Cairo, however; those with trains or waterpipes could not be bought.

Ibrahim urged us on through the dusk and into the night. Lights ahead indicated the large town of Damanhur, but before reaching it, we made a sharp turn into the Behera Canal, which would take us to Cairo. Hectic barge and felucca traffic from Alexandria via canal joined us here. Still Ibrahim wanted us to continue and, since Irving could see just enough with help from the moon, we groped on our way apprehensively.

We kept at this seemingly perilous game until a bridge loomed ahead. Four or five men were laboring to shut off and then separate the large water main that crossed on the bridge. The maneuverable *Yankee* with a good motor could usually get through bridges ahead of the feluccas. But she must dodge the oncoming craft.

Once through no one stopped. Not a single light was shown ashore or afloat, but all vessels piled on toward the next barrier. This type of complete blackout navigation was hair-raising. The traffic consisted of powered barges northbound and southbound, tugs towing strings of barges in both directions, feluccas sailing south against the current, and feluccas drifting north broadside to the currents and barely maintaining steerageway.

Though it was midnight now, we were all on deck peering into the darkness. No one spoke unless to call out, "Skipper, do you see that felucca ahead?"

"Back her down!" he would shout from the bowsprit. "He's smack in the middle of the channel. Give him a blast on the horn."

Slowly a heavily loaded craft would drift closer to one side or the other and *Yankee* would nip by somehow. We never turned on our running lights or even considered our good searchlight. This perilous game had to be played by the local rules. Not only would "cheating" have blinded our night vision, but it would have blinded others. It was almost too exciting, but in a couple of hours another bridge stopped us. The relief we felt told us how tense we had been. Though we got involved in this risky business more than just the one night, we never felt there was any technique to it that could be learned. It just seemed to be a wild gamble.

On our fourth day we advanced about 200 yards toward Cairo. The first bridge opened at ten and we progressed 100 yards to the next one, which opened at 12:30; 100 yards more to the third bridge which would open at midnight. So that day we investigated Damanhur, one of the largest cities of the Delta, with a population of 100,000. We explored the narrow streets, past the innumerable tiny shops tucked close together, down one or two broad traffic-less avenues, meeting water buffalo on their way to the river, and marveling at the camels. These were almost as fascinating as the feluccas and I never tired of watching or photographing either. I was expecially enchanted that day with some that went loping along under such huge loads of straw that it looked as though the straw were self-propelled, except for a rather snake-like head sticking out in front and those great, squashy round feet padding along underneath. Camels were used everywhere in Egypt, almost exclusively for carrying. As Irving said, they were not so dumb as to let themselves be harnessed to plows or carts, but limited their services to the weights on their backs. Four hundred pounds

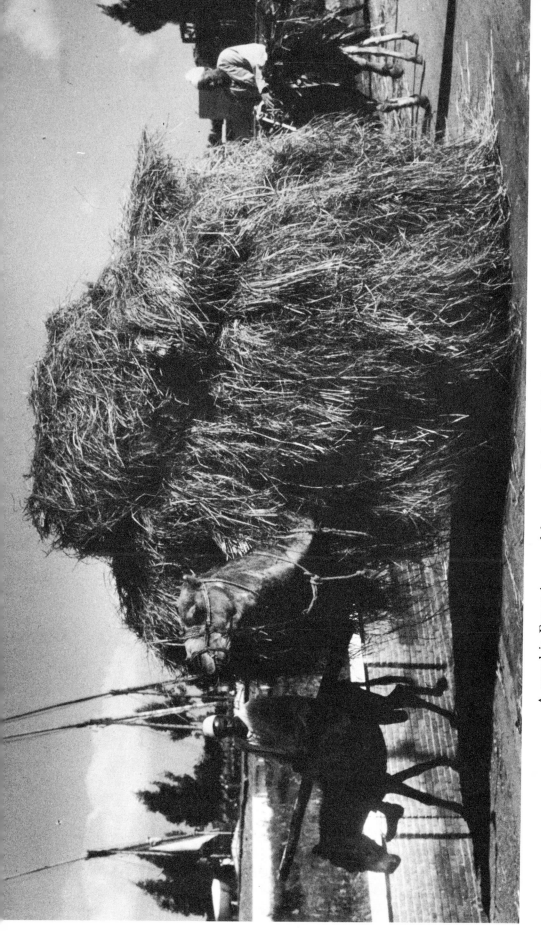

A camel in Egypt is as useful as a truck in the United States. They carry every sort of load and look disdainfully superior to the lowly donkey.

was an average load, though a camel could carry 600 pounds for short periods. Some of them swayed like bridesmaids and swished the cargo of straw like a combination bustle and train. A policeman appeared and ordered us to stop taking pictures. Now, why shouldn't we photograph camels? But we couldn't make our point in Arabic. An American yacht was so different from anything covered by police or officials' instructions that they really didn't know what to do about her. In such cases, the impulse of petty officials everywhere is to prohibit *something*.

Damanhur is a big cotton depot and we saw thousands of bales stored in open lots and warehouses. The whole business has shifted since the 1950's from British to local management. Egyptian long staple cotton is the country's prime export. It has made me dissatisfied with all other cottons, for it seems to resist dirt and creasing, is easy to wash and iron and feels smooth and silky. I found that cotton blouses were the best present to take home from Egypt.

I was encouraged to see plenty of fresh vegetables for sale in Damanhur, but Ibrahim seemed to have trouble finding eggs. We were still eating American-style bread from Alex and looked doubtfully at the common Egyptian kind, round and squashy, tan with brown freckles.

We were almost too involved in the present to think of the past here in the Delta. Though this broad triangle, sixty miles on the sea side, has been the most important part of the country in many periods, and though it has always been the most prosperous, no ancient monuments rise there today. The past is literally buried under the layers of alluvium brought by the Nile.

As soon as one begins to think about what the Nile has done, the whole story of Egypt follows. South of the Delta, the very narrow band of arable soil that borders the river is called "The Cultivation," and its cultivators are the fellahin (peasants) who make up a large proportion of the 27,000,000 people who live in an area not much larger than Maryland. In ancient times the population at its greatest was probably 5,000,000 and even then every bit of soil that could produce was in use. On either side of this narrow strip lie the deserts: the Libyan Desert to the west, the Arabian to the east.

Only in the triangle of the Nile mouths did the country expand, and this area, reaching upstream to ancient Memphis, thirteen miles above modern Cairo, was Lower Egypt. To the south, all that 800-mile-long, narrow valley was Upper Egypt. So different were the conditions of life in these two regions that there were always two kingdoms, even though during most of ancient times one pharaoh ruled over both, wearing the dual crown of

Upper and Lower Egypt. It was a splendid crown of most remarkable design: the tall, white, conical cap of Upper Egypt superimposed on the broad, high-sided, flat-topped red crown of Lower Egypt. In the Early Dynastic Period and the Old Kingdom, from about 3200 to 2280 B.C., the Pharaoh ruled in Memphis. Archeologists have found extensive material from which they can recreate that long-ago civilization, but much, much more evidence, which they would love to unearth, has disappeared in the alluvial Delta.

Even when the capital moved upstream (which we always found difficult to think of as *south*), the Delta never became unimportant, for here was access to the outer world. With this exception, Egypt was marvelously protected geographically from that outer world by its flanking deserts and the wildness of Black Africa south of the Cataracts. In its isolation, the great and distinctive civilization was able to develop for the most part undisturbed. Geography greatly determined the character of this civilization and water was the key. In order to live, the Egyptian must get the water of the Nile to his fields. Each man was downstream from someone else, and cooperation and organization were absolutely necessary. A strong central government was the answer and this Egypt had in its best periods. The elongated shape of the country made it harder to manage than the same area in compact form, but the river helped in transportation and communication. This marvelous water highway provided a fair current coming downstream and almost always a northerly wind to help vessels upstream. The *Yankee* would benefit just as the sailors had 5000 years ago.

From the regularity of the Nile's annual flooding, from the need to define land boundaries as the floods changed appearances, and from the necessity of controlling and distributing the life-giving water, arose many of Egypt's great achievements. In that rainless country of clear skies, astronomers recognized order in the heavens, and Egyptologists date the beginning of the 365-day calendar as early as 4241 B.C. Then these early scientists progressed to valid conclusions on the movements of the stars, to noting yearly phenomena like the rising of Sirius and the coming of the flood, to measuring that flood, to surveying land, and on to writing, record-keeping, inventories, census, and property valuation for taxes—as great a feature of Egyptian life as of our own. The scribe and the tax collector are the most familiar human subjects in paintings and sculpture. The man who could read and write was respected and might rise to high position.

The special geography of their country also influenced Egyptian thinking in matters beyond scientific knowledge. Outside their narrow land of habitation, the inhospitable desert to the west must have seemed like infinity. Into that unknown where the sun sank daily, they believed, their souls would sail on after death. As the practical, orderly, traditional Egyptian mind followed that thought, it built up a detailed concept of the after life and made elaborate provisions. Since the tombs were to furnish the dead with everything the living could imagine their wanting, these tombs with their paintings, sculptures, models, and inscriptions have revealed to us in great detail the life of the country. They have also associated Egypt and death in our minds. And yet they picture how much the Egyptian enjoyed life: his family, his hunting and fishing, his lands and possessions, and the joys of nature in a climate which kept him outdoors.

Though the long, closed valley provided the isolation for the development of Egypt's civilization, there were a few small and hazardous exits by the caravan routes to the Red Sea and to the four or five oases in the Libyan desert, and there was the one real doorway, the Delta. The coastal Libyans to the west drifted in at some periods, invaded at others. To the northeast there was contact with Syrians, Hittites, and the Lebanese. Since the valley provided the people with practically no wood, they went overseas for it. Egyptian ships with decks, cabin, oars, and sails made deepsea voyages to Byblos on the Lebanon coast 3000 years before Christ. Zoser, who preceded Cheops of the Great Pyramid, built river ships 170 feet long and sent a fleet of forty vessels to Lebanon. To the north, Crete was accessible, and in the 16th century B.C. it developed a civilization of its own, which owed much to Egyptian influences. At about the same time even the Sardinians also appear in numerous inscriptions. The final blow to independence came in the 6th century B.C. when the Assyrians invaded via the Delta. Later from the north came Greek and Roman conquerors. In a few more centuries, an Arab culture moved in from the east and is there still. Perhaps when Nasser today shakes his fist toward Israel, Syria, and Jordan, he remembers when the pharaohs of an imperial age marched across these lands and set up their markers on the distant Euphrates.

Since the Delta was exposed to outside influences and the rest of Egypt was not, it is easy to see why Lower and Upper Egypt were so different. For the *Yankee* they turned out to be absolutely different too. Our confused, bewildered, and frustrating cruising struggles north of Cairo were to change, thank Heaven, to serene and sensible progress once the *Yankee* sailed into the single southward course of the Nile. The reasons in our case had nothing to do with Egypt's history, but they were good reasons as we shall see. However, we had no promise of that change now and wondered if we could stand four months of delays, blundering policemen, crowding feluccas, and unlighted night-time traffic.

Our fifth Delta day started at midnight. The railroad bridge opened and we carried on again in pitch darkness—for only one rather scary hour, however. Neither *Yankee* nor feluccas showed a light and the moon was obscured; headlights of trucks on the highway were often blinding and distances were impossible, for me at least, to judge. As usual a bridge brought us to a stop. By this time we had a companion, a small, very old steam tug, which we named *Charlie*. Six men were aboard and our interest was mutual. Sometimes it was an advantage to lie up alongside, but not if we were to leeward when *Charlie* got up steam and showered soot; once an all-night argument went on aboard. Anyway, we had no choice, because our speeds were about the same and locks and bridges kept us together.

At 8:30 A.M. the familiar operations began—water pipes laboriously closed, barriers lowered, bridge opened, *Yankee* and *Charlie* through ahead of the following feluccas and dodging the oncoming ones. Our progress was good through a lock, but by the dam beyond, a dredge barred the way, and above it a dozen feluccas were tied up at right angles to the bank, stuck in the middle of the canal all hard aground. Everyone except the *Yankee* expected to wait till the dredge stopped operating for the day, but Ibrahim recognized a chance for baksheesh, and the dredge obliged. The feluccas were stuck too hard to benefit, but *Charlie* followed us as we worked past their bows in shallower and shallower water. Near the last felucca we too stuck. We tried all our usual maneuvers with engine and lines to shore, but there just wasn't enough water. Then the dam came to our assistance. One outlet was closed and the water slowly rose, but not enough. So a second opening was closed and we got the six inches we needed. With this increased depth, the feluccas could move just enough to let us past. A little further on we had a bridge to wait for from noon till six, and half hour later another bridge stopped us for the night. It was really discouraging to look at the map. We had covered less than half the distance to Cairo and this was the end of the fifth day.

The sixth day's progress was no better. Our first lock is memorable because we shared it with the whole bloated carcass of a donkey. The bridge near Tewfikia stopped us at 10 A.M. and would not open till midnight. That fourteen-hour wait was the record. We walked to the nearby railroad station and tried to phone Cairo. The man at the switchboard demanded our passports before placing the call. Nearby, a butcher shop consisted of a leg of some animal hanging from a tree. But all Egypt would not be as uninspiring as this, we were sure. It couldn't be. Walking back to the *Yankee* we counted forty feluccas waiting above the bridge.

That day Ibrahim did not feel like eating: sick during the night, he told us. I claim a certain distinction. They say Americans sooner or later always get sick on Egyptian food. Here my American cooking had made an Egyptian sick!

The seventh day started at midnight. A great sweep of felucca sails followed us through the bridge, a magnificent sight of sails astern, like great white-winged birds skimming the river in the moonlight. Before long *Charlie* signaled us to stop and we tied up alongside. To our surprise we found ourselves under way at 5:30, still lashed to *Charlie*, who took us to the nine-o'clock-opening bridge. At the next lock we waited till one. It would take days for all the feluccas to get through. I think they must figure about twelve days from Alexandria to Cairo. They need all their Moslem resignation which leaves schedules to Allah.

Now the unbelievable happened. For thirteen miles we advanced with no stops. It felt like a runaway. The shores seemed to be rushing by. At last a bridge appeared and the unbelievable continued. It opened immediately. Our experience of recent days made us appreciate this marvel as we never could have before. Not another bridge till almost dark. That day had cut down the distance to Cairo enormously.

And the eighth was our last day of the "emotional route." In fact, it was an emotional day. After the first bridge we made real progress again, and the second bridge did not involve a long wait. By three we were at the Cairo Barrage and the lock which would put us into the Nile. We knew the story of the city's bridges. The three would open at 2 A.M., 3 A.M., and 4 A.M. successively. We could have put our masts down and gone under them, but that is no trifling job and we would surely want to raise them while we were at the Yacht Club, for photography with a Cairo background was important. After our recent ordeals we were braced for the 2 to 4 A.M. passage through the city.

Now Ibrahim informed us we could not get through this lock and its bridge with our masts up. They must come down. This was not what we had been told by Mr. Couvaris, but Ibrahim was in no doubt. So we tackled the inevitable, and in a hurry. It seemed this lock would open very soon and if we didn't get right in, the feluccas astern would be only too eager. The mast lowering was a familiar procedure though not so very easy. We slacked off turnbuckles, pushed out cotter pins, laid protecting canvas over varnish, rigged the aluminum gangway as a derrick, set up the tackle to the bow, and altogether made a real tangle of our neatly rigged ship. Slowly the masts slanted down. Nothing can hurry that step when the pull must be controlled and the heavy spars gently eased. But they were lying horizontal as the lock opened. The rigging was in a mess all over the deck, but our clearance was now eleven feet instead of sixty.

The water in the lock rose, the forward gates were ready to open and now what did we see?! The bridge at that end was lifting! What had Ibrahim told us? We could have gone through with masts up! Ibrahim became very busy and seemed to forget all his English. If we had been reconciled to a 2 to 4 A.M. passage through Cairo, he had not. He intended to get the *Yankee* there that night. Next day he offered Irving some sort of apology.

Well, the deed was done and since it was, we were only too pleased to get there too. The city was waiting ahead not only with its wonders, but with mail, with Winfield Parks, the *National Geographic* photographer who was to join us, and with a special Egyptian friend, Ahmed Fahmy. We passed the outskirts, the warehouses, and the factories. Then someone cried, "The pyramids!" There they were off to starboard, so tremendous and impressive that it was hard to realize they were twenty miles distant. The lovely Cairo Tower with its casing of wide concrete mesh rose over the city. Tall minarets scraped the sky. It was nearly dark and the heavy city traffic shone its myriad lights.

The first bridge looked too low for eleven feet. Had we folded our masts for nothing? We crept at it with the utmost caution, Irving in the bow to judge the height and call back orders to me at the wheel and engine controls. We slipped under untouched as traffic poured over unaware of a little American vessel. We passed lines of houseboats, numerous rowing clubs, left Gezira Island to port, advanced under the next bridge more confidently, and under the third at our regular speed. Tall modern buildings loomed white to port. One in circular tiers, the new broadcasting building, seemed to extend over the river. A Shepheard's Hotel sign said "Cairo" in its own way. Irving spotted the Yacht Club float and the *Yankee* sidled up to it. A young man answered our call in perfect English and seemed to know exactly where we wanted our lines to go. That was Sherif Mazhar, the son of the Commodore and almost a fixture at the Yacht Club. To our amazement they both seemed to know the *Yankee*, though they had no idea she was within thousands of miles. We felt really welcome.

By ten o'clock we were dining in a friend's beautiful apartment, admiring valuable rugs and Chinese vases, eating off the finest china, savoring fish pastries, tenderloin, and souffle. The world of the feluccas, the obdurate bridges, and Ibrahim's ruses was far, far away.

chapter III

≈

Cairo

≈ The city of Cairo does not date
back to Ancient Egypt, but was founded
in Arab times in 969 A.D. Its most famous
lord was the Crusaders' great enemy,
Saladin, in the twelfth century. I found
very few books that covered all of
Egypt's history. Most of them dealt
either with ancient times or the problems
of the present, and before becoming interested in the country I certainly
couldn't have explained what happened
between the eras of Cleopatra and Napoleon. The pleasantest way to find out
is to go to the Sound and Light show at
the Citadel which tells the story of the
Egypt of the Arabs. Saladin built this
great fort above Cairo on the Mokattam
Hills from which the fine limestone for
the Pyramids had once been quarried.
In 1517 Egypt became part of the Ottoman Empire. Through these centuries
despotic sultans, Mamelukes, and pashas
came and went, and the orderliness of

Ancient Egypt gave way to violence and sometimes anarchy.

After the brief Napoleonic invasion a remarkable Albanian, Mohammed Ali, seized control in 1803 from the Turkish governor and treacherously massacred the Mameluke beys and their followers, 480 in all, who
had assembled in the Citadel at his invitation. He was the founder of the
dynasty which ended with Farouk. Through this period Eurpoean and in-
dustrial influences reached the land. In 1869 the Suez Canal was opened
with great pomp in the presence of such guests of the Khedive Ismail as
the Empress Eugénie, the Emperor of Austria, and the Crown Prince of
Prussia. The charming Eugénie made a tour of Egypt which took her beyond Aswan to view the great temple of Abu Simbel. Verdi composed the
opera *Aïda* for the occasion. Now we sat in the Citadel and heard the stirring music of the great *March* pour out into the desert air. Then Egypt's
story moved up to the present. In 1952 a disgraced Farouk sailed away
peaceably and Nasser was one of the Army group which then took control.

In one corner of old Cairo are the ornate tombs of the Mamelukes,
as rich and fanciful and exotic as anything in the Orient. Nearby rise the
straight, squarish, modern workers' apartments. Mosques of every period
dominate each quarter of the city, their lofty minarets of distinctive shapes.
The museums of Ancient Egypt, Islamic art, and Coptic art collect the
treasures of Egypt's greatness. From the days of Farouk and his dynastic
predecessors there remain the names of Shepheard's Hotel and Groppi's
Tearoom, and the shop windows which, however, no longer show the
finest of imports. Balconies enclosed with wood "filigree," *mashrabia*, and
the occasional sight of a veiled woman recall the days of the wealthy merchants, the rich trade of Cairo, the secluded life of the harems. Then the
smooth, modern lines of the riverside Nile Hilton bring us to the present,
and the striking originality of design in the Cairo Tower seems to take us
into the future.

These are the signposts of Cairo. Among them spreads the daily life of
the overcrowded city: the dense metropolitan traffic with none of the horse
cabs of Alexandria, the fruit sellers with mountains of oranges, the vegetable
stalls with the freshest produce, the ragged men who perhaps are trying to
make a living off baksheesh for watching a car, the young women with
short, tight skirts and Cleopatra make-up, the early morning parade of
camels to the slaughterhouse, their sides painted with a cerise marking, the
long shiny cars of diplomats and ministers, the newspaper kiosks with peri-
odicals in a dozen languages, the pictures of Nasser in every shop or office,
and one last typically Cairene sight, the boy on the bicycle with a four-

foot square tray of the round Egyptian bread balanced on his head. As he pedals through the worst traffic, he steadies this broad load with one hand, weaving in and out, dodging pedestrians, timing the stop lights. When he reaches a real impasse, Irving observed that he speaks a couple of words and everyone makes way or gives him a steadying hand. Then on he slithers again.

With a week to spend, we glimpsed many sides of this fascinating capital. Our most wonderful experience came out of Ancient Egypt: the Sound and Light show at the pyramids. It is given in different languages on different nights. Lights skillfully smooth over the time-jagged sides of the huge geometric structures and illumine the Sphinx like a great old actress so that the broken nose never shows. We see them in their early magnificence, the bright stars of the desert sky behind them, the sea of desert sand stretching beyond the horizon, and a sense of infinite time comes over us. When the voice says, "I have seen the pharaohs, I have seen Alexander. . . ." the moments of history and most of all our own presence seem reduced to near nothingness. For a spellbound hour the lights work their changes and emphasis on the four objects before us and the voice moves the long story of Ancient Egypt through our minds. The whole Christian era seems brief. Emotion and meaning have been breathed into inanimate objects, which will never again seem just triangular designs and a crouching human-headed lion. Incidentally, it was not Napoleon who shot the nose off the Sphinx, as guides enjoy telling you; it was the Turks.

A later daylight visit brought other impressions. We arrived at the camel yard opposite the old Mena House, so full of Victorian atmosphere, just as a whole busload of tourists were starting out on every available camel. Helen Hokinson ladies, thin-lipped businessmen, and expansive Rotarians with flowing Lawrence of Arabia headdresses were jolting to their steeds' strange gait on the road to the pyramids. We knew we would look just as funny, but that didn't spoil our amusement. Later a particularly pudgy, white-skinned lady in flowered chiffon dismounted from her camel and, somehow separated from her group, nearly in tears of bewilderment rushed to our waiting car, which looked like a familiar haven, and uttered the forlorn cry, "Take me to the Hilton." At last our driver found her group for her.

The chance to ride a camel, even a pyramid camel, is well worth appearing ridiculous. One mounts while he is folded up close to the ground. Then with four great separate lurches he rises to his full height. Bright-colored woolen tassels make three or four broad necklaces and more tas-

Donna Grosvenor and her camel seem to be laughing at the same joke. (*Zacher*)

Win Parks called our little donkey driver Nefertiti, for she lived at Tell-el-Amarna where that beautiful queen had graced the court of Akhnaton. In her red dress and bare feet she flitted through a free and happy childhood still too young to hide her beauty under the folds of a black *mylaya*.

sels flap from the decorative saddle bags. A few blue beads at his brow avert the Evil Eye. The camel driver trots alongside reciting his stock of tourist phrases, "The Campbells are coming!" "Heigh-o, Silver!" and "Isn't this just wonderful?" Then he volunteers to take a picture of you with your own camera. He is familiar with every make, every adjustment, and when all ready to push the button calls out, "Say cheese!" The sublime pyramids look down. But it is fun, and a picture of yourself as a camel rider posed against the pyramid-Sphinx background, taken by a man with the old equipment of wooden tripod, big square camera, and black cloth over his head, is the souvenir of all souvenirs.

This mood vanishes entirely on a visit to the inner chamber of the Great Pyramid. Statistics of its size are staggering. In the space covered by the base could be placed the cathedrals of Florence, Milan, St. Peter's of Rome, Westminster Abbey, and St. Paul's. Nine-tenths of Egypt's farms take up less than half the 13.1 acres covered by what is still the world's largest man-made masonry object. 2,300,000 stone blocks averaging 2½ tons each, some as much as 40 tons, were used to construct this pyramid of Cheops about 2650 B.C. It was built 481 feet high (the top 31 feet are now missing), and the peak was originally gilded to shine in the rays of the sun.

Just as impressive as its size is the construction of the Great Pyramid. Local stone forms the inner structure over a core of rock whose exact size has never been determined. (I have read that there is now a plan to x-ray the pyramid.) The whole vast exterior was smoothly cased in the fine quality white Tura limestone from the Mokattam Hills behind modern Cairo and, to quote the great American archaeologist, James Breasted, "Some of the masonry finish is so fine that blocks weighing tons are set together with seams of considerable length showing a joint of 1/10,000 of an inch and involving edges and surfaces equal to optician's work of the present day, but on a scale of acres instead of feet or yards of material." In the nineteenth century the pyramid was found to be so mathematically accurate that there was less than 7.9 inches of inequality in its 756 foot square. Since that time, as more and more exact measurement has been possible, the wonder has increased. Maximum error in all angles involved is 6/100 of one degree!

We climbed up the now rough exterior to the only modern entrance and started down toward the center of the pyramid. This corridor originally led to a deep underground tomb chamber in the rock which was almost completed when the plans changed. So our direction changed to a steep climb uncomfortably stooped way over, with headroom of about forty inches. This corridor would have led to the second nearly completed chamber, but again the plans changed and access was blocked off. So continuing at the same steep angle, we straightened up to ascend the Grand Gallery 153 feet long and 28 feet high, stopping often to admire the smooth beautifully fitted stone. This third and last plan led into the great burial chamber where the huge granite sarcophagus of the pharaoh still stands, lidless and empty. It must have been built into the pyramid, for it is about an inch too wide to get out any of the corridors.

"I'm glad this place is lighted now," Irving said. "When I came in 1928 I had to pay the guide fifty cents every time to light a little magnesium flare that burned five seconds. This time I intend to look as long as I want."

This is not a place to hurry away from, for one needs time and quiet to absorb the wonder of its structure and age. It had been hot and stuffy in the corridors, but here there was space, for the chamber is 34 by 17 feet and 19 feet high. And there seemed to be fresh air. Two slim air channels were constructed to the exterior of the pyramid either for ventilation or for the coming and going of the soul: explanations differ. They were still in operation without repair after 46 centuries! Another marvel of construction which we read about, but could not see, was that above the 400-ton ceiling of nine blocks of granite were five separate compartments, four with flat ceilings and the highest with a pointed roof, all built into the very center of this huge structure to ease the pressure of the tons of rock above the ceiling. As our eyes adapted to the dimness, we could see the rosy color in the granite which had come from the Aswan quarries 600 miles upstream.

How was it all possible? A hundred thousand men worked twenty years, we are told. That constituted a rush job, for all had to be completed before the pharaoh's death. Some people imagine Moses' Israelites toiling here under the lash of pharaoh's overseers, but Moses came probably 1500 years later. It is not even likely that slaves provided all the labor, for though every man in Egypt was subject to the pharaoh's call they were not considered his slaves. Organization is the explanation for the tremendous achievement. Stonecutters and masons worked at their specialized tasks. Unskilled labor hewed the stone from the quarries. Carpenters built ramps; shipwrights built boats and rafts. Most of the limestone was floated across the river at the time of highest flood when the least moving by land was necessary and when farm work came to a stop. On land there were only rollers, sledges, ramps and the strength of thousands of men hauling on palm fiber ropes. I was amazed to learn that the use of the pulley was unknown, for I had so often seen how it would multiply the power of a *Yankee* crew pulling the ship off a hard grounding. Iron came to Egypt only in Roman times, so all the stone work was done with copper saws aided by abrasive powder. The big blocks of granite were quarried by driving in dry wooden wedges and wetting them so their swelling would split the rock. But difficult as all these operations were with the knowledge and tools at hand, Egyptian stone workers were masters.

These explanations we could follow, but it took all our powers of imagination to try to picture the whole glorious scene here at Giza when everything was new and shining and animated with the majesty of the god-king, the ritual of priests, the honored participation of royalty, vizier, chancellors, and nobles, and the presence of the people, believers all. Then the pyramid stood not alone, but dominant above surrounding temples, the finely built covered causeway to the river, and the great mortuary temple at the landing stage, all of it a magnificent architectural ensemble covering acres. There was color, too, and music, contributing to an unequalled scene of ceremony in this undistracting desert setting under the clear Egyptian sky.

"Take me to the Hilton" was sometimes our request too. This new, attractively decorated, well-run hotel is an enormous convenience with its shops, hairdresser, newsstand, post office, bank, and most of all the Ibis Cafe, a very American coffee shop with young Egyptian or Greek waitresses. It was such a blessing to be able to get a short, simple meal at any time of day that I did not care how Americanized the setting was.

At the other extreme the bazaar of Khan el Khalili is as exotic as its name and half as old as Cairo. Roofed over, a maze of alleyways leads one under old arches and wood-filigree balconies past innumerable tiny shops, children hammering on brass, country women looking at thin gold ornaments by the hour, men smoking water pipes anywhere from one to five feet in height, carpets spread for display at the slightest sign of interest, awnings with more holes than canvas, every sort of load on women's heads, miles of cloth for sale, a smattering of tourists, a small bunch of goats with the fatal cerise mark on their side showing they are on their way to slaughter, a few well organized shops pretending to have fixed prices, "antiquities" of recent manufacture, sticky pastries and appetizing-looking crusty concoctions, a Vespa scooter entirely out of place scattering pedestrians, boys darting about with swinging trays of tiny cups of Turkish coffee to relax a customer or accompany hours of tête-à-tête at a little table, displays of silver anklets, inlaid boxes, leather hassocks—the whole scene a direct descendant of the medieval bazaars of this corner of the Mediterranean where

East and West exchange.

In this same part of Old Cairo stand the mosque and university of Al Azhar, the world center of Moslem learning since 988. Here in a courtyard we saw pupils sitting at the feet of a teacher with beard, turban, and yellow robe. Until very recent times practically all learning centered around the Koran, but now faculties of civil law and science have been opened.

In the same 24 hours that we marveled at the age and dignity of Al Azhar, we marveled at Wafaa Kamel, the belly dancer of the Pearl of the Sahara, a night club in a great, rich Arab tent where we dined at low brass tables on delicious food, hard to identify. Belly dance is really a poor name for the magnificent performance of a star dancer, but that seems to be the accepted term. The dance was erotic and the costume skimpy, but Wafaa must have loved to dance or she could never have put on such a dazzling, exhausting performance. When we thought it was practically over, it was only half through, and at the end she was gleaming with perspiration, but her black eyes were still fiery, her broad smile still flashing, her black hair still tossing, all with such vitality that I felt she could hardly come to a stop but would have to dance till she fell. Her special musicians played their peculiar instruments with a weird, monotonous, but exciting whine.

We met many Egyptians for whom the only word was "charming:" professional men and their wives; an Egyptian Henry Luce and Clare Booth; the doyen of Egyptian actors; the most popular movie actress, Fatin Hama-mah, who was simple, friendly, and wore the least make-up at the party; and one of the most active women in Egypt, Aziza Hussein, whose husband had been Ambassador to Washington, who had served as President of the Cairo Woman's Club, and who had been brought up by a father who believed in education and freedom for women before many girls attended the university. Aziza Hussein had just returned from an international family planning conference in Singapore. Egypt does not need us to tell them they are over-populated. Dr. Mazhar was giving newspaper interviews about The Pill. Women's groups in the villages of Lower Egypt were eager for information on birth control. After the Singapore conference Mme. Hussein had been asked to talk to men's groups in the villages about sterilization of men who already had families of two or three. A plunge into this subject was frightening even to such a confident and capable woman, but she was amazed at the excellent reception she got and the men's understanding of the seriousness of this problem. The present population of 27,000,000 is increasing so fast that all the new land made cultivable by the work of the Aswan High Dam will merely provide the same amount of food per person that now leaves millions constantly undernourished, even with tremendous shipments from the United States. Population control is Egypt's greatest problem.

Some of our own problems were still with us: the navigation of the Nile through the whole length of Egypt, the question of official permissions, the availability of food supplies, and the need for a guide-interpreter.

Irving continued to inquire in every direction for a chart, or even a good map of the river. In the end the very best we could get was in the 1929 Baedeker (still the best guide to Egypt), a treasure loaned us by Dr. Mazhar. Its maps were small scale and far from a skipper's ideal, but they did give place names and distances, and show some islands, even if they were miles away from their actual present location.

Some sort of guide-interpreter we would definitely need. Irving had no intention of taking a pilot, for the *Yankee* was too completely different from any Nile vessel for a pilot to understand our needs, limitations, and capabilities. Besides, such a man, if he existed at all, would not speak English. This person also would be our shipmate for four months, in the confines of a small boat. I had braced myself for a university student and only hoped that he would be more understanding than a young man the Tourist Bureau provided one day, who did speak English and dress well, but who knew less about the tombs of Sakkara than we did, who liked to drive fast and play the radio, and who thought of the United States in Hollywood terms. I was not very optimistic about our Egyptian shipmate. Maybe he would leave his things around and never make his bunk and I would have to cook special food for him. Would our usual pleasant mealtimes be strained by his presence? I had better expect the worst.

But the best was what we got: a charming friend, perfect shipmate, a true gentleman—Ahmed Fahmy. A lucky chain of circumstances, not an official assignment, brought him to the *Yankee*, and, though we didn't know it immediately, the success of the cruise was then assured. Ahmed was in his late forties, educated at Cambridge, a star cricketer, a linguist, a bachelor, a man of the world, and an admirer of our country. His father had been an early exponent of Egypt's independence whose name was respected throughout the country.

Ahmed understood immediately that what the *Yankee* needed was not any particular permit for river sailing. No such thing existed. But we did need an official blessing, and this should come from the present influential Minister of Culture and National Guidance, Dr. Hatem. In addition to any reputation the *Yankee* might have, we had the advantage of working with

Ahmed Fahmy points out how a porous water jar set in the sand can cause a garden to sprout around it.

the *National Geographic* magazine on this cruise, and a staff photographer would be aboard. Since Dr. Hatem was concerned with public relations, with Egypt's image abroad and with tourism, the advantages of attractive *Geographic* pictures reaching millions of people all over the world would surely appeal to him. So Ahmed arranged for us to meet Dr. Hatem at a diplomatic reception at the Hilton held to celebrate the signing that day of the plans for moving Abu Simbel. The man we met was dark, a bit heavy, with large brown eyes which seemed to take in everything around him and still concentrate on the immediate person. He said he would like to visit the *Yankee*.

For that visit, Dr. Hatem arrived with an entourage of reporters and photographers. The picture of him chatting with Irving in our after cabin was a better ship's passport than any written forms. He was a delightful visitor, interested in the ship and in our way of life, so completely strange to him. Our bookcases struck a more familiar note and those keen eyes didn't miss a title, especially on the subject of Egypt on which there were many volumes. In fact, he asked what our reading list was and went off with a copy, a list originally made up by a Dutch archaeologist friend who was an expert on the Middle East. Next day a splendid present arrived with Dr. Hatem's card—a further selection of excellent books on Egypt. Nothing could have pleased us more.

As he was about to leave he spoke the most gracious phrase, "What can I do for you?" We left it to Ahmed to answer and the first result was the use of a Russian-built Army helicopter to get pictures of the *Yankee* under full sail off Cairo.

After this personal encounter, Ahmed made further arrangements for us to appear on TV, speak over the radio, give newspaper interviews, and pose for pictures—a small price for the great advantage of an official accolade for the *Yankee*.

Even Ahmed did not know all the answers to my questions about provisions up the Nile. The *Yankee* was loaded with canned goods, but what could I get along the way? Would even all this load of canned food be enough if six of us drew on it day after day? Ahmed's married brother thought we'd find very little and sent us a large supplement of rice, flour, sugar, and spaghetti. Dr. Mazhar was sure we wouldn't starve. Sherif introduced us to *foul* (pronounced *fool*), the poor man's basic food all over the country, rather like baked beans. I bought a mountain of fresh supplies, and put food uncertainties out of my mind. I had done all I could.

On November 16th we were ready to leave Cairo. Sheridan had gone back to Athens, Ibrahim to Alexandria. In addition to the Nelsons and Ahmed, Winfield Parks, staff photographer of the *National Geographic*, moved into the forward quarters. Win was not tall, but he was dark and handsome. In fact, when he and Ahmed went ashore together he was taken for the Egyptian and addressed in Arabic, and Ahmed was considered the uncomprehending American. Win had a little game of fitting his appearance to the country where he was working by just slight changes in clothes and face so as to draw as little attention as possible to himself as he went about his work. Now a black moustache with downswept corners turned him into a likely Arab. For all his natural flair, his genius for photography, his newspaper years of "front page" drama, his artistic sense, his natural daring, Win was as pleasant, agreeable, and considerate a shipmate as ever sailed in the *Yankee*. He could keep us spellbound after dinner with tales of chasing gangsters or fighting for scoops or telling the opposition where to get off, but on the *Yankee* he kept his quarters neat, never monopolized the bathroom (mark of a good yachtsman), acted as though he liked everything I cooked, and quickly caught on to what the skipper needed in a good hand.

Ahmed told us later that the Cairo Yacht Club members shook their heads over our bold venture, especially our independent departure without guns, pilot, or servants. Many said we would never make it. But all that was in Arabic, and they smiled and gave a cheer as we pulled away from the dock. Cairo had provided fun and excitement, but we were glad to be off on our own again and at last away from crowded canals, bridges, and locks, heading south up the Nile.

Win Parks put on his *galabia* and fez and took his water pipe into the Nubian desert, making what seemed to us the "compleat Arab."

chapter IV

≈ Cairo Through Beni Suef

≈

We spent our first night south of Cairo tied to the landing of Farouk's old palace, one of many we would see scattered about the country. Next morning we passed beneath our last bridge for a week and raised the masts; future bridges would open and we would not lower the masts again till we were back here. The next was our first full day on the Nile and this was a different world from the Delta—not so rich, not so fertile, not so busy, the narrow world of the river. My greatest surprise in Egypt was the beauty of the country. The great monuments of the past were all I had been able to picture of Egypt. I expected a long river with great deserts on either side, but nothing had told me of the color and loveliness of the valley.

Where the land is fertile, where the river floods or irrigation helps, the soil is a rich, dark taupe color. The greens are a shining green like the rice fields of

Bali and the date palms attract the eye vertically from all the horizontals of the small fields to their graceful tops responding to the breeze. The mud brick houses color into the landscape so naturally that they seem to have grown here. Of course they almost did, being made of the earth itself. Sometimes an individual touch shows in a pattern of mud brick open-work, fan-shaped above the door. Sometimes a grape-vine grows over the door-way, but it is almost always a dusty one in this rainless country. The whole scene is one of mellow, natural beauty seldom disturbed by mechanization. In fact, the combination of river, green fields, and distant desert is the same which the Egyptian of 5000 years ago knew and loved.

The people blend too. We got used to the men in their long *galabias*, which are cool and dignified. All men wear something on their heads, some-times the fez, more often a hastily-wound turban. The orthodox turban winds around the head seven times, long enough to serve as a shroud. The women float by in their black draperies. They seem submissive and anony-mous. They carry everything on their heads, the most common burden being the pottery water jar with broad base and small neck to keep the water from spilling. Their faces are gentle and smooth with soft, feminine fea-tures. Many wear anklets and bracelets of silver or gold. This is their wealth.

The animals complete the scene—the ineffable camels with their peculiar motion, the gun-metal water buffalo with skin-and-bone haunches, the dun-colored cattle. Cattle and buffalo are yoked far apart to the wooden plows with the shallow wooden share, just like those of pharaonic times. The lowly herds of sheep and goats drift across the scene. The hardy little gray-white donkeys carry men whose legs always seem disproportionately long.

The tombs tell us how much the ancient Egyptian enjoyed the wildlife of the land, for the artists picture in charming and accurate detail the birds of the marshes, the fish in the river—no longer so plentiful—the hunting dog, and the household cat. In those days there was still wild game to hunt: lions, panthers, gazelles, hippopotami. A pharaoh was expected to be a mighty hunter and his biggest successes were recorded on temple walls. Nobles also followed the kingly sport. In quieter mood, they enjoyed the charming gardens and orchards which we know from pretty models of domestic scenes.

On the river the white sails of the feluccas are always in sight, little ones ferrying east and west, the great swooping triangular sails traveling north and south. There are usually a few of these vessels tied up to the bank astern of us at night. They start out with the first light about 5:30 and

Irving and I sit up in bed to watch them through the stern windows. With stone cargoes, they have only a few inches of freeboard. Others are piled to a height of twelve feet with even rows of four thousand pale gray or pink pots. Hundreds more pots hang over the side skillfully stowed in huge nets which often touch the water. Sometimes a golden stack of fine straw held together with a coating of sugar cane juice—like a high-style head-dress with hair spray—is so neat and smooth that it looks like a huge bar of gold bullion. Another sort of straw stack is just as high, but of ragged outline.

On two mornings we had early fog. In the middle of breakfast preparations, I would look out the galley window and see a little ferry breaking out of the mist, loaded down with huddled Arabs, their fierce dark faces going by so close that I thought an oar might come in the window—a great, heavy, unpainted oar with no shape to it, just a little concession of flattening for a blade. On many mornings these close-passing ferries seemed part of my galley operations. Perhaps curiosity about our strange boat brought them closer than they needed to come.

The early inhabitants of this river country were of course boatmen. Their first craft were made of bundles of papyrus, but even in the earliest dynasties they began to build deepsea ships. In time, the steering oar changed to a tiller and improvements showed in the rig of sails and staying of masts, many of which could be lowered like *Yankee*'s. It was primarily for good ship's timbers of cedar that the Egyptians first ventured to the Lebanon coast. Their ships knew that sea lane centuries before the days of empire, when around 1300 B.C. whole fleets of troopships carried Egyptian armies there and brought back cargoes of tribute from the conquered.

Warships, however, were only a part of the vast amount of shipbuilding through the ages. Trading vessels plied the "Great Green," as the ancients called the Mediterranean. They explored the coasts and the Greek Islands. I can believe that some of them reached islands farther west, perhaps even Gibraltar. The famous expeditions to Punt (modern Somaliland) began with the building of ships on the shores of the Red Sea.

But on the Nile itself the Egyptians were in their element. The pleasant sounds of shipbuilding were natural to those shores. I don't remember reading anything about roads in Egypt. The river was everyone's highway, for every sort of useful craft: fishing boats, little ferries, farm boats for carrying cattle, grain, stone, and sand; heavy barges up to 200 feet long freighting tons of granite from Aswan, boats for duck-hunting in the marshes, for fish-spearing, family boats, the endless variety of useful,

A Nile ferryboat's capacity seems to have no limit. One passenger rides "steerage"—aboard the rudder.

everyday boats, forever evolving changes as boats will, to take men and their materials from here to there.

We see them all pictured on the walls of tombs, the special boats as well. The pharaoh's barge bears its royal standard, its throne and musicians. The rich man's private galley is second only to the royal yacht. Each has a kitchen boat following. The funerary boats are distinguished by their high bows and sterns. The Sacred Bark of Amon is even more gorgeous, sheathed in gold with a shrine amidships, gold rams' heads and crowned serpents gleaming. I was especially pleased to read, "The man 'without boat' is listed in the writings of ancient Egypt as among the unfortunates of the earth—the hungry, the naked, the orphan." Irving approved too of the sunboat in which the souls of the dead would travel across the sky. "At least they had a ship in their afterlife," he said appreciatively. The *Yankee* was following some marvelous ancestors.

We all began to learn the ways of river life. Our long boathook was carved with marks for sounding at five, six, and seven feet and we marked another pole in the same way so that Win and Ahmed could sound on either side. We were finding our way by Irving's general knowledge of rivers—curving away from the shallows that back up the points, watching for any informative signs on the surface of the water, sounding to locate the channel as it wandered back and forth across the river, asking a farmer on the bank or a felucca skipper.

Irving would bring the *Yankee* within hailing distance and Ahmed would call across to the other boat with the proper greeting, "Marhab be el raies" ("Greetings, Captain"), and then ask where the channel crossed. Sometimes, quite lost on the little Baedeker map, we just wanted to know where we were, a village name that we might locate and thereby measure our progress.

One sight along the bank was becoming very familiar—the shaduf. From the beginning of agriculture in Egypt, from the time the wandering herdsmen were first tempted to stop on the shores of the Nile, water had to be lifted from the river to the fields. For thousands of years it was carried— back-breaking work. Then about 1650 B.C., the foreign overlords, the Hyksos, introduced the shaduf. It is still the simplest and most common means of raising water. At the present height of the Nile bank, it took three men, each lifting the same water six or eight feet for a total lift of about 20 feet. The device used resembles the well sweep of early New England. A hide bucket is suspended from one end of the sweep while at the other end, to conterbalance the water, is a great lump of dried mud.

The ancient shaduf raises water from the Nile to irrigate the fields. Three men chant and the sweeps creak as each leather bucket lifts the water to the next level.

The first man pours his bucketful of water from the river into a ditch behind him, where it runs back into a pool, from which the second man's bucket scoops it up to the next level. On the third rise, the water is dumped into a channel running to the fields. The rhythmic dipping and lifting makes silence impossible, and so we always hear a song or at least a chant as the men perform their age-old task.

It was so pleasant on the river that we were in no hurry to get anywhere, but the town of Beni Suef was not far ahead. Like Damanhur, it numbered 100,000 inhabitants, though it seemed about a third that size. As soon as we moored, Ahmed went ashore and came back saying we were expected for tea at the nearby house of the young mayor, Major Sharkawi. Beni Suef had a broad new avenue for its waterfront, with modern street lights, a big new sports stadium, a fine Club House and grounds, and a new waterfront house for the mayor. Maj. Sharkawi was an energetic administrator, an Army man, a man of the New Egypt.

Mrs. Sharkawi had energy too. Up to date in a dark skirt and red pullover and cardigan, she was a cordial, jolly hostess. In a drawing room of gilt French-style furniture, she served us an ample tea, introduced two of her five children, and made us feel like real friends. When we had eaten all we should, a special treat arrived, the last thing in the world we would have expected—popcorn!

The mayor arranged for us to go the next day to the Faiyum, the largest oasis in Egypt. The most important god of this "province" in ancient times was Sobek of the crocodile head. He was still important more than 2000 years later when the Greek overlords of Egypt called this place by the mouth-filling name of Crocodilopolis. In modern times, crocodiles have vanished from the Nile below Aswan at the First Cataract.

The Faiyum is a depression in the Libyan Desert shaped like a huge maple leaf with its stem to the east. We drove in along this stem, which connects it with the Nile valley. In fact this basin, roughly some forty or fifty miles in diameter, was in ancient times and still is watered by the Nile. Over 4000 years ago, the whole area was covered by a lake when the Nile in flood rushed through the narrow stem we were now entering. Then during the Twelfth Dynasty, about 1800 B.C. some sort of ancient regulators were installed across this entrance so the flood waters could be retained for release during the dry summer. Recent calculations determine that the flow of the Nile below here could thus be doubled during three months of its lowest period each year.

Several modern dams across the Nile now regulate the river, so the

Faiyum's Lake Kurun has been allowed to recede from 73 feet above sea level to 144 feet below. While the lake is still some 25 miles long and four to six miles wide, a vast area that used to be flooded has been made available for farming. Joseph's River, the Bar Yusuf (partly canalized), still brings the necessary Nile water from above the dam at Assiut over 200 miles to the south. Entering the Faiyum via the stem, as in ancient times, the water now spreads through a network of irrigation canals to all parts of the old lake bottom. The sloping land descends in large crescents toward Lake Kurun in the northwest.

We drove directly to the town of Medinet el Faiyum and called on the General Secretary of the Province Government, Mr. Anis Diab, a tall, handsome man with curling moustache. In his spacious office he served us tiny cups of Turkish coffee and made us feel very welcome. His English was excellent, and we were interested to hear he had spent five months in Boston while his little daughter was being treated at Children's Hospital for a kidney disease. Mr. Diab gave us an English-speaking guide in the person of the Rev. Adub Habeeb, a Coptic Christian pastor who was to show us the sights of the Faiyum, from a model chicken farm to the Middle Kingdom pyramids.

In this part of Egypt we were meeting the Middle Kingdom, 2050 to 1786 B.C. We had already seen the greatest survivals of the Old Kingdom at Giza and would see more of it in the nearby Memphis area on our way downstream. That splendid period had ended with the 90-year reign, the longest in history, of Pepi II, who lived to over a hundred. But in his old age he no longer had the vigor needed to maintain the strength of the Old Kingdom, and then for nearly 300 years, known as the First Intermediate Period, the country suffered severely from dissension of rival nobles and outright anarchy. All the stability, law, order, and productivity of the Old Kingdom crumbled away.

But powers of recuperation were still in the people and eventually a strong pharaoh, Amenemhet I, united the country again and a second glorious era began, the years of the Middle Kingdom. Once again Egypt prospered. Expeditions were sent down the Red Sea to Punt. Mines were reopened and the southern border was advanced to the Second Cataract, where a great fort was built. Traveling in the *Yankee*, we could appreciate how extensive that domain was, for the Second Cataract, the head of Nile navigation across the border in the Sudan, was our final objective. From there, 4000 years ago, fast messengers brought word of the measurements of the rising Nile so that adequate preparations could be made downstream. All these activities were evidence of sound administration the length of the country. But probably the greatest accomplishment of the period was Amenemhet III's vast drainage and irrigation work at the Faiyum, which with the consequent agricultural expansion raised the prospertiy of the country as a whole. The population was then about 2,000,000.

Back along the entrance canal, we drove in our Buick along the palm-shaded macadam road. Try as we did, no trace of the ancient "regulators" could we see. A small dam, a modern lock, yes, and many Twelfth Dynasty ruins, including a large pyramid of Amenemhet IV at Hawara. This pyramid had the most complicated arrangements of any for protecting its tomb against robbers. But of all the pyramids and tombs of Egypt only one has ever been found untouched, that of Tutankhamon. Here at Hawara the deep-descending corridors changed direction four times, and three enormous stone trap doors should have safeguarded the burial chamber successfully. But the wealth of royal tombs was so great that human greed overcame any barrier, and tomb robbing has been an Egyptian accomplishment for 5000 years.

It was not always criminals who robbed the tombs. In periods of distress, extreme want would drive the poor man to dig for some of the wealth he knew was hidden close by. Sometimes the robbers were the tomb builders or officials, who knew the secrets of the construction. In the hugh Hawara pyramid, for example, it is known that only the outer of the three trap doors was ever dropped. Even the pharaohs did their share, appropriating stones and decorations from the monuments of their predecessors. "Perpetual care" was a hollow phrase then as now. These pyramids near the Faiyum with their ponderous trickery were some of the last. As the pharaohs realized that no amount of stone would guarantee an undisturbed burial, they ceased to build such conspicuous tombs and sought an afterlife security by digging deep into rock cliffs.

We left our car at the roadside between the green irrigated fields and walked over desert sand toward the remains of the huge old structure. No longer its whole 190 feet high, it has lost its limestone covering. A desert fox raced across our path. The pyramid was excavated and thoroughly reported on in the 1890's by one of the great early Egyptologists, Sir Flinders Petrie, with whose name we were going to become quite familiar. But since that time its entrance has filled with sand, like other early tombs which have been thoroughly studied but which would not repay the effort and expense of keeping them open longer. So we knew only from reading that the sepulchre chamber under this mound was 22 feet long, eight feet wide, and six feet high, cut from a single block of the hardest quartzite weighing 110 tons. It had no door and the only access was through a roofing stone weighing 45 tons. Even that did not prevent pillage.

Close by, little is left of the "Labyrinth," a name given by Herodotus in the fifth century B.C. to the enormous palace-temple-administration building from which Amenemhet III directed the affairs of his realm. Its size and construction are a reflection of the organization of the Middle Kingdom. Government departments, officials of every rank, reports from near and far, tax records, surveys, engineering projects all converged here in a period of strong, centralized, and complex government. This was a magnificent building of twelve courts and 3000 rooms, the roofs all of stone and the walls covered with sculpture. It was still standing and considered one of Egypt's greatest wonders when the Greek geographer, Strabo, visited here in Roman times. But then the new masters of Egypt used it as a quarry for their own building activities. However, it was the only structure not a temple which survived that long.

We drove on across a farmer's dream of perfect land, which yields three or more crops a year, depending on what is planted, with no time out for winter, rain, or flood. Much pumping is needed to the fields two or three feet above canal level. Win would shout, "Stop, there's a picture" whenever the photogenic waterwheels or laboring cows appeared, endlessly pumping irrigation water.

The slope of the land is so gradual that only by noticing which way the canal water ran could we be sure we were heading for the lake. Around a last bend, there it was, a true inland sea with only evaporation for an outlet. So large we couldn't see the other end, it is today a salt lake and will become even saltier as the years go by.

In the modern countryside were great pink dovecotes, not the single rounded cones such as we had seen in the Delta, but large many-turreted structures—highrise dove apartment houses. At any disturbance, hundreds of doves would take to the air protesting, circle briefly, and return reassured. We asked if Egyptians ate so many doves, but were told that the birds were kept as much for fertilizer from their droppings as for their meat. It seems, however, that this is a mistaken effort, as the birds do more direct damage to the crops than indirect benefit. But dovecotes seem to be an established part of village life and we saw them even in the new agricultural centers.

We were proudly shown some new government rest houses, but we were much more interested in a grist mill of the most primitive type. Women were bringing in on their heads heavy baskets of coarse grain. As they

Dovecotes in Egypt are like big apartment houses for myriads of birds. Wealthy Egyptians raise the birds mainly to provide fertilizer for family vegetable gardens. The black *mylaya* which shrouds an Egyptian woman makes her an accentuated moving shape in the landscape rather than a human figure.

waited their turns, the black-draped figures folded to the ground by their baskets, not a merry, gossiping lot, but tired and patient. At a sign from the miller, a woman would empty her grain between the heavy millstones driven by the power of the Faiyum's falling water. Old wooden waterwheels turned, worn wooden gears and shafts transferred the power to the rotating stones. It hardly seemed there could be a nail, wire, or piece of iron in any part. The scene came right out of the Old Testament. It was probably at some such place that Joseph had the bags of grain filled for his brothers to take back to their famine-struck Land of Canaan.

It was late when we returned to the *Yankee*. After dark there were almost no lights in the villages we drove through, but the lively town of Beni Suef was all electricity and activity. In one day we had seen evidence of the continuous life of the Faiyum from the times of the pharaohs to the bright hopes of the New Egypt.

Our friend, the mayor, asked next morning if we had any other requests and seemed so willing to grant any wish that I thought I might as well try out on him the inquiry with which I had had no previous success. Were there any of the fine Arab horses in his area? Of course, the best!

So in midmorning, as we were having Turkish coffee in the sun on the verandah of the Club, a gentleman rode up on a beautiful black mare, followed by grooms leading two other horses and by four unprepossessing characters who seemed to me to have nothing to do with fine horses. The gentleman was wearing not riding breeches, but a light blue *galabia* of a material about as heavy as denim, the first handsome *galabia* I had seen since our pilot's pinstripe. I have no idea how long we watched the stirring performance as we were not conscious of time, but only of the beautiful, perfectly trained animals who performed for us. The four men turned out to be the horses' musicians, and with flutes and strange instruments they set up a continuous piercing sort of wail that would have driven any Western horse frantic. But these lovely Arabs danced in time to the weird music, their shorter, rounder ears held prettily forward, necks arched, knees lifting high; light, lively, compact animals, not nervous or wild, but fiery and alert. It was beautiful riding, training, and control. At the end of each horse's performance, he bowed down on his forelegs and held that unnatural position until signaled to rise. Mr. Sharkawi's four-year-old son, Mustafa, in bright blue hand-knitted suit, was placed on one of the horses, carefully watched by the owner and lightly held by the groom, but he sat the lively horse like a man. I asked through Ahmed if the owner, the gentleman, had ridden when he was that young. He re-

68

Local Arabian horses, trained here for centuries, obviously love to dance.

plied that his father had loved fine horses and that he had been in the saddle long before he could remember.

After that performance, visits to a trade school and a rug weaving factory seemed tame. But schools are going up all over Egypt, in a determined effort to reduce the 73% illiteracy of the people.

We sailed after lunch, literally sailed, because the Nile was wide here, and with our southerly course the wind was astern. Win and I clambered from the bowsprit onto a moving barge to take pictures of the *Yankee* with everything set: main, mizzen, mule, and the red and white striped Genoa jib. Feluccas were following with their great sails straining. Win included in his picture a few of the barge's crew on their craft watching the *Yankee*, making a good foreground for his picture. I of course copied.

But now Irving had to get us back aboard *Yankee*. As he tells it:

With *Yankee* and barge both making several knots against the current, it was bound to be tricky. The river had now become shallow, which always caused erratic steering. Still I had to recover Exy and Win, so under both sail and power I maneuvered *Yankee* toward the barge's stern.

"Ahmed, stand by with fenders," I shouted. "Doc, you catch the cameras so they can grab with both hands when they jump aboard." Meanwhile *Yankee* seemed to want to slalom. Our photographers chose a short moment of quiet and leapt aboard successfully.

Before dark we were tied up to the bank near a village composed of just six widely spaced houses, each under its small shade tree. The people did not come down to look at us, but went about their simple tasks, the women in their black *mylayas*, a donkey, cow and buffalo under the trees, a well where the pottery jugs were filled. The lovely late afternoon light gave way to a glowing Nile sunset. Then a sliver of moon climbed over the spars of the feluccas astern, one of them with a cooking fire burning. Darkness fell. Dogs barked. We sat down to a roast of lamb, the last of our Cairo fresh meat. Win looked at his watch and across to Victor, "Dad, can I have the camel tonight?" Cairo really wasn't very far in miles.

chapter V

≈ An Egyptian Village

≈

We were pulling away from the bank next morning when we noticed something strange going on under the trees. From a five-foot-high tripod a black shape was suspended and a woman was jerking it back and forth.

"What is that black thing and what is she doing, Ahmed?"

"It's a goatskin and she's making butter," Ahmed informed us.

"Who are they and what are they doing?" the woman probably asked when the departing *Yankee* stopped, turned around, and pushed her bow into the bank again. This was our first sight of Egyptian churning. The farmers must be expert at skinning goats, and the skins must be strong and tough, for we saw them put to many uses, the equivalent of our indispensable plastic bags and bottles. I may add that we didn't try the butter, probably made from buffalo milk.

We had observed with interest that

The sakia is an advance on the shaduf. Animals instead of men provide the power. They turn a geared wheel which turns the vertical wheel with its loop of pots dipping water from the river and spilling it into an irrigation ditch at the top of the bank. (*Zacher*)

there was more than one way of raising water from the river. The ages-old shaduf is the simplest and most common means. But whereas the shaduf is arduous toil for man, the waterwheel or sakia shifts the work to cow or camel. It might be considered a modern improvement, as it does not appear in the ancient tomb paintings. The sakia is a beautiful old mechanism, fascinating to watch. The principle is that of the mill wheel, but the scoops, instead of being part of the rim, are twenty or thirty pottery jugs securely lashed to a loose loop of rope that runs over a vertical wheel. At the bottom the jugs dip under water and fill, then rise with the rotating rim, and, as they curve over the top, drop their water into the irrigation ditch at the height of the river bank. This vertical wheel is geared at the top to a horizontal one which is turned by a circle-plodding animal. The sakia is a lovely sight, compounded of the hand-hewn wheel, the hand-lashed buckets, the sound and sight of falling water, the slowness of the circling beasts, the creaking of wooden gears. A small boy is usually stationed at the sakia to see that the blindfolded animals keep going. It's a dull job, so we sometimes saw the animals at rest and the boy asleep.

About lunchtime a barge by the east bank looked like a convenient place for tying up, and we thought we'd explore the village. So far we had viewed the villages only from the stream. Sharom was very poor, very dirty, and full of flies. Even Ahmed seemed to think we really shouldn't be seeing this, and certainly no official would have sent us here. But the *Yankee* had the great advantage of being able to stop anywhere. We had the time and the curiosity.

Everyone was very close to the dirt of streets, floors, mud walls: animals, children in the dirt, hens making nests in the dirt. We felt like shrinking away from people and buildings in spite of ourselves. Most of the women covered their faces at our approach. There were some oranges and limes for sale and small, dirty, rotting tomatoes. A leg of veal (I guess) hung completely obscured by flies. Even the mosque seemed no better than the rest of the town. The happiest people in the village were the little girls. Not yet shrouded in black or subject to all the Moslem restrictions which apply during the years they might attract men, the little girls ran free in their shapeless, somewhat ragged, ankle-length dresses, usually red. They were pretty little girls, with their big brown eyes, smooth olive skin, and delicate hands. I was startled, however, at one task for those delicate hands. A water buffalo had dropped a large cake on a sandy path. While it was still steaming, a couple of little girls rushed gleefully to it and moulded it into shape to dry for fuel.

Seeing this poor village made us realize what Egypt is up against. Progress had begun in the form of a well and electricity, not in the houses of course, but as some bare bulb street lights. Sharom was the village I always had in mind as I asked questions through the following months.

"How do you ever know where to start?" I asked American missionaries.

"Well, we start on illiteracy," they answered.

"Do the people want to learn to read and write?"

"Many of them do. Of course the Moslem fatalism and resignation work against it. Moslems believe that three things are foreordained—a man's worldly success or failure, the size of his family, the time of his death. That attitude does not make people ambitious to get ahead.

"As for the living conditions that bother you, the dirt and the flies—the sun is a great healer and purifier. If it weren't for the Egyptian sun shining on them through almost every day, life would be even more precarious. And as for the dark, mud houses—people are outdoors practically all the daylight hours. The houses are just for the night."

I slowly learned more about the life of the fellahin, the Egyptian peasants, many of them the direct descendants of the ancients, with none of the Arab blood that came into Egypt within a generation after the death of the Prophet in 632. In some respects their way of life has not changed in thousands of years. Wooden plows, the methods of yoking and harnessing, the ways of drawing, lifting and redirecting water, the making of mud-bricks, the navigation of the Nile, the planting and harvesting—it is all much the same.

In ancient times the peasant was of course at the bottom of the ladder below king, priests, nobles, army, government officials, scribes, and artisans in their descending ranks. Like a serf he was usually attached to the land and its owner. But he was not a slave as captives of war were. Perhaps his lot was not too bad. In the scenes of everyday life as we find them carved on tomb walls, we see the peasants working under the overseer, that inevitable Egyptian character, in fields and vineyards. The peasant's lot undoubtedly depended largely on the particular overseer or proprietor he worked for. The landowner had certain responsibilities toward his peasants as well as rights over them. Now, we could not help thinking how good life in this beautiful valley could be if the population were at most a fifth of its present size.

But if the peasant had a fairly good life in ancient times, he surely did not in succeeding centuries. He was exploited, oppressed, and neglected under Arab and Ottoman rule. Even in Egypt's nineteenth-century westernization, the enlightenment, benefits, and wealth went to the upper classes. The rapidly growing numbers of fellahin did not touch the social conscience any more than did the Welsh miner or child laborer in the mills of the nineteenth-century industrialists. In fact, in Egypt children were especially good at cotton picking, and a large young family could work for parents who might be old or debilitated by chronic disease by their 30's. But the Moslem resignation that held them back also helped them to endure.

One of their greatest misfortunes was the corvée or forced labor of Turkish times. A "recruiting officer" would descend on a village and commandeer a certain number of young men for the army or for government building projects. Mothers would even blind their children to save them from the corvée. Blindness from ophthalmia is a common affliction in all villages, and is one of the government's prime targets now. But when we consider all the deprivation and suffering of the villages, we still have to realize that the miraculously good things in human nature are here too—love, family affection, sympathy, respect, hope, and resilience.

Nature has often been cruel in this beautiful valley, hemming it in by the uninhabitable deserts. There have been years when the Nile did not flood and renew the fields—extremely rare, but a terrible calamity. Another catastrophe, remembered nearly as long, is the almost unknown phenomenon of rain. Built for a dry climate, the mud bricks of the houses would soften and collapse. Structures safely placed above flood water are unprepared for water coming from above. Our familiar, cleansing rain must be as destructive as a tornado.

But even in this society, which seems to offer so little choice or opportunity, there are all kinds of change and unevenness. The older men learned the Koran as little boys: reciting, repeating, chanting in the school by the mosque. They performed the prescribed rituals of prayer—the preliminary ablutions, the correct placing of the feet and hands, even the position of the fingers; the use of the prayer rug or its approved substitute. They hoped to make their pilgrimage to Mecca. They lived within the strictest dictates of family life often till they were middle-aged, following the old rules, though these often led to quarrels over division of land, conflicts between parents and in-laws, extreme demands of filial duty, and the seclusion of women between childhood and well-settled matronly years.

Now their sons and grandsons are not so strict. Many boys wear Western clothes and go to Government schools. Some go off to the city, for one of many possible reasons: father may be too strict; brothers may have got all the land; returned city boys may tell of excitement and better money; a bright boy may want more education; the wife that is chosen for him may not be one he wants; the religious observances may seem tedious. And so village life begins to break up, not all at once, not everywhere, not evenly. Conservatives and traditionalists hold out. Family ties are strong. Religious training started young and is almost bred into people. Probably village life was never static, but changes come faster now.

The Government is trying to build a future for its millions. The foreigners have been expelled and the profits of the cotton crop and the Suez Canal now go to Egypt. The enormous land holdings have been divided up and many a fellah is at last out of debt and has enough land to live on. The Aswan High Dam will provide more arable land. Schooling will replace child labor. Clinics offer medical service to groups of five villages. Most Egyptians we met, rich or poor, dispossessed landowner, Government official, or undernourished fellah, wanted this same bright future for Egypt and its people, even though their ideas of means to this end might vary. But the goal will not be easy to reach in this modern world of haves and have-nots, of quarreling allies, of emerging nations, racial conflicts, and all the problems so familiar to us in the overcrowded world of imperfect human nature.

Gradually we were identifying ourselves with Egypt. The poor, dirty village of Sharom had shocked us into facing Egypt's gigantic problems and they were never out of mind entirely no matter how beautiful the scene, how impressive the ancient monument, how happy the cruise.

chapter VI

≈

Beni Suef
to Tell-
El-Amarna

≈

Minia is one of the more important Nile towns, especially as a cotton
center. That afternoon we came alongside the riverbank by the so-called Yacht
Club; it was really a rowing club. On
shore stood a little pavilion with Coca
Cola signs. Egypt has eliminated nearly
all consumer goods from hard currency
areas, needing every bit of exchange for
machinery and industry, but Coca Cola
is one of the few exceptions and the red
sign looked familiar, even with "Coca
Cola" written in Arabic.

Ahmed disappeared ashore and came
back with a report that we were to become accustomed to. "There's an old
friend of mine here, chap I went to
school with, and he'd like us to come up
to his house to tea and see what we want
to do tomorrow." Ahmed's friends, who
were practically family, were all over
Egypt and they always treated the
"Yankees" as though we were not much

more distantly related. This was Rauf Shadi, another good-looking charming Egyptian, with an attractive wife and a handsome little son, Amr; a daughter was away in school in Alexandria. Tea was served in an English garden where three or four dogs romped on the pleasant lawn. The Shadi family had been big landowners but their acreage had been greatly cut down in the land reform. Rauf was still in agriculture, however, and uttered no complaints.

We returned later to the big house for dinner. The buffet offered duck (shot that afternoon), steak, vegetables, a delicious rice dish, and for dessert kounafa, a sort of delicate shredded wheat and honey mixture. The finishing touch was pomegranate seeds floating in rose water!

Next morning Ahmed shepherded us to the Governorate of the province and again we went through the pleasant ritual of Turkish coffee. Mr. Shadi had been there earlier, and we were met by the local archaeologist, Michael Adly, and supplied with a station wagon. Among the "courthouse crowd" we met the *galabia*-clad, gentle-looking old mayor of Ashmunein, who invited us for tea later. This red carpet treatment, magically produced by Ahmed, is not our usual style elsewhere, but it was especially welcome in Egypt. We were spared the trail of clamorous "baksheesh" followers, the unwanted volunteer guides, the sellers of fake antiquities, beads, and skull caps, the requests for cigarettes, and the problem of whom to tip when and how much. We were seeing a new side of Egypt, and in this case we didn't mind being shielded from reality.

After a slow start through the crowded town, we enjoyed the mellow countryside. Once we passed a long row of houses with women jerking their goatskin churns in front of each one—and did not have to ask what they were doing. Mike, our archaeologist-guide, would not have been interested anyway, for this plump, smiling young man was much more concerned with the past than with the present. He took personal pride in every antiquity in Minia Province and seemed to feel personally honored to be associated with one of Egypt's most famous pharaohs, the controversial Akhnaton. We drove across the broad farmland onto the edge of the desert, and then climbed on foot to a boundary stela of this pharaoh's special domain.

Stela is a term of the Egyptologists for a commemorative stone, usually a vertical rectangle set into a wall, and carved with a picture or hieroglyphic inscription. Some are a part of temple architecture, others are stone signboards commemorating a special event, giving notice of some royal decree, or marking a particular site. Funerary stelae, of course, belong with tombs and tell of the deeds or importance of the dead person.

On temple wall sunken relief has survived the millenia to show us clear inscriptions and scenes of pharaohs and gods.

Here, under the protection of a slightly overhanging cliff, we could clearly recognize the outlines of the young pharaoh, Akhnaton, his beautiful wife, Nefertiti, and their daughters, carved in the fourteenth century B.C. Mike deciphered some of the hieroglyphics, but explained that this was only a scant introduction to what we would see and all he would tell us next day.

Then we drove further on the narrow hardtop road through the desert to Tuna-el-Gebel, and jumped more than a thousand years into Ptolemaic times, the period when the Greeks ruled Egypt. Alexander the Great had conquered the country, established the city which bears his name, and pushed eastward to his early death. In the division of his empire, Egypt fell to the general Ptolemy, who with his descendants ruled the country for 300 years. This Ptolemaic period was not an unhappy time for Egypt, and in religious matters the Greeks tolerantly imposed only a slight veneer onto the interesting culture they found.

There is no town now at Tuna-el-Gebel, merely a little rest house built originally for the archaeologists who excavated the fascinating ruins nearby. In 1919 the French scholar G. Lefebvre uncovered the tomb of Petosiris, which looks like a pretty little temple, nicely proportioned with its eight-columned front. The walls are covered with a record of Petosiris and how he and his peers lived. The scenes are still clear, with even some of the color remaining, of his workmen in the fields, his overseer tallying cattle, his grapevines heavy for the picking, his cow giving birth to a calf. Mike led us around the walls lovingly describing each familiar picture, translating the inscriptions in his special sing-song English, and making vivid for us this old, old biography.

Behind this building were lesser house tombs without the fascinating and informative decoration of Petosiris'. Mike particularly wanted us to visit Isidora's house, and told us her pathetic, romantic tale. Her father was a High Priest and she made the mistake of falling in love with a man of the people. Going to meet him one night, she was drowned in the Nile. Her father was very angry, but at the insistence of the people made a fine "funerary bed" for her. We climbed the marble steps to the entrance hall with shell design overhead and Mike indicated a small room to our left. There lay Isidora's mummy! We were staggered. After hearing her little story, to see her, Isidora herself, right here after 2000 years! The mummy wrappings were gone, but the brown skeleton and brown flesh, very dried out, were there with teeth, toes and fingers. It was one thing to see the famous mummies of a few pharaohs in the Cairo Museum, but it was something else to find a young heroine lying at our feet. Her father was in another room, but we

The mounds of Moslem family tombs in the vast cemetery near Minia are the echo in a different culture of the tombs of Ancient Egypt.

didn't feel much affection for him.

Mike was to amaze us still more, however. He led us to a building half buried in sand with a steel door which was unlocked by the gaffir, the guardian. This was the Ibitatium, an underground layout of streets and cross streets which had been excavated only a dozen years before; Mike himself had been on the project. Once an opening was found and the sand dug away, the streets were high and open, and no stooping was necessary. In this vast subterranean complex were buried not humans, but mummified ibises and baboons! Preserved in their little covered sarcophagi of bronze, stone, wood, or pottery, they were set by the thousands in niches in the walls. This was almost too strange to believe, even when Mike and the gaffir would open a little coffin and bring out a specially well-preserved specimen.

"There is one man buried here, and I will show you his tomb," Mike said, and we followed close behind him in the soft sand and semi-darkness. He led us to a small trap door, pulled it up, and started down a ladder ahead of us with only his flashlight to give any illumination. In the center of this sizable, deeper chamber, a human-size sarcophagus of stone contained the remains of the priest who had specialized in mummifying the birds and baboons. Several of them were buried with him.

It was all so unnatural, unearthly, and haunted that we did not doubt Mike even when he pointed out a corridor disappearing beyond the electric lights and said that it was believed to extend eight miles to the ruins at Ashmunein, the Greek Hermopolis. From very ancient times this was·the center of worship of the god Thoth with the ibis head. This Egyptian deity represented wisdom, writing, invention, languages, and the divisions of time. He was the patron of the scribes and therefore especially venerated by the ancient Egyptians, who had an extremely high regard for the written word, often endowing the mere outlines with magic properties. All those miles and miles of inscriptions that we would see before we left this country, and the many more miles we would never see, were a credit to Thoth. There is undoubtedly even more ancient material to be excavated under the Ptolemaic remains at Hermopolis.

Somehow the monkey or baboon became associated with Thoth and the ibis, but it would have grieved the wise god to see to what extremes his misled worshippers went in building the Ibitatium. I think it must have been the baboon association that led to such foolishness, because surely they are more mischievous than wise.

As we drove from Tuna-el-Gebel toward Ashmunein, we stopped to inspect two colossal baboon statues eighteen feet high. These are now held together by scaffolding having fallen and broken in the 1927 earthquake. Many of the granite columns of the agora (market place) at Ashmunein fell at that time, but others stand against the sky. The *galabia*-clad guards here carry shotguns and look rather fierce, while the village women do their washing in pools among the ruins. Mike pointed out the trefoil base of the sacred spot for baboon rites.

Then the guards indicated that we should go to the mayor's house. The station wagon left the ruins and the hardtop road, and seeming much too big, squirmed among the mudbrick houses of the large and lively village. We pulled up in front of the two-storied yellow plastered house of the mayor. He had expected us earlier and had been obliged to leave, but had told the armed guards to make sure we came to tea. So we sat on chintz-covered chairs with uneven springs, in a barnlike parlor, and were served biscuits and tea by a tall man who looked like a brigand. In *galabia* and turban, in a very belligerent style, he passed cookies and made the rounds with a little teapot, aiming it as though it were a gun at each empty cup. But I felt he was doing his best to treat us properly at the injunction of his master, the kindly-looking old man we had met that morning. Nasser looked down upon us from the wall with his sharky smile.

Mrs. Shadi told me that Minia had had a hairdresser for the last two years, and made an appointment for me next morning. He was not very quick, but he seemed to have all the business he could want, and I thought he could be considered a small private enterpriser in this socialist state. Two ladies already there were in Western dress and speaking French, but before I left two other customers came in shrouded in black and wearing anklets! It would hardly seem worthwhile having one's hair done if it was to be hidden under a black veil, but perhaps it was admired at home.

Mike rode along next day to show us the tombs at Beni Hassan. The men explored farther than Mildred and I did, and for an hour we were alone on board, tied up to the bank at the end of the village. It was the only trying hour I spent on the Nile. The *Yankee* had attracted all the small and teenage boys in Beni Hassan, and they were pests. They clamored for baksheesh, asked for cigarettes, felt of stanchions, jingled the lifelines, climbed on the rubrail, peered in the windows, and hung on the anchor rope. They were delighted if one of us would appear and order them off, so there was no use doing that except under the most severe provocation, such as a long pole coming in the forward porthole (too bad it couldn't hook anything), or hands on the boathook. This was all such small-time annoyance that it never seemed worthwhile to play our trump, which always worked like an ace. That was to bring the Very pistol on deck. This shoots only a signal flare, but looks terrifying with its big barrel, and the mere sight of it has always eliminated this sort of nuisance.

I am always sorry when I pass up an excursion. Through the years I have missed just a few good ones. A tourist who never weakens needs to be made of iron, and sometimes I am made of putty. So it is for Irving to tell of his visit to the Beni Hassan tombs:

~

Skirting the mudbrick walls, we slanted up the mountainside. A stiff half hour brought us to a row of thirty-nine tombs cut straight back into the vertical cliff wall. Steel protective doors were unlocked, and there our torches picked out the famous relief carvings cut into the solid rock walls. They had been only recently uncovered, after having been plastered and painted over by early Christians who lived and worshipped in these ancient tombs. Today these are among Egypt's best pictorial sources of information on ancient village life. Colorful ceremonies, showing us their specialized funeral practices, are depicted. But I particularly liked the agile dancing girls and the life-like heavyweight wrestlers. On the way back we skirted the village with the feeling that it was just too poor to bear looking at.

If a traveler can read only one book before visiting Egypt, I think that book should be James Breasted's classic, *A History of Egypt*. He leads the reader down the long line of history so that events fall into place and the pharaohs take on individuality. I suppose the favorite you pick reveals something about yourself. Mine was Thutmose III, a magnificent leader, a brave fighter, and a great ruler of the empire when it extended from beyond modern Khartoum to the Euphrates. To his ninetieth year he went campaigning to hold his vast domains together, and even in his mummy the fine drawn features show a man of keen intelligence.

But many particularly admire that interesting ruler, Akhnaton, sometimes called the first heretic or the first individual in history. Fourteen centuries B.C., he followed my hero by four generations and inherited the responsibility of holding together Egypt's vast empire. Moreover, he came to the throne at a time when the priesthood was very wealthy and powerful. So many gods were represented by jealous priests that the people found it hard to satisfy all the demands for sacrifices and contributions. The most powerful High Priest in the kingdom presided in the great Temple of Amon at Thebes (now Luxor) and his influence extended deep into politics as well as into religious matters.

The young, idealistic king took brave and drastic measures for the right as he saw it. He proclaimed an end to the worship of multiple gods, including the great Amon, closed their temples, dismissed their priests, and had their names obliterated in the thousands of places where they appeared on temple walls and in tombs. What the popular reaction was, how he succeeded in such a clean sweep, what confusion and disintegration this religious revolution brought about, is not fully described for us. But the young king carried out his convictions. The old capital at Thebes with all its reminders of Amon-worship became unbearable to him, and he resolved to break with the past in a more worldly way and move the capital away from all the associations he detested. He would build a new city where none had been, beautify it, and dedicate it to the One God in whom he believed, Aton, the beneficient sun. To him Aton was the source of all life and the benefactor of all men, guardian of mankind. Light and truth, concepts to which he came back again and again, proceeded from Aton. His thoughts traveled centuries ahead toward knowledge and science, and they penetrated deep into mysticism. He cannot be called the product of his time; he was a prophet.

The place he chose to build his beautiful city, Akhetaton ("Horizon of Aton"), was 300 miles north of Thebes, where the limestone cliffs curve away from the Nile. It was a beautiful city of palaces, gardens, light and sunshine, "great in loveliness, mistress of pleasant ceremonies, rich in possessions." It was a dream city, the creation of its inspired ruler, but it hardly outlived him. For it was founded on spirit alone and not on the realities of this world. While Akhnaton lit a light that shone way ahead of his time, he turned away from all the needs of his people, the advice of his counselors of state, the warnings of his generals, the pleas from the outposts. Nothing mattered but his vision of light and truth. He ruled for seventeen years, and then Akhetaton was abandoned, Aton worship was forgotten, and his name and his god's were obliterated as he had obliterated Amon's. The old priests came back, the capital returned to Thebes, the generals and statesmen picked up the pieces, the people returned to their familiar rites and the prophet was cursed as a criminal—which indeed he was, from some points of view. His dreams were too lofty for this world and the good vanished with the visionary.

The name of Akhetaton was wiped out then, and the village on the east bank of the river, near the barely discernible foundations of the ancient royal city, was given the present Arab name of Tell-El-Amarna. Mike went ashore to get donkeys for us to ride to the cliffs, where tombs of Akhnaton's courtiers are the only artistic remains of the period outside of museums.

There were more than enough donkeys with their owners on the bank and Mike expected trouble in making his choices for us. In the crush of business, arms and sticks were flailing about, and even after decisions were made the arguing and hitting would start up again. Our gentle Mike was shoving and thrusting in the melee. Finally we were all mounted and riding through the village. Saddles were cushions which had developed the shape of a donkey's back. My donkey was the only one with a bridle and reins, but we each had a donkey driver about ten years old. Win's was a pretty little girl with lovely teeth and smile, soft brown eyes, and a sweet manner. We called her Nefertiti. Like the little boys, she kept a near-running pace but managed to watch all of us and bestow her pretty smile with every glance.

It wasn't a long ride, just through the village, across that definite line where all green stops, and about a mile into the desert. At the foot of the cliffs we left our mounts and climbed to where the long-robed gaffir with gun, keys, and Coleman lantern was ready to unlock the great steel doors to the best tombs. The Department of Archaeology doesn't allow anyone in here without permission. Mike led us to the wall carvings of Akhnaton, his lovely Queen Nefertiti, his little daughters, his swift chariot, with the rays of the sacred sun reaching down to all. Horses, chariots, and people were all quite clear and Mike "read" the inscriptions to us. Akhnaton was his hero and he believed the world today would be better for his leadership. The carvings at Tell-El-Amarna have a life and realism and immediacy quite different from other Egyptian styles. In the young king's desire for truth and light, he encouraged the artists of his court to look clearly and represent with reality the people and things around them. That court 3200 years ago must have offered an unusual freedom to artists and craftsmen, a real joy to spirits that were kindred to their ruler's.

The chambers were high and wide. The strong beam of the lantern held high illuminated the old carvings. Win posed little "Nefertiti" just inside its rays, and her eyes reflected her fears inside the great tomb which she had probably never visited before. For me, there was a world of difference between turning the pages to find Fig. 157 in a book on Egypt and being right here in the *Yankee*, riding a donkey to the cliffs, climbing to the tombs, and following Mike around the walls. This was not just learning and seeing, but feeling as well.

chapter VII

Assiut and Balliana

In a ten mile stretch south of Tell-El-Amarna, the *Yankee* found the Nile scene quite changed. The land no longer spread out flat on either side. Steep rock cliffs of Gebel Abu Foda rose to an average height of 400 feet on the port hand. There were many dark rectangles of open tombs in the cliff wall, but as none were closed with steel doors, I presumed that they had either been fully investigated or long since robbed.

Then we noticed long ropes hanging here and there and tiny figures on the face of the cliff. Black splotches, like thrown inkwells, pockmarked the white-faced limestone. Careful study with the binoculars gave us the clue.

"I know what the story is," Irving said. "Those dangling men are drilling the rock and placing more black powder charges in their mountainside quarry. The black spots show where previous charges were set off."

Close by we now saw camel-loads of gleaming white limestone rock approaching the river where it was stacked in the holds of feluccas. This was cliffside mining.

A strong wind had come up, and our blue sky for once had clouded over. Ahmed told us how, on his first ocean voyage to England, he used to think the steward's daily greeting of "Fine day, sir" was absurd. Fine days are the rule in Egypt. Nowhere have I seen such a perfect climate as the Nile valley's in winter. The days are summery without being too hot and the nights are cool to cold. The light for photography can be depended on day after day, and in the late afternoon it takes on a special quality that mellows and deepens the whole scene beyond its midday quality. Sunsets sometimes had real postcard colors, sometimes just furnished a gentle pink to lavender glow to set off the silhouettes of palm trees and homing workers. Then we found there was a sort of second sunset in the afterglow, when the light seemed to brighten again with a change of effect that we always watched for and always marveled at. Moonlight on the river was lovely too, but the nights were usually too cold to make us want to linger on deck.

With plenty of time and a suitable boat, we felt somewhat related to the dahabias. A wealthy Victorian family would take one of these house-boats and set out with parents, children, nanny and governess, Nile captain and crew. The dahabias were as much as 100 feet long and carried sail on two masts. When the wind dropped or came from ahead, the crew would row with long heavy sweeps. Curious arrangements for a dozen or more oarsman were seen well forward, where a low deck had removable hatches concealing long low seats. Rowing these huge dahabias hour after hour seems like the final faint echo of the galley slaves.

The spacious quarters built the ships up high above the water, but they drew very little below. Sometimes two or three would travel in company, meet and part, exchange dinners and teas. The cook and stewards provisioned the ships and must have somehow served ample Victorian meals. I wondered how they planned, how much fresh food they bought, what kind of meat they got, and whether supplies sometimes ran low. The dahabias had arrangements in some towns to use the local bakers' ovens and would work all night to put in a stock of bread that would last a week or so till the next baking town. We liked to speculate on dahabia life, the ladies in long skirts, the lord-and-master gentlemen, the decorous romances of the Nile, the floating bits of England in a strange land.

One fascinating source of information on dahabia life is an account of a voyage in 1874, *A Thousand Miles up the Nile* by Amelia Edwards. On her travels Miss Edwards brought along a drawing board, a most observing eye, a ready pen, and a keen intelligence. An early amateur archaeologist, in writing her book she has lured many others to Egypt and to the inexhaustible study of its past. What began as a pleasure trip for her became an absorbing study, and on returning to England she founded the Egypt Exploration Fund and the Chair of Egyptology at London University. We later met the present incumbent. When we found travelers who were seriously interested in Egypt and well informed and who could talk creditably with archaeologists, they always knew "Amelia". In her clear, intelligent record she still travels with those who want to know Egypt, and her long-skirted ghost has joined those of the pharaohs around the tombs and ruined temples.

Emerging from the lock at the Assiut Dam, we found two dahabias tied up by the town. The best place for us to moor was alongisde one of them. Only a caretaker was living aboard, but he was happy to take our lines and have the *Yankee* for company. Then Ahmed found that he knew the owner of the other dahabia, that it was still livable and, though it no longer traveled up and down the Nile, that it served as a riverside cottage where its owner, Mr. Khayat, entertained his friends. Ahmed came back—of course, we were now saying—with an invitation for us to come over for a drink. White paneled walls, rows of cabin doors down a long corridor, dining room with Victorian sideboard, drawing room with bric-a-brac, comfortable chairs and intriguing photographs of family and friends, bells everywhere to ring for service, and aft a large semicircular cabin with tall wardrobes, large hat shelves, and curving windows instead of portholes at the stern—the whole thing was a period piece.

≈

The next day was Thanksgiving and I had been wondering for days how I was going to get a turkey. Ahmed seemed to be sure there would be one in Assiut, but we had arrived too late on Wednesday to get one that day. I urged Ahmed to try to locate a turkey as early as possible. My anxieties did not do justice to Ahmed's resourcefulness and connections. In mid-morning he reported that a turkey would arrive—and it would arrive all cooked! This was indeed a cause for thanksgiving on my part.

About one o'clock a twelve-pound bird was delivered on a platter, shining brown and hot, surrounded by delicious Egyptian rice. Roasted sweet potatoes came from one of the street vendors. I had only to cook fresh beans and open a can of cranberry sauce. With the turkey had come about two dozen little doughnut-shaped sweets which we enjoyed to the vanishing point. On subsequent New England Thanksgivings I will always remember Assiut and Ahmed's kind friend.

Assiut was the largest town in Upper Egypt until Aswan's recent rapid growth and also had a large proportion of the Coptic population. Egypt's Copts are the descendants of the Christians to whom St. Mark brought the Gospel and who were not later converted to Islam. Comprising seven per cent of the population, they are, on the whole, a proud, hard-working, and noticeably prosperous group. Copts have often held important offices in government and have been outstanding business men. However, the present national constitution states that Islam is the religion of the country, so the Copts may come up against discrimination before long.

While Irving filled our tanks with good drinking water from a convenient pipe on shore, I went marketing with Ahmed. When we were in Minia, a servant of the Shadis had bought fresh food for us, but that was gone now. We set off with horse and carriage on a marketing expedition as interesting as any in my experience of the Orient or Europe. The stuffing was breaking out of the carriage seats in places. Our driver was very dark and wore an old sun helmet. A small boy in dirty *galabia* rode with him. A little green felt duck outlined in yellow blanket-stitch was tacked on the back of the driver's seat. I wondered who could have made that duck.

We would see much more of Assiut on our return journey. Its name is hardly changed from the ancient Egyptian, Siut. In those days it was the capital of the nome (province) sacred to Wep-wawet, the wolf of the desert. The adaptable Greeks therefore called the town Lycopolis, incorporating their word for wolf. The cultivated area is broad here, extending 12½ miles altogether from the Libyan or western desert to the Arabian desert to the east. The town had always been an important terminus of the caravan route to three important oases in the Libyan Desert.

On a drive around town with the Director of Youth and Recreation, he had showed us the grounds of the new University and many imposing mansions of formerly wealthy families; most of the houses now stand empty or have been converted to other uses, but they are magnificent even in their decline. We had met the Americans at the Presbyterian Mission school and hospital which had served Assiut for many years. It was a well run institution which represented a large investment in both money and dedicated effort, but the school and most of its land had now been taken over by the Egyptian Government and no one could say how long it would last in its divided form. The missionaries, however, some of them second generation in Egypt, did not seem perturbed. The mission had weathered troubles in the past, and they intended to go on with their work as long as they were allowed to stay.

Assiut is a busy, crowded town. Women in black, quite a few of them veiled; urchins at every elbow; traffic of horse cabs, donkeys, camels; hundreds of patient people sitting with their bundles on the railroad platform and around the station; a huge dummy of a rocket eighty feet high in the station square with a couple of recumbent shapes asleep below it; tiny niches of barber shops; camera shops (mostly for identification photos); a man being shaved in the street; scores of orange vendors with carts piled high; carts selling hot roasted sweet potatoes; jewelry shop windows filled with thin gold jewelry dangling behind the glass and closely examined by women and little girls; an open space for a Shell gas station; the flat round bread piled on trays carried on boys' heads; a few overweight women in Western dress, occasional men in Western suits, but mostly a population of black *mylayas, galabias,* carelessly twisted turbans, brown felt skullcaps and fezes—that is Assiut.

The butcher shop was literally a hole in the wall, with a clamoring crowd in front of it, but somehow Ahmed and I succeeded in buying a couple of legs of lambs in the melee. That is one cut of meat that is always easy to recognize. Fruit and vegetables were plentiful—big, delicious oranges, bananas, grapefruit, carrots, beans, peas, zucchini, perfect tomatoes, and the best cucumbers I have ever eaten, with no bitterness to them at all. Lettuce and raw cabbage have a bad reputation in Egypt so I never served them, for our good health was essential to the Nile trip. Tomatoes I always peeled.

"I'm sorry to drag you around for all this shopping, Ahmed. It always takes longer than you think," I said apologetically. "I can't imagine how I could do it alone." As in the Orient, I could point, of course, and I could have learned to count in Arabic, but there is something overwhelming and even a bit frightening at times in the rough crowds of Arab towns.

"I'm enjoying it really. I've never done this sort of thing and I'm learning," protested Ahmed. What a nice reply! "We'll try the Co-op for the other things."

The Cooperative stores are government-run and newly built, not exactly gleaming, but more orderly than the "independent groceries" which despite a fairly good front usually reach far back into darkness, dust, and mouldy merchandise. What the Co-op may have is never certain, but this day we were delighted to get six dozen eggs. Egyptian eggs are very small, and outside of Cairo cost between two and three cents apiece, and I never got a bad one. We also picked up some of the crackers flavored with cumin which we had found very good. We never tried to buy meat in the Co-ops, for there were always long, long lines of customers and the meat never looked very appealing. We finished our shopping and Ahmed went through the slow process of paying. The clerk laboriously made out the sales slip in duplicate, Ahmed took them both to the cashier for further notation and the filing of one, paid, got his change and returned with the other to the clerk who checked it intently, put it somewhere, and finally handed us our purchases. We returned to the *Yankee* with the carriage loaded to capacity front and back. Meanwhile, the laundry had been delivered, well done and cheap.

There was one more job before we left Assiut. The kind-faced old caretaker on the dahabia alongside had a thickly bandaged finger which he wanted Victor to look at. He had cut off the end of it accidentally, and had had one treatment at the hospital, but without knowing that Victor was a doctor, seemed to feel that our foreign treatment would be good for his finger. Victor of course did a professional job, and the old man's pride in his handsome bandage and gratitude to us shone from his eyes plainer than all his words. We shoved off and resumed our course southward.

We sighted the bridge at Sohag at 1:30, just in time to watch it close! When could we expect it to open again? We tied up and found all offices closed till four o'clock. By that time Ahmed had made some official connections, but it hardly seemed worth going on at that hour. The officials graciously sent word they would open the bridge any time we wished, so we said 6:30 A.M.

A big side-wheeler, the *Kased Kheir*, came downstream and tied up on the other side of the bridge. With the glasses we could make out the beautiful gold scroll work on her paddle boxes and her old-style elegance. She had once been Farouk's river yacht, but was now in the tourist business.

Passing through the bridge soon after 6:30 the next morning, we had a better look at the handsome *Kased Kheir* and then went on to our objective, the town of Balliana, which we reached by 12:30. Word of our coming had been sent ahead and, as usual, people there had expected us earlier. Against a 2-knot current our progress was about 6 m.p.h., whereas people ashore always expected the *Yankee* to do about 20. However, we were in time for a very pleasant visit with the mayor in his office, over tall glasses of delicious fresh orange juice instead of the usual Turkish coffee. We then piled into a car he provided and drove the eight miles to the rest house by the Temple of Abydos where lunch was served.

There we met one of the most remarkable people in Egypt, Om Seti, a stalwart old girl with short, straight, sparse hair, shapeless dress, heavy sandals and a bright green bandanna. The British occasionally produce a dauntless woman who in some far corner of the earth becomes a stronger and truer disciple of an Eastern religion than its local adherents, or an etymologist more at home in a jungle than the natives themselves, or a desert traveler more enduring than an Arab, or an archaeologist closer to the men of antiquity than their own descendants. These remarkable women have often been scoffed at, but they rise to a true, if eccentric, greatness which commands the respect of the conventional world. Such a one was Om Seti, meaning Mother of Seti, for she had named her son after the great pharaoh whom she most admired.

Now over sixty, plain and indifferent to clothes (but not more so than many tweedy Englishwomen), Om Seti had come to Egypt thirty years before as the wife of an Egyptian teacher. She was soon attached to the momentous archaeological digging near the great pyramids and Sakkara, and she refers offhand to a long camel ride when her son was three weeks old, and when he played around the pyramid tombs. The son is now grown and working in oil-rich Kuwait, and she and the husband have long since been divorced.

The real love affair of Om Seti's life has been with Egypt and with Seti I, who lived fourteen centuries before Christ. She has never left this country since she first arrived, has become an Egyptian citizen, and for the last eight years has lived in the village of Arabeh El Madfouna close by the great temple of Abydos. She now holds an archaeological post under the Egyptian Government.

With Om Seti as our guide, we would be shown the temple to the greatest possible advantage. Breasted has called it the "noblest monument of Egyptian art still surviving in the land." An outstanding Chicago archaeologist whom we met later had devoted years of his life to other great temples, but said that Abydos was the one he would most want to see.

In the desert to the north we could discern the grave mounds of a time much much older than the New Kingdom time of Seti. Since the First Dynasty Abydos had been considered the most important burial place in Egypt because here Osiris himself was believed interred. At first the great pre-pyramid pharaohs were buried here. Then nobles too were brought to rest near Osiris, the Lord of the Underworld. In later years, those who could not be entombed at Abydos often had their mummies brought here,

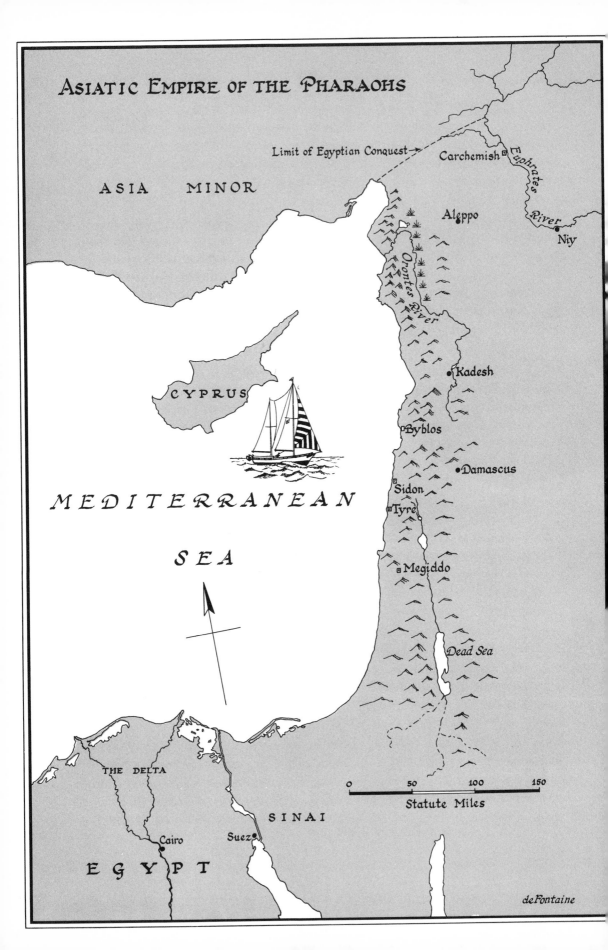

to derive the benefits of coming close to Osiris before they were placed in their own permanent tombs elsewhere. Abydos is the oldest continually sacred place we know of in Egypt. I was tempted to walk across the desert to those most ancient graves, but Om Seti told me I would find nothing except the outline which was just as visible from a distance. Besides, there was much to admire in Seti's temple, which has stood here 3300 years.

Following Akhnaton, the dreamer, who had let his empire reach the brink of disintegration through neglect, and his young son Tutankhamon, who had ruled only a few years before an early death, the great general Horemheb became pharaoh. Horemheb managed to pull the kingdom together again, restore the temples of Amon, obliterate all reference to Akhnaton and Aton, reorganize the government, codify new laws, develop new sources of revenue, set up a strong administration, and even leave a reputation as a reasonable sort of humanitarian. But he was not able to reestablish Egypt's power abroad as it had extended in the glorious days of Thutmose III, who had set his boundary markers on the banks of the Euphrates.

After a brief reign by the elderly Ramses I, the brave and capable Seti I took up the task where Horemheb had left off. In the great old manner he led his armies into Palestine (this may have been close to the time of the Exodus), reasserted Egypt's power, collected tribute, fought decisive battles, and staged a triumphal return. The celebrations extending from the eastern border of the Delta all the way to Thebes (still ahead of us upstream), were such as Egypt had not seen for two generations. Seti did not reestablish Egyptian supremacy all the way to the Euphrates, but he collected tribute from vassals as far as the Orontes—especially the valuable timber from Lebanon, which again arrived in Egyptian ships for all the needs of this unforested country. He also quelled Libyan disturbances to the west and Nubian rebellion to the south, continued work on the great temples at Luxor and Karnak, laid out his own royal tomb, and at Abydos built the splendid temple to Osiris. Om Seti had certainly chosen no minor hero.

She led us around "her" temple, pointing out the beauty of some of the finest relief carving in Egypt, which showed Seti making offerings to Osiris and presenting the image of truth, with representations of the graceful sun boat in which souls traveled to Osiris' Kingdom of the Dead, and innumerable minor charming bits which she loved. With an encyclopedia of Egyptology in her head, she could answer our questions, straighten out the fragmentary knowledge we had acquired, and read off the lines of hieroglyphs as if they were the daily newspaper, and yet she never hesitated to say when she didn't know the answer. As we admired the sureness of line in the sculpture, Om Seti pointed out, "This is called 'relief en creux.' You can see it is different from bas relief. That wears down more readily and would probably not have stood the ages so well. This is a sunken relief. Its highest surfaces are just flush with the wall and its deepest cutting goes in several inches. You will see this all over Egypt."

Aside from splendid figures of gods and pharaohs, the walls showed scenes from everyday life, and Om Seti particularly pointed out a butchering episode where the figures, being of lowly people, were shown in the round. "The Egyptians could give a three-dimensional quality to their figures, you see," she said. "But it was their convention as far back as we know anything of them to show faces and bodies in profile, but eyes and shoulders facing front. Some of today's artists have come around to the same method of portraying what they know is there and want to show, not just what a viewer can see from his one position. This style did not make their drawing any less skillful or less observant of reality. In fact, I think it enabled them to tell us more about a subject." We did find that the more we looked at Egyptian art, the less we were bothered by this traditional style.

It was here that for the first time we experienced the incomparable sensation of walking into a hypostyle hall, among the tremendous, awe-inspiring columns so huge and overpowering that they make a mere human feel tiny and insignificant. "Hypostyle," a word which one meets constantly in guidebooks, simply means "upon columns." The hypostyle hall, beyond the outer courts, was the first part of the temple roofed over, the huge ceiling slabs resting upon the columns.

If the modern visitor to the temple, with no belief in the old gods, feels as though he were something microscopic, what awe and perhaps fear must have stirred the people of old as they brought their offerings to the gates. Coming no farther than the courtyard, dressed in their whitest linen garments, they would watch the king and priests enter the enormous hall and move into the broad shadows. Even the king, I think, needed strong nerves to perform his part with composure among twenty-four immense close placed columns.

In this temple there are two great halls. In the first one, about 150 by 36 feet, stand 24 columns in pairs with papyrus bud capitals. Priestly processions would move down the aisles, through the seven doors and into the second hall, with its 36 great columns marking the way to the seven sanctuaries behind. Om Seti, I am sure, could put it all back 3300 years and in her mind's eye witness the great ceremonies that took place in such a colossal setting. Where we marveled at the lovely remains of red and blue color on the fine reliefs, she could see all the bright colors, the long-gone woodwork, the splendid costumes with much white predominating, the regal figure of the king wearing the high double crown of Upper and Lower Egypt, the slender figure of his son who became the famous Ramses II, and most of all the rich glitter of gold so lavishly used on walls and statues, doors, screens, ornaments, jewels, and clothes. Only the greatest, most absolute kings with unlimited wealth in people and gold and the most powerful priesthood could conceive and erect buildings on this scale. Our first experience of one of Egypt's great temples had been deeply impressive.

We drove away from Abydos with the sunset light spreading over the desert around the temple and then over the little fields divided by irrigation ditches, interrupted by the temporary huts of golden straw, and quietly animated at this time of day by the homeward-bound figures of men and beasts. For several miles our eyes rested on almost nothing that wouldn't have looked the same 3300 years ago. It was dark when we reached the outskirts of town.

That night we were invited for dinner by a charming young man, Makram Habashi, whom we had met at the mayor's office. Ahmed, Win, and Victor decided to dress in the handsome *galabias* of beautiful Egyptian cotton which they had had made in Minia. When they climbed up the river bank in the dark ahead of Mildred, Irving, and me in Western clothes, they found Makram, the mayor and the chief of police waiting for them with the car. At the approach of the *galabia*-clad figures, these latter thought they were about to be approached with some petition and tried to ignore the importuners. By the time we arrived all of them were laughing at each other. If the party needed any ice-breaker, this was it.

A large and pleasant apartment was tucked away on a canal-side street where we would never have expected to find the nicely furnished rooms with welcome open fire, an attractive roof garden for shaded meals in summer, and to our great surprise a blue-tiled bathroom like an American advertisement. Everyone spoke English except Makram's mother, a devout, conservative lady of the old school, dressed in black with a small black bandanna hiding all her hair, a severe effect offset by a warm, kindly smile and hospitable manner. Dinner started with an Egyptian specialty, kishk, a soup made from yogurt and wheat with crusty fried croutons floating on top. Next came scalloped veal, fresh peas, and then marvelous little roasted pigeons stuffed with the same flavorful rice which had accompanied our Thanksgiving turkey. Dessert was a large and perfect creme caramel. I know that all this excellence was due to Madame Habashi's personal supervision in the kitchen.

Next morning we were shown Balliana's cotton ginning mill. But first in the manager's office we were served Turkish coffee, in dainty cups handed around by a smiling giant who used to be part of Farouk's guard. I gather he is now employed as much for his grand stature as for his skill with coffee cups.

None of us had ever seen Eli Whitney's invention at work in our own country, but I doubt if the scene there is as attractive as in Balliana. Long rows of young, black-clad girls stand behind the machines as though each were playing on the keyboard of a clavichord. Most of them are pretty and willing to smile at visitors, and they giggle among themselves. The mill works around the clock, but only one shift has girls, and I was surprised to find even this feminine labor force in Upper Egypt. I got the impression the girls were really enjoying their "careers." Yachtsmen all know the quality of the long staple Egyptian cotton which before synthetics made the best and most expensive sails. Exported in bales, it was the foundation of many large fortunes in Egypt. Now the textile is woven here too. The cloth of ancient times was linen. Wool was considered debased, at least around the temples. Silk came in with the Persians, and cotton was introduced in Roman times.

chapter VIII

Nag Hamadi
to Luxor

We progressed upstream from Balliana in the afternoon and next morning went through the lock by the Nag Hamadi barrage in company with a felucca loaded high with straw. Irving always helps another boat whenever there is a chance or a need, so we towed the felucca out of the lock till it could again catch the wind in the river. Otherwise her crew must go ashore, harness themselves to towing lines, and pull the boat upstream till they can get aboard and set her sails. A felucca sailor has a hard life, climbing aloft on the picturesque but awkward yards, some as long as 130 feet. It was always a marvel how they climbed and handled sail at the same time and also managed their *galabias*. One hand for yourself and one for the ship is usually a foolish idea under sail where both hands are generally needed for the ship. But on the Nile, what hand for the *galabia?* The teeth have to help out at

99

times by holding up the hem.

The tillers on the great unpainted rudders take all a man's weight when the sails are pulling. There is no such thing as a bunk below—just a place on deck to roll up, and in what on these cold nights? There is no galley stove, no galley, just some cold food—beans, onions, and dry bread—or sometimes a small fire in a sandbox on deck. And what is the felucca economy? One is usually owned by several people, often related, but it was plain to see that whatever the fee for cargo carrying, there was not much profit in it. Still, Irving or any sailor would say that life was better out on the river than tied to a little plot of land. Some of the feluccas had fancifully painted bows, and perhaps the men who thus lovingly ornamented their ships were the ones who found satisfaction in the life of the Nile, saw the beauty in the passing scene, and felt the joy in being afloat that any craft can offer to one who responds to it.

No flight of imagination could attribute such sensitive feelings to the delegation which met us at Nag Hamadi: small-town officials well down in the ranks of bureaucracy. There were ten of them who never left us for the duration of our stay. First they led us to the former palace of Prince Yussef Kamal, an uncle of Farouk, and, shoving about and often standing in front of us, made it somewhat difficult for us to see what they were pointing out—the carved Moorish arches, the red and blue divan covers, the carved openwork doors, arabesque inlay of ivory and mother-of-pearl, the huge, handsome brass braziers for heat, and the prince's possessions left behind. He had been a famous big-game hunter and, though his guns had of course disappeared, our escorts brandished the remaining spears, his dress sword, and, laughing uproariously, one lone golf club.

Our escorts were not very gracious either over coffee served on the palace verandah, but lolled about in the peeling wicker chairs talking loudly. We appreciated them more, however, in the excited crowd celebrating the festival of a local sheikh, or holy man. The streets were so jammed with the mob that our two cars could barely progress, horns held down the whole time. We soon got out of them and our hosts ran interference to get us onto a rise of ground from which we could take pictures. A sea of people seethed below us, the young ones jumping up and down in a sort of dance, everyone shouting, sometimes "Nasser, Nasser, Nasser, Nasser, Nasser," holding his picture aloft, waving canes, and one young man holding high his most valuable possession, a big radio. Best of all were the camels decked with bright tassels, gaudy neck scarves, and carrying in big square baskets on their backs ten or a dozen gaily dressed children in holiday spirits. Dust

Feluccas' bows are sometimes fancifully painted. The steel strut in the foreground is one of *Yankee*'s two "tail feathers" which hold up her fiber glass dinghy and hold down the mizzenmast backstays.

hung in the air, and we were grateful for the rise of ground which kept us out of the crush while we could take in the excitement.

Our guides got us out of the crowd with the tactics that had got us in, and took us to visit the large sugar mill of Nag Hamadi. Surely the capable looking manager was rather bewildered at our arrival, since this was the month the mill was regularly closed for overhaul before the cutting of the cane. And surely our hosts must have known this. But the futil visit was carried off by a round of Cokes out of the bottle in the manager's office, and we were led on to the Club for lunch.

We were really ready to get back aboard the *Yankee* and be on our way, but lunch ashore seemed to be required. Little did we realize that lunch would involve a two-hour wait by the side of the swimming pool, which with the clubhouse dated back to the days of British management of the sugar mill. The kitchen apparently didn't start its preparations till guests arrived. For an hour we did our best conversationally, but hunger and time induced a glassy-eyed torpor. Every few minutes one man would rouse himself and say to us loudly and emphatically, "Welcome." We would force a smile of acknowledgement. Then all of us would relapse.

Time apparently was nothing to our hosts. What were their working hours? What work would all ten of them be doing if they were not entertaining us? Then we learned that they had understood we were coming the night before, had gone through this same preparation at the Club and eaten the dinner without us. It didn't seem to matter. We almost felt that nothing mattered by the time we sat down to spaghetti, chicken, canned peas, a salad (uneaten), and fruit.

I tried to sort out in my mind the right place in the scheme of things for the wealthy departed prince, the seething mob in the streets, the British families who had lived in the compound by the Club, and the well-intentioned but boorish new officials. I found no quick or easy answer, but it certainly felt good to be back on the *Yankee* and out in the river.

Shortly before dark, the unusual formation of a sort of bay appeared to port and we went to have a look, sounding our way and always getting plenty of water. A big irrigation ditch cut into the shore and Irving kept going till we were actually in that ditch, still afloat.

"How about tying up here for the night, Ahmed? The *Yankee* in an irrigation ditch would be something new."

Ahmed looked worried. It was farther from a village and any authority than he liked. A lone Arab squatted on the bank. In other parts of the world we like the lonely spots.

"I don't think it would be advisable, Skipper," Ahmed objected uncertainly. He always felt responsible for our safety. Maybe one Arab could suddenly become fifty. "These people are so terribly poor," he explained. "They might take just anything, whether they wanted it or not or even knew the use of it. There is no protection here. A raid could happen." Could it or was he unnecessarily worried? We had no way of judging, but we didn't want to give Ahmed a sleepless night, so we moved out into the river and anchored.

It was strange that that should have been the night when we all roused in alarm as a vessel collided with the *Yankee*. Ahmed and Irving with the Very pistol got on deck at the same moment, in time to see hands reach out of the blackness to our stanchions.

"What do you want?" Ahmed called out in Arabic as Win and Victor appeared to back up our defense.

If they were marauders, they were easily intimidated. "We just wanted to see what it was," came the gruff reply. It was plain enough that the *Yankee* was a boat at anchor. No collision was necessary to find that out. The boatload drifted away and we went back to bed, but I'm sure Ahmed didn't go to sleep immediately.

≈

Here the Nile takes a course almost due east, making its farthest reach toward the Red Sea. From the provincial capital of Kena the old routes start through the Eastern Desert, and at the time of the pilgrimage to Mecca this is a crowded place. In the Middle Kingdom gold was brought in to Koptos, just a little farther south, from the mines in the Eastern Desert. The vizier of the nome himself was sent to convoy it with a strong military escort. Even earlier the caravans to the harbor of Wadi Gasus had established wells and stations on the five-day desert crossing. Here too the caravans formed for expeditions to the Red Sea shore, whence they set out for the fabulous land of Punt, now called the Somali Coast. On their return, the Loptos people would be the first to glimpse the treasures of incense, ivory, panther skins, even seedlings of unfamiliar trees and plants, and hear tales of strange fish, wild animals, and the primitive black people who lived in grass huts.

At our Kena mooring we had front row seats for an interesting late afternoon show when the women came to the river for water. An empty jug would be balanced horizontally on the head; a full one just slightly tilted from the vertical. Our calculations made a full one hold about three gallons and weigh between 30 and 35 pounds. Since the women have developed strong neck muscles and are used to walking, the chore wouldn't be bad if it weren't for the costume. But the yardage of black *mylaya* must be held around the person and over the head at all times, even when rinsing out a jug in the river, filling it, adjusting the doughnut-shaped rag on top of the head, and raising the heavy jug to sit on it. The operation isn't so difficult if a friend is handy to set the jug on one's head, but often it has to be done alone.

We also watched some washing going on, but saw no soap. The clothes were dipped and sloshed about and then wrung out. In many villages where clean filtered water has been piped to a central faucet, the people still prefer to get the more flavorful untreated water of the Nile, and we could testify that the river was used for every imaginable purpose.

"I'm going to get some cheesecake pictures from the bowsprit," Win announced. "Cheesecake of ankles!" He wouldn't get anything more. At least the ankles were set off by interesting silver anklets.

We understood that Kena was a center of pottery, so on Ahmed's usual prompt visit to headquarters he expressed our wish to see the potters. The mayor was not very eager to have us do so, as the proposed "factory" where the potters will work is not yet built and they are still carrying on in their own mudbrick houses. He would much rather have had us visit an agricultural experiment station. It took all Ahmed's powers of persuasion to convince him that we really wanted to see the pottery making, that we would even insist, after all the felucca loads we had seen, that we enjoyed and admired that side of Egypt, that they should not try to hide things of interest, that some backward methods would in fact show us why they were ambitious to modernize, and that in pictures this would look like art to admire rather than a primitive method to be despised. So a car and driver appeared.

We found the potters scattered through a village behind Kena, and and one was a particular joy to watch. An assistant brought in the clay, pounded the air out of it, and kept the potter supplied with water. The potter sat with his back to the dark wall, a long shaft of light slanting in from a high opening. His foot worked the treadle that turned his wheel, and his long slender fingers quickly shaped the damp clay into lovely forms, a process that always seems miraculous to me. With perfect timing of feet and hands, skillful drawing out of his material, and a cut with one motion of a string, a perfect pot was made in a minute or two and set beside dozens of others. The next one was already forming on the wheel. The slender young potter had an interesting, sensitive face with high cheekbones and pointed eye brows. His small white turban set off the rich color of his skin and almost shone against the dark background.

We drove to the end of the village to see the firing process. Stoked with straw, the ovens gave off great puffs of thick black smoke and cast infernal light on the stokers.

Then we went dutifully to see the experimental farm, but no one was working there that afternoon, and the various fields growing quietly by themselves had none of the appeal of the potters at their wheels.

In the morning we took the *Yankee* across the river to the village, where we could get donkeys for the three-mile ride to the Temple of Dendera. We advanced from the fields of bright green and dark earth over the line into the desert. Ahead rose the imposing temple entrance gate and the front of massive columns, and as a backdrop in this part of the valley are the lovely pinkish desert mountains.

Since this temple was sacred especially to Hathor, the ceremonies here must have been joyful, since among her many attributes as goddess of the sky, mother figure, and nurse of the king, she was also the goddess of happiness and love, in whom the Greeks found an identity with their Aphrodite. The Egyptian pantheon includes a tremendous variety of gods. The earliest religious thinking was naturally animistic. When some animal attribute seemed greater than human, like the swiftness of the hawk, the beneficence of the cow, the fierceness of the wolf, or the deadliness of the crocodile, the Egyptians would graft these animals' heads onto manlike figures to portray their deities. Through the centuries they continued to identify certain gods with certain localities and men felt a particular attachment to their own. A few gods became "national": Osiris of the Underworld; Amon, the Sun; Hathor, the mother; Horus, the good son. But on the whole the gods' attributes and functions overlapped in a great confusion, and since the ancients never felt the need to straighten out their thinking in these matters, we found that the more we learned about the gods, the less we approached any order or consistency.

As we discussed alternate interpretations, we approached the entrance gate, which rose 70 feet high. We were studying its inscriptions when long-robed figures surprisingly appeared, bearing trays of teacups and two bright blue enamel teapots. So before going any farther we found ourselves seated incongruously on some ruins in the forecourt, teacups in hand. But the refreshment was a welcome finish to the donkey ride.

The Temple of Dendera is one of the best preserved in Egypt, its present Ptolemaic form built on the foundations of a temple of the Old Kingdom (2280-2780 B.C.) and subsequent structures. Its seven-foot diam-

eter columns do not have the usual lotus or papyrus capitals, but are
called sistrum columns and are surmounted by the face of Hathor. The sistrum was a musical instrument rather like a rattle, usually carried by
women, and its shape was easily adapted to a column.

This enormous hall was roofed with sculptured stone, still clearly
showing the ancients' explanations of the heavens: Nut, goddess of the sky,
pictures of the Zodiac, sun boats, and figures of the stars and the hours,
differentiated for day and night. Beyond another hall, antechambers and corridors led to the sanctuary 300 feet from the entrance door of the first hall.
Not only were there many side storerooms, treasuries, and chapels, but at
Dendera there were passages and chambers within the outer walls at different levels. Here temple valuables and ceremonial objects were probably
kept.

As the guide led us farther and farther into the temple he pointed out
carvings in three tiers covering all the walls. Their extent was so vast that
I wished someone could have given me a figure for their total length if
extended in a straight line. Whatever it was, it called up a picture of an
army of sculptors with noisy chisels hammering out the designs of scores
of artists, supervised by priests and overseers. But this was just the decorative part of the temple. There had to be the architects and their army of
builders, and before them the quarriers and movers of this tremendous
weight of stone, and behind all of them the people who fed them, the economy that supported them. Looking at the magnitude of the result, we pon-
dered the logistics.

The guide had now brought us to one of the innermost chambers, and
we saw a hole in the stone floor about three and a half feet square where a
large slab had been removed. Into this hole the guardian with his lanter
proceeded to descend, indicating that we should follow. At the foot of a
ladder each of us squeezed through an even smaller opening. The lantern
light did not extend very far, our feet groped for what we could not see,
the air was hot and stale, and I was glad I was not last in line. We were
in a crypt-like passage which extended within the thickness of the walls
around most of the inner temple, and at three different levels, to a total of
32 chambers, which were just widenings of the corridors. Not all are open
to visitors, but this one is shown for the excellence of its carvings, especially a beautiful hawk, symbol of Horus, whose plumage was so finely
carved that the two-foot bird seemed to be cut in bronze rather than stone.
Perhaps this especially gifted carver was making his masterpiece for Hathor, mother of Horus, in gratitude or hope for her blessings; now apprecia-

tion was reaching back to him from twentieth-century admirers.

Once more in the open air, we walked around the temple to see on its outer wall one of the few representations of Cleopatra, here shown with her and Caesar's little son, Caesarion. The sculpture is disappointingly conventional and so does not reveal to us the living beauty of this femme fatale. Off to the right, Cleopatra's pool, with stone sides and descending steps, was far from ruined and would still be lovely if cleared of vegetation and filled with water.

We next climbed a stone staircase of many turns within the temple to the roof, where one chamber ceiling displays the only known Egyptian representation of the Zodiac in circular form, a very handsome composition. The present ceiling, however, is only a plaster copy, because the original was removed as a gift to a royal lady—from the Khedive Ismail to the Empress Eugénie at the time of the Suez Canal opening celebrations. It can now be seen in the Louvre.

The view from this lofty roof equalled for me all the art and wonder of the temple. Having been for many weeks a sailor on the Nile and observed its valley from the river, I now for the first time had the broader view that height gives. Behind me rose the pink-tinged mountains above the pale tan of desert sand; off to the side at some distance the eggshell domes of Moslem tombs; then before me the land of the living cut into fields of vibrant green, or soft gray with the flowers of the *foul* bean, or light yellow with a fodder crop. Here and there the golden straw color of shacks and temporary walls interrupted the cultivation. In a round brown area the sakia turned to raise water. Trunks of date palms rose very straight to their plumy waving crests, and toward the river the dark mud houses made distant lines. Then the stream of the Nile wound through the plain with only shiny white dots indicating the great sails of the feluccas. On the far bank, only desert reached to the eastern plateau. It was not only a lovely view, but one which within a comprehensible scope told the whole story of life on the Nile.

Our visit to Dendera had a pleasant conclusion, for there was a little rest house near the temple and we had brought our lunch. So without tedious waiting or polite conversation we could sit down to a simple picnic at a table on a shaded patio and look back at the whole impressive structure of the well-proportioned temple. Then our donkeys jogged us back to the *Yankee*.

Though we had enjoyed seeing the potters of Kena, we were not quite satisfied. The pots they made were both larger and smaller than the most common variety, the ones we saw every day on the women's heads. But what interested us even more was that we had observed them as cargoes the whole length of the Nile. They were even more intriguing than the smooth golden loaves of straw or the dangerously heavy loads of stone. The cargoes of pots were piled as neat as a supermarket display. The mounds of creamy or grayish pink, round bases outward, rose precariously high above the deck. Then hundreds more, carefully arranged to carry the maximum load, were slung in great rope nets below either side of the ship, almost touching the water. Not one more pot could be added anywhere, we were sure. Counting and estimating repeatedly as these marvelous cargoes floated by, we figured that a large felucca carried over 4000. We were determined to find the source of the ballas, the Egyptian word for pot.

It was the town of El Ballas (Pottsville to us) just south of Kena on the west bank. Many feluccas were loading from a vast outlay of pots lying on the shore. These arrived in bags of rope net hanging on either side of a camel's hump. The ungainly animal would jolt down the bank and at the proper command would perform his remarkable folding operation in four extreme tilts until his stomach rested on the ground and his burden was at an easy height for unloading. Then his forty-four pots were laid out in neat rows. After watching this lively scene for a while we were ready to start inland to find the end of the pot trail.

Ahmed recognized a look of authority on the face of a rather slight older man in a neat dark *galabia* and clean white turban who was about to board a small sailing ferry, and persuaded him to put off his trip and be our guide. Ahmed chose well, because our mentor was no mere hanger-on, but immediately took charge of our small expedition. So we set out, watching our footing on the little raised paths, between the fields, and then through a sizable village. It was a two-mile hike to the potteries and reminded me of many hikes on South Sea islands, except that the date palms would have to change to coconuts and the camels to pigs.

If it hadn't been for our guide, I think the children of El Ballas would have mobbed us, but he could lay about him in good style, both verbally and with stick. The day was pleasantly summery, but not too hot. We passed beyond the village and followed the unloaded camels along the desert road, meeting the loaded camels carrying their pots to the beach. I was actually beginning to notice differences in camels; young and old, dark and light, even pinkish, springy and plodding. The tails are as interesting as the feet—rather feathery hair growing out from a center stalk. The tails aren't very long, and some are in much better shape than others. All the faces and

We met vast loads of pots drifting down river with the current to markets along the way. To accommodate a cargo of 4000 many were slung in nets touching the water on either side.

teeth still looked wicked to me and many wore muzzles.

The potters and the firing pits were no different from those at Kena, but here we were close to the mountains from which the clay is dug and could see in nature the very same colors which we had observed in the high-piled cargoes. We were finally satisfied on this subject.

On the homeward walk I fell into the sort of trance that eliminates time and distance, my steps unconsciously keeping time to the gentle clatter of the pots in the camel bags and the other daily nosies of Egypt falling on my ears. After a while the thinking process intruded, and I began to enumerate the sounds of Egypt: the whipping sound of cloth when a *galabia* figure ran, the distinctive bells of horse or camel or donkey, the creaking of the sakia, the singing chant of men bending rhythmically to haul up water by the shaduf weights, the other chants for heaving and hauling as when men pulled the feluccas, the horses' hooves on the streets of the towns, the radio noise which might unexpectedly proceed from a felucca or a mudbrick house or from under a *galabia*-clad arm, the call to prayer from a minaret, the heehaw of a donkey, and the still fascinating and bewildering sound of the Arabic language.

We might have got to Luxor that night if we hadn't lingered at El Ballas. But though the famous city tempted, none of us was averse to one more quiet night at anchor just out of the channel of the Nile.

chapter IX

≈

Luxor

≈

"We're coming into Luxor," someone called down the hatch, so I stopped sweeping the cabin floor and rushed on deck. A tree-lined avenue, a few large houses, the Savoy Hotel and terrace, then the great Temple of Luxor just back from the river, the Edwardian Winter Palace Hotel with its curved driveway, the modern facade of the New Winter Palace building beside it—along this waterfront the *Yankee* looked for a berth. We were offered a fine one by a float at the foot of a stone stairway to the street, by the line of shops adjoining the Winter Palace, but far enough from the street for privacy. A newsboy was inspired to run down to our landing, and we bought everything he had in English, our first newsprint in over a month.

The Nelsons were leaving us here after six weeks on board and were heading farther south to Khartoum and Kenya. Soon due to take their place was Ted

Zacher of Hartford who had sailed around the world with us before the war in our Schooner *Yankee*. He arrived with a lot of overweight in movie and still cameras, lenses, light bulbs, and film, as he was going to help Irving take movies for lectures.

Luxor, which the Greeks called Thebes, offers a view of Egypt at the height of its greatness as an empire, from the sixteenth through the eleventh centuries before Christ. From all the remains here of temples, tombs, carvings, and inscriptions, Egyptologists can bring to life this glorious period in great detail. Lesser visitors reconstruct it more or less completely depending on their knowledge and their imagination. Many an amateur archaeologist has spent happy months around the ruins without any of the professional's ambition to "publish," that final step in archaeological success. It is surprising how often a passion for Egyptology originates in a person's early years and lasts a lifetime. But if one had no archaeological knowledge at all, there would still be a thrill in just looking here.

Amon was the king of the gods in the days of Theban glory, and in his magnificent temple at Karnak, just north of modern Luxor, were enacted the most splendid ceremonies of Ancient Egypt. Nowhere else were as-sembled such treasures, such displays, such pageantry. As the empire and the pharaoh increased in wealth and power, the priests of Amon kept pace, so that at one time they owned the majority of the slaves and temple property in all Egypt. Their great temple was the center of its own domain of land and herds, farmers and herdsmen, treasures of gold, silver, fine textiles, incense, and storerooms of grain; craftsmen and artists spent productive lifetimes em-bellishing the edifice of the god. Scribes, overseers, managers, and adminis-trators carried on the big business of the temple, and finally a priesthood over all mere temple workers became so powerful that it could make and unmake kings and eventually exercised the supreme temporal power as pharaoh-priest. The revolt against Amon by the heretic king, Akhnaton, foreshadowed the downfall of the god; his earthly representatives eventually achieved such exaggerated splendor that they toppled of their own weight. Thebes was the witness to the days of Amon's greatest glory and the days of the mightiest emperor pharaohs—Thutmose I, Thutmose III, Queen Hatshepsut, Seti I, and Ramses II.

This was the era when conquering kings returned from their Asiatic campaigns with hundreds of captives and the spoils of war, the defeated leaders hanging head downward from the bow of the emperor's boat, the cargoes of tribute to swell the treasuries of king and gods, and the victorious army marching in triumph. The cheering population, nobles and commoners

From the pylons of Luxor Temple an avenue of sphinxes leads to the Temple of Karnak. Excavation continues here where hundreds of stone sphinxes have already been unearthed. (*Zacher*)

both, felt themselves to be the privileged metropolitans of the greatest country in the world.

We commoners of the twentieth century A.D. felt privileged enough when the mayor offered us his carriage, drawn by a harness pair, for the half hour drive to Karnak. This is the largest religious building in the world (though the Labyrinth at the Faiyum was even larger). Its walls enclose 62 acres of temples. Six or seven of Europe's largest cathedrals would easily fit in that space. Our carriage rolled along the tree-lined riverside avenue. Then after a turn inland, we reached the outer entrance of the temple, where in flood time the pharaoh had alighted from his boat at the temple quay. From this spot once a year the statue of Amon, borne by his priests, would embark on the Nile for his annual visit to Luxor to meet Mut, the divine mother, in that temple. His boat gleamed with gold and bright colors and trappings. Other sacred boats joined the procession. The king took part, like his people waiting for some oracular pronouncement from Amon. Ten days later the god returned to Karnak, as excited festive crowds followed along the bank. At another season, for the Festival of the Valley, Amon again left Karnak and crossed the river to the temples on the west bank. Egypt's temple festivals are described as of great splendour. When they were launched upon the river the production must have surpassed all others, for drama seems to gain a greater dimension on the water. I remembered the Thailand procession of royal barges on the Bangkok River, the gaiety of the theater afloat at Coblenz on the Rhine, and the solemnity when Churchill's body was borne on the Thames. Amon's stage managers were masters of their art.

The avenue of ram statues led from the place of the pharaoh's quay to the entrance between the loftiest temple pylons in all Egypt, great wedge-shaped structures each 142 feet high, 370 feet wide and 50 feet thick at their bases. In the eight shallow recesses on the outside of the pylons stood the overtowering flagpoles of tall cedars brought from Lebanon especially for this purpose.

The pylons served several purposes. They made imposing gate posts for the great door, often decorated in gold, and the outer wall around the temple grounds. Their carving commemorated the proud deeds of the pharaoh who erected them. They supported huge flag staffs, framed the obelisks before them, and in all announced the greatness of the temple they guarded.

To enter this greatest hall of ancient times, where one wanders microscopically among close set columns of enormous height and girth, is an awesome experience. I think Champollion expressed it best saying that the "architects thought in terms of men a hundred feet tall." After these introductory impressions, the visitor views reliefs of battles, gods, and kings on the surrounding walls, goes on to explore side chambers and sanctuaries to find the statues which have survived the ages, and to admire the beautiful obelisk of Queen Hatshepsut, 97 feet of pink Aswan granite standing where she raised it 3500 years ago. Never again would I glance casually at the obelisks in other parts of the world. Having seen this one in the Temple of Amon, all other obelisks would remind me of Karnak.

With the preferential treatment that Ahmed's winged words always seemed to bring about, we were shown around Karnak by the resident Egyptian archaeologist. He opened some closed areas for us, showed us a whole field of granite blocks (still within the temple walls) laid out for further study, and led us to a lovely little pavilion all of alabaster. He showed us the sacred lake, whose sides were built of vertically-set huge stones, and the enormous granite Scarab that is said to bring children to childless women who run around it. He helped us visualize the temple in the various stages of its building over a period of seventeen centuries, starting about 2000 B.C. But Karnak is so vast and overwhelming that it requires many visits, at different times of day. Baedeker in hand, I would follow the explanations of the inscriptions up and down the walls, delighted when an illustration matched a piece of my knowledge of Egyptian history. "Templing" with Baedeker is a fascinating game best played alone.

Irving and Win climbed the highest pylons to take pictures. Ted and Win twice got up early to capture dawn over Karnak. The memory I like best is of a late afternoon visit when I felt more than usually awed by the huge, superhuman columns. I thought I was all alone in the shadows of the hypostyle hall. Then a fox ran across my path, probably a temple dweller.

Mixed with my exalted memories of Karnak are recollections of my most everyday concerns. It seemed as though I was often looking at a relief of a battle some Pharaoh fought while wondering with half my mind how I would cook those skinny ribs of veal, or a chicken which was likely to be tough even though it weighed only a pound and a half.

The towering presence of those ancient monuments seems not to affect all life in Luxor. I was quite surprised to find influence of tourism so negligible in one of the greatest sightseeing areas of the world. At the waterfront and near the hotels there are shops offering second-rate curios, antiquities (almost never genuine), and souvenirs. There is an inefficient Tourist Bureau and a barely passable ladies' hairdresser. There are the eternally persistent hawkers, urchin or aged, selling "mummy beads" (whatever they

Egyptian temple pylons here at Edfu are of overpowering size, filled with musty rooms and dark worn stone stairs. Irving, on top, looks over the green valley to the desert mountains beyond. (*Zacher*)

are), scarabs, and little pharaonic figures. But back from the waterfront the daily existence of Luxor is a scene of poverty dreary beyond our understanding.

In the dusty post office we wondered who were the men crowding around the window pushing crumply-looking letters over each others' heads and shoulders? Whom were they writing to and about what? To a student son in Cairo? To a landlord? To a creditor? It would be easy for any of us to give a plausible explanation of each person in an American post office line. But I felt hopelessly far from understanding the lives of these people. I fell back on studying details. All the men wore shoes, heavy ones, carelessly fitted. Women more often wore rough sandals or went barefoot. Some were squatting on the sidewalk across the way, endlessly shifting and tucking and rearranging their shapeless *mylayas*. In front of me a post office employee, squatting on the floor, was trying to make holes with a big, long nail through a three-inch stack of papers so that he could string them together. What was the life of these townspeople? What did they eat?

I was back at the usual question. What were we going to eat? Marketing here was easy enough so that I could even manage without Ahmed at times. Excellent oranges cost six cents a dozen. Beans, zucchini, eggplant, carrots, and two-foot diameter cabbages gave me good choice. But for meat I needed help. The unidentifiable hunks of lean and fat at which an open air butcher was hacking away looked impossible to me. But, as usual, Ahmed had a friend. He was Osman Ghaleb, the host, manager, skipper, and probably former owner of the Government steamer *Delta* which cruised mostly between Luxor and Aswan. He not only ordered meat for me, but invited all of us to dinner on board the *Delta* and thoughtfully sent me cakes and rolls baked by his chef.

The dinner party aboard the *Delta* was a congenial affair. We were a mixture assembled from many directions: our own *Yankee* group, a charming Churchillian Englishman and his wife who wintered in Luxor every year, a British engineer whose firm had been expelled from the country at the time of the Suez crisis, but who had chosen to come back and work for the Egyptian Government—a most unusual move. After dinner we joined the regular passengers and met the two charming and poised young hostesses who traveled in the *Delta*. Nabila was a tall, graceful young woman who had studied archaeology at the University of Cairo, who spoke excellent English, and who led the shore excursions to ancient monuments. Mimi was small and appealing, but far from helpless, and equal to the endless demands made on a hostess. When we got to know her better, she told us of the variety of her trials, amusing, infuriating, and as difficult as dealing with the sudden death of a passenger. I marveled at her skill in handling her tourists.

Various people in Luxor came to tea on the *Yankee*, and we had some good talk in the after cabin. There were our friends from the *Delta*, a TV crowd from New York, visitors from the American mission, a couple from Larchmont who were attracted to the boat herself, and callers from "Chicago House," the American archaeological headquarters which had been established by the great James Breasted. If we had done nothing else it would have been pleasant just to stay aboard the *Yankee* in Luxor and see who came over the gangplank.

We often dined ashore at the Winter Palace. More than the dinners there, however, I enjoyed midmorning coffee on the back terrace by the garden, with the sun pouring down, not a bit too hot, just delightfully warming in that pleasant setting. An equally good time of day was the sunset hour on the front verandah, when people would gather to look across the river, usually in silence, at the beauty of the coloring constantly changing above the distant mountains behind the Valley of the Kings. The river would darken, a felucca would drift by, the afterglow would revive, and then darkness would descend on one of the most thrilling views on earth. This natural beauty had not changed with the centuries or—as one must think in Egypt—in the millennia. To the ancients, so concerned with the afterlife, here to the west beyond the pink mountains and the endless desert the soul would naturally find eternity and his way to the great world of the dead.

chapter X

≈

Thebes
West

≈

The *Yankee* was our Nile ferry
to the west bank for visiting the Valley
of the Kings and the great mortuary
temples. We just cast off the dock lines,
motored across the river, let go the anchor, and rowed ashore in the dinghy.

The two rulers whose tombs we
were to visit, Queen Hatshepsut and
Thutmose III, particularly interested me.
We must go back to the founder of the
Seventeenth Dynasty, Ahmose, about
1580 B.C., who begins the period of the
New Kingdom or empire. Ahmose drove
out the foreign Hyksos rulers and after
him Thutmose I built up an empire that
extended to the Euphrates. During his
Dynasty, the Eighteenth, tribute flowed
in from all the lands between. To quote
Breasted: "Phoenician galleys, such as the
upper Nile had never seen before, delighted the eyes of the curious crowd at
the docks of Thebes; and from these
landed whole cargoes of the finest stuffs

of Phoenicia, gold and silver vessels of magnificent workmanship, from the cunning hand of the Tyrian artificer or the workshops of distant Asia Minor, Cyprus, Crete and Aegean islands; exquisite furniture of carved ivory, delicate wrought ebony, chariots mounted with gold and electrum, and bronze implements of war; besides these, fine horses for the pharaoh's stables and untold quantities of the best that the fields, gardens, vineyards, orchards, and pastures of Asia produced."

Even before Thutmose I died, an old man, the succession to the throne became so confused that historians have never straightened out the sequence of events to their final satisfaction. But there is no doubt that about 1500 B.C. Queen Hatshepsut was the ruler of Egypt and all its empire. She is called all at once "king's daughter, king's sister, god's wife, and king's great wife"! However, she does seem to be directly descended from the first rulers of the New Kingdom, those strong Theban lords who had driven out the foreign rulers. In the midst of all the rivalry for the throne, she decided to strengthen her claim by announcing that she was also the daughter of the great god Amon and that, as pharaoh, she was a man! As Hatshepsut, however, she never pretended not to be a woman. All these claims still speak forth from the sculptured walls of her temple.

But nothing else gives us the impression that Hapshepsut was a masculine sort of woman. Her maneuvering around the court intrigues sounds feminine. Though statues of pharaohs are more stereotyped than candid, the likenesses of Hatshepsut are not at all manly or overpowering. On the contrary, her small features suggest a woman rather delicate, intelligent, pretty but determined. "Beautiful and gifted" she has been described. I was of course particularly charmed by one description: "Hatshepsut adjusted the affairs of the Two Lands by reason of her designs; Egypt was made to labour with bowed head for her, the excellent seed of the god, who came forth from him. The bow-cable of the South, the mooring-stake of the southerners, the excellent stern-cable of the Northland is she; the mistress of command whose plans are excellent, who satisfies the Two Regions when she speaks." As she is likened to a Nile boat, perhaps this is the first time a boat is called "she."

Hatshepsut ruled firmly, although not aggressively, and held the loyalty of courtiers so prominent that we know them still as individuals: Hapuseneb, vizier and High Priest of Amon; Ineni, overseer of the gold and silver treasury, later succeeded by Thutiy; Nehsi, chief treasurer. But most important among them was Senenmut, often referred to as her great architect, but more likely a sort of Prime Minister, who had many responsibilities in administrating and planning for more than buildings alone. Hatshepsut also

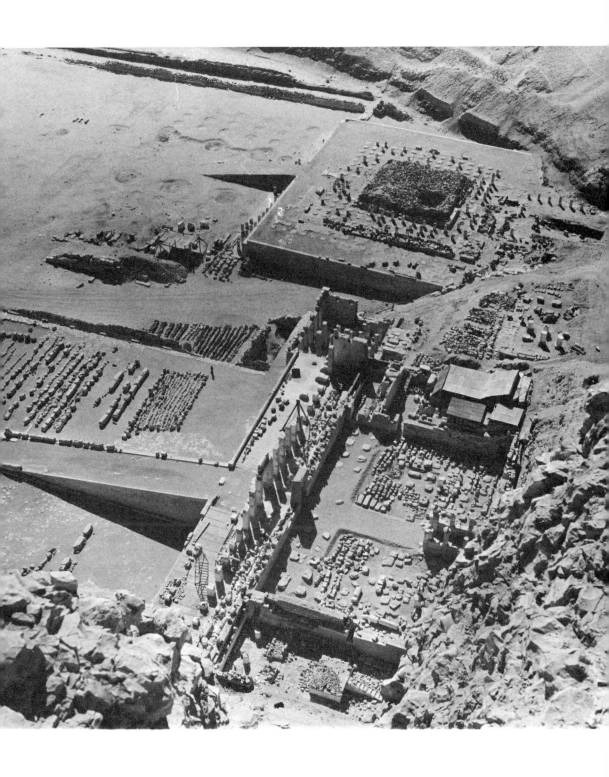

The layout of Hatshepsut's Temple seen from the cliffs above looks like the world's biggest jigsaw puzzle, a challenge to archaeologists who are trying to rebuild the upper stories.

entrusted him with the education of her little daughter, Nefrure, and their whole association was so close and so interdependent that it seems to me Senenmut may very likely have been the love of her life and not simply a consort selected for political reasons. Together they planned the temple which I thought the most beautiful in Egypt; for me it expresses their relationship and is not just the monument to a lonely queen. There is little in Egypt that can be called romantic, but Hatshepsut is a possibility.

Hatshepsut fittingly practiced the arts of peace. She never led armies, and the empire that Thutmose I had won might not have held together if her reign had lasted more than fifteen or twenty years. But for that length of time revenues continued to pour in from Nubia and from far-off Syria-Palestine. One famous accomplishment of her reign was the great expedition to Punt, which had not seen an Egyptian ship for many years. Amon had asked her, she said, for myrrh trees to beautify the terraces of the temple, but her ships brought back much, much more. We were especially interested to learn that the ships may have traveled from the Nile to the Red Sea by a canal across from the eastern Delta. Such a canal was believed to have been dug in the Middle Kingdom and perhaps it had been brought back into use. The five ships shown going down the Nile from Thebes are the same which appear in the Red Sea and again homeward-bound up the Nile. There is no mention of a caravan or a transshipment. We saw the whole story of this voyage on the walls of her temple.

The queen is also famous for her obelisks, one of which still stands within the Karnak temple enclosure. Its mate lies fallen nearby. These were 97½ feet high and weighed nearly 350 tons each. The queen had their tops sheathed with electrum, a silver-gold metal, so that their high-shining beauty was seen from both sides of the river. One relief shows the almost incredible freighting of two of her obelisks from Aswan, 200 miles south, where they were quarried. They are shown lying end to end on a huge barge towed by thirty galleys rowed by 950 oarsmen! We later saw an unfinished obelisk at Aswan still in the bedrock and marveled at the quarrying itself, as well as at the problem of transportation. The boats could be brought close in at flood time, of course, but the moving of hundreds of tons of a granite monolith, which was done again and again in pharaonic times, still staggers the imagination.

A less spectacular, but characteristic accomplishment of the queen's reign was the steady restoration of the temples of her ancestors, which had suffered much damage during the period of Hyksos rule. The archaeologists are grateful to her for saving buildings of earlier times. She was putting her house in order, mending the broken pieces, strengthening the weak places, and with imagination and taste making it more beautiful than she had found it—the natural inclination of a woman who was also a queen.

As I mentioned earlier, my Number One hero of ancient Egypt is Thutmose III. I know it is not the fashion now to have a military, empire-building hero. At least war was quite different in that time; the largest army Egypt ever sent forth was probably less than 20,000 men. Courage and a strong right arm, endurance and the ability to inspire loyalty, plus intelligent planning, brought Thutmose success in the field. He also held together capably an empire that reached from the Third Cataract to the Euphrates. He was successful at sea as well as on land and maintained a steadfast determination to keep Egypt supreme after victory. He did not stop with one act of heroism as Ramses II did, but won his battles, followed them up, pushed on farther. His hold never slackened.

Thutmose III's first significant appearance at the age of eighteen was dramatic. At that time, this son of the great Thutmose I by a concubine was a young priest in the Temple of Amon at Karnak. (Thutmose II seems to have been a timid youth who reigned for a short time with Hatshepsut as regent.) On an important feast day, when the image of Amon was being carried into the temple court with multitudes watching, the god suddenly stopped before the young priest, raised him up, and had him placed in the "Station of the King." Such was Amon's will—or the will of the powerful priestly faction.

He ruled for some time, but then in the rivalry of court factions was obliged to accept as co-regent Hatshepsut, who was actually in a line of stronger, legitimate descent. Queen Hatshepsut was supreme and undisputed ruler of Egypt until her death about fifteen years later. But those years of eclipse gave Thutmose time to mature, learn, and prepare for the day when he would take power. When he again mounted the throne, it was to rule for fifty-four of Egypt's most glorious years, extending her power to the limits of their civilized world.

Thutmose III's Theban forebears had protected their borders from further invasion by pushing Egypt's power to the northeast into Syria-Palestine. But although Thutmose I had placed his boundary marker on the distant Euphrates, during Queen Hatshepsut's reign no Egyptian army had marched in that direction. Now revolt was stirring under the leadership of the most powerful of numerous small kings, the King of Kadesh.

At the head of the first army to enter southern Palestine for many years, Thutmose III, young and ambitious, advanced in strength, acknowledging allegiance and receiving tribute as he went. Megiddo is nearly 400 miles from Egypt's border, and I wish we had a daily account of that march. Such accounts were strictly kept, but they have not survived. Thutmose approached his foe, decided on his strategy against advice, and took a chance on the direct approach through a narrow pass, though it strung out his army dangerously. This bold risk was something the enemy had not expected and the Egyptians funneled unopposed into the Plain of Esdraelon, where they could bring all their force to bear. Thutmose, in his gleaming chariot of gold and silver, led the onslaught and drove the enemy in flight into the fortress until the gates closed. On a temple wall we saw a relief showing the last of the craven enemy being ignominiously pulled in over the wall by their comrades.

Pressing the attack with the same vigor would have gained the fort. "Would that the army of his majesty had not set their hearts upon looting the chattels of those enemies, for they would have captured Megiddo at that moment, while the vile enemy of Kadesh and the vile enemy of this town were being hoisted up." But military opportunities have been lost like this through the ages because of irresistible plunder. So Megiddo had to be taken by siege. When it finally fell, the spoils were enormous: 924 chariots including those of the kings of Kadesh and Megiddo, 2238 horses, 200 suits of armor, the splendid tent of the King of Kadesh, 4500 cattle, a whole harvest of grain, furniture of the royal household, the King's scepter, statues of silver, gold, and lapis lazuli, and quantities of plain gold and silver.

It was the Egyptians and not the locals who did the harvesting that year. Some must have been left behind to guard all the loot, for Thutmose pushed on north to more victories, built Egyptian forts, and turned back only when the fighting season of the summer months came to an end. We know of the triumph of their return home and the parade of spoil and captives through Thebes.

In the spring Thutmose and his men set out again. That campaign and the next year's met no serious opposition. The chastened vassals sent in their required tribute and, as long as they stirred up no trouble, were left to run their own affairs. Princely children were taken to Egypt for an education—indoctrination more likely—at pharaoh's court.

But Thutmose's eyes were on a goal beyond Megiddo. Farther north he intended to conquer Kadesh itself, subdue the country of the Naharin beyond, and push on to the Euphrates. To subdue the whole area he must control the seacoast. So on his fourth campaign Thutmose set out with a fleet and proved to understand and command sea power as many of history's great generals, Napoleon for instance, did not. He showed remarkable diplomacy too, in making an advantageous treaty with the big commerical Phoenician port of Tyre, which probably cared more about business and its own security than about its allies.

It was not till the next season, however, that, having come again by sea, Thutmose carried the attack to Kadesh itself. The mighty fortress stood as an island between two rivers, with a connecting canal and even an inner moat. This time we have no record of Thutmose's strategy or details of the battle, but we know Kadesh fell. Then he subdued coastal ports as necessary, and with the approach of winter sailed home, making more than the usual arrangements for tribute and submission. From now on he expected dockyards and supplies for his ships as well as for his army. Undoubtedly Egyptian officers stayed behind to carry out preparations for the return of the fleet.

It was on the eighth campaign that the Egyptian army passed beyond the mountains of Lebanon and conquered Aleppo 100 miles inland. Then Carchemish 100 miles farther on the Euphrates fell. Thutmose crossed that farthest river and set up his boundary stone on the east bank, outdistancing his father's on the nearer shore. He turned south and subdued the river city of Niy and then, hearing that a herd of 120 elephants was nearby, he topped off his victorious year with a bit of sport. At one critical moment he was saved from a charging elephant by his old friend and companion in arms, General Amenemhab, who of course records this great moment on the walls of his tomb.

Thutmose's greatest ambition had now been achieved, but in the years to follow this tireless warrior returned nine more times at the head of his armies to hold what he had won. Revolts and conspiracies of princely states could make no headway as long as Thutmose and his army continued strong. Egypt's power and supremacy were recognized far beyond the penetration of his armies. Gifts and recognition came from peoples hardly known to Egypt: the Hittites of Asia Minor, the far-off Babylonians, and the island peoples of Cyprus and Greece. The pharaoh might have claimed that he had conquered the world.

Meanwhile there were more expeditions to Punt. The southern border was secured beyond the Third Cataract, and the Middle Kingdom temples and forts guarding the Second Cataract were restored. Gold was brought in

Donna Grosvenor and I enjoyed our donkeys in the Valley of the Kings.
(*Zacher*)

from the mines of Nubia, and the important caravan route from Koptos toward the Red Sea was established and secure. The great old fighter was 71 when he campaigned for the last time to the northeast. Egypt was at the pinnacle of her power and Thutmose III had brought her there by his own ability.

The Valley of the Kings, two miles from the river, well beyond the cultivation, is a narrow, steep-sided cut into the desert cliffs. This far into the uknown the great funeral processions carried their pharaohs to elaborate tombs prepared for them under their own direction. Everything that a pharaoh or nobleman might need in the afterlife was assembled in his tomb: furniture, food, chariot, royal insignia, jewelry. What could not actually be placed in the tomb was provided for in statues, paintings, and inscriptions. The statue of the man himself represented him at the height of his powers and little figures of servants stood ready to obey his commands. His family, his possessions, his boat, his house and lands were often shown on the walls. His overseer appeared, keeping the field laborers at work. His grapes were harvested, his cows milked. Hunting and boating scenes made sure he would enjoy the recreations that had been his pleasures in this life. And in addition to pictures and sculptures, inscriptions told of his great deeds, his integrity and courage, his praiseworthy behavior. "I was the poor man's vizier who does not accept the bribe of the guilty." Other inscriptions charted his course through the world of the dead, explained the formalities and requirements to be met. Gods and goddesses looked down from the walls: Horus, the Hawk; maternal Hathor of the cow head, Thot and Ptah who were the patrons of understanding, learning, and art; Anubis with a jackal or dog's head, the great funerary god; and always Osiris, ruler of the underworld, before whom the heart is weighed against the feather of truth and man's life is judged.

But whatever the chronology and whatever the details, the ancient Egyptians told us a great deal about themselves in their tombs and temples. The scribe's office was honorable and respected and the written word had an importance and even a power of its own. We could appreciate that as we admired the decorative quality of the hieroglyphs. Some of them even became familiar: the symbols for life, for man, for sun. But the lines and lines of symbols were beautiful in themselves. When we had an archaeological guide we were often lulled by the repetitive explanations stringing together phrases which became familiar: "The king makes an offering to Amon. He smells a lotus flower while seated at his funerary banquet. The priest wears the sacred leopard skin. Anubis brings the soul to judgment. The forelock of youth. The beard of royalty. The sun boat crosses the heavens. Nut swallows the sun. The crown of Upper and Lower Egypt. Hathor the mother of Horus. Isis and Osiris." These multiple and variously described deities were old friends by this time, and we felt at home in the tombs in their company.

The final burial chamber with its stone sarcophagus was far inside the tomb. Steep ramps led down into the earth. Some passages came to dead ends. False doors and deep, broad pits had been constructed to thwart grave robbers, all in vain. The tremendous wealth in gold and jewels, alabaster, ebony, lapis lazuli, turquoise, ivory, furniture and ornaments from the unrobbed tomb of nineteen-year-old Tutankhamon, rather an unimportant king, has given the world a suggestion of the treasure that other tombs held. The Tutankhamon display in the Cairo Museum was unbelievably sumptuous, even without a large part of that tomb's contents which was on display in the United States. Here in the tomb itself we could see the inner of his three coffins, mummiform of wood covered with gold with multicolored inlay, fitting over the only mummy in Egypt which still lies where it was buried.

We visited other tombs: Seti I's vast chambers, with marvelous color in the painting, and pictures of afterworld punishments; the tomb of Ramses VI with its huge broken sarcophagus and astronomical decorations; Horemhab's with the detailed reliefs. Then we were very fortunate to be admitted to Queen Nefertari's, which is not open to the public because seepage in the plaster is damaging the wall paintings. It is to be hoped that some modern technique can preserve these walls, as the decorations here are the most charming in all the tombs.

By now fairly transported back through the centuries, we walked into a startling scene. An American TV crew employed by the U.A.R. Government was shooting a film. From the glaringly lighted chamber came a sharp voice at television pressure, "Move that camera over here. Light a little higher. Light on the queen. Shoot!" Making our way around tripods, ducking under the beams of sunguns, avoiding the frantic crew, we tried to identify Nefertari. "Ten feet of film left. Got a good god? Who's that? Amon? OK, he'll do."

The TV men were generous in sharing their professional light with the *Yankee* photographers, while Mildred and I escaped down a corridor. On its walls were painted figures of the loveliest Egyptian ladies of the court of 3200 years ago. Their beautifully draped dresses, in colors still bright and

The Temple of Dendera is tremendously impressive in both the size of its columns and the miles of inscriptions. Heads of the goddess Hathor top the 24 pillars of the Great Hypostyle Hall. *(Parks)*

Yankee would curl an especially big bow wave in shallow water. Ahmed calls out "Six feet . . . five feet," as he sounds to find the deep water channel in the shifting sands of the river bed.   *(Parks)*

Towering canvas catches a following breeze. With gunwales awash, heavily laden naggars — popularly called feluccas — ply the Beheira Canal, part of the Nile Delta's maze of waterways. Sometimes a whole fleet of feluccas would come sailing toward us. These are deep-laden with building stone for Alexandria.   *(Schreider)*

My first sight in the morning out the galley window would often be mist-shrouded fishing boats. *(Parks)*

Yankee herself was a misty, perhaps incredible, vision to a young farmer feeding his cow and water buffalo soon after sunrise. *(Parks)*

The last delta lock before Cairo was a busy place for *Yankee*. Masts had to be lowered quickly, using our aluminum gangplank with block and tackle to the bow to control the descent of the spars. *(Parks)*

(See over)

Closer to the river than most, Luxor Temple proclaimed to the approaching *Yankee* the glory of Egypt's empire at its height. Of vast size, it is not seriously affected by the presence within its walls of the Mosque of Abu'l Haggag, from whose window this picture was taken. *(Parks)*

High on the cliff above Queen Hatshepsut's Temple, Irving aimed his camera on the ruins. Next it followed our eyes over the desert, cultivated fields of green, and the winding Nile. *(Parks)*

Below in *Yankee*'s great cabin Irving and I were at home. Outside we were in Egypt sharing the river with the strange craft of the Nile. This combination is the charm of *Yankee* life.   *(Parks)*

In the Temple at Abydos, Irving, Mildred Nelson, and I follow Om Seti's reading of the cartouches, or names, of 76 pharaohs. Ranging from Menes, the first to unite Upper and Lower Egypt, to Seti I 3000 years later, this inscription has been of enormous value to historians.   *(Parks)*

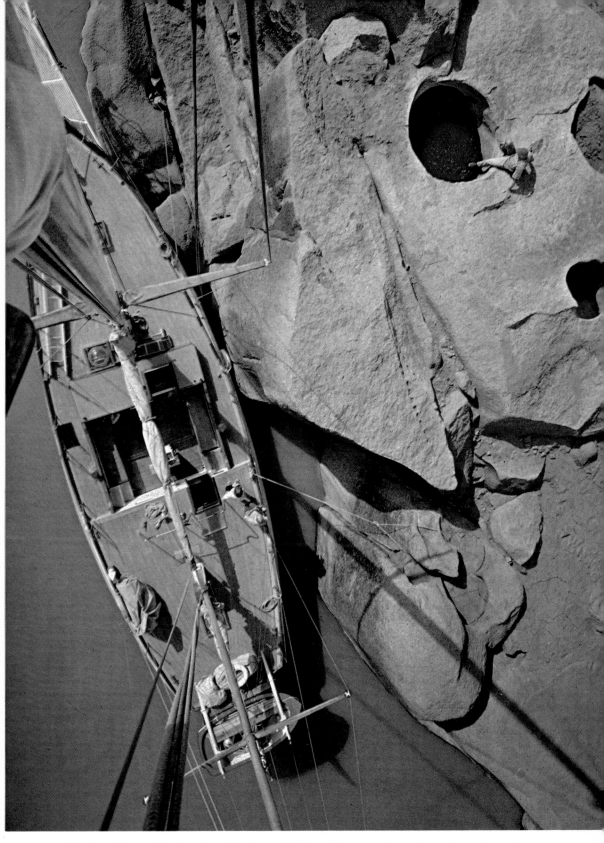

Yankee ties to Elephantine Island at the First Cataract where in ancient times the Lord of the Elephantine controlled the narrow waterway and the lands to the south. Aswan granite, the pharaohs' finest building stone, was cut by drilling a line of holes and plugging them with wood. Swelling when wet, they would split the rock. The big round holes were made by natural scouring action of the Nile in flood.   *(Parks)*

Ambarkab's final festival. Nubians came by felucca to celebrate their sheik's (a local saint) tomb, the women in their brightest colors and the men ready to dance day and night. Soon all these people will be moved out of Nubia and Ambarkab will be under the waters of Lake Nasser.   *(Parks)*

(See over)

Yankee sails the lonely desert where ripples of water meet ripples of sand.   *(Parks)*

Feluccas moor by nosing into the bank just as *Yankee* often does. We always marveled at the life of these craft and the agility of their sailors aloft on sparks 130 feet long. Occasionally a man would shorten his *galabia* by seizing the hem in his teeth.   *(Grosvenor)*

Ahmed helped me bargain for a water pipe at Assiut and a crowd gathered.
(Parks)

Christmas in Egypt for Irving, Ahmed, Ted, and me, with Win taking the picture.
The turkey from the Aswan market, the Christmas tree made by Ted, and Win's
book of cartoons, "Irving and Exy Sail the Nile," made it a celebration.   *(Parks)*

A 15-foot wall from which Irving was photographing at KasrIbrim gave way, crashing rocks on top of him after his fall. Donna Grosvenor and I could only use water and disinfectant until medical help arrived. *(Parks)*

Dr. Samir Shalek Farag at the left took 16 stitches in Irving's head and returned him to the sagging bed of the desert hospital. The local police felt more cheerful than his *Yankee* shipmates. *(Parks)*

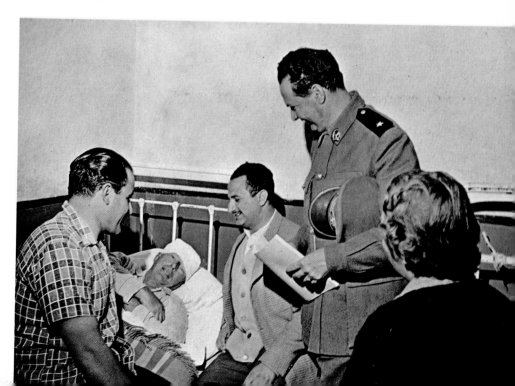

Irving sails the *Yankee* ashore at Abu Simbel and drops Donna Grosvenor off the bowsprit without getting her feet wet.   *(Parks)*

true, must have been made of the sheerest fabrics. What style and care and grooming! The elegance of fashion crossed the centuries and confirmed what designers claim: that the best clothes never lose their beauty, regardless of changing fashion.

Following our guide farther into the tomb, we found some of the lights were out. Everyone should bring a good powerful flashlight to the Valley of the Kings. Though he thought he knew his way, he suddenly stepped over a two-foot drop. We were often exasperated at the inattention to the most obvious demands of tourism. Egypt wants tourists and has some of the greatest attractions in the world, but it doesn't supply lighting adequate to much lesser attractions. How many times we tried to make out inscriptions on a dim wall, with a small area brilliantly lit by the gaffir's Coleman lantern held high, the rest in obscurity. At Karnak I had even been shown around one small temple by the light of a homemade beeswax candle. There were great holes in the floor there, of which the guide kindly warned me, real leg-breakers. And another day, at the Valley of the Kings, I bribed my way into the tomb of Ramses III particularly because of the fascinating descriptions Baedeker gave of ten little side chambers showing "baking, slaughtering and cooking scenes; two rows of ships in the upper row with sails set, lower row sails furled; kneeling Nile god; king's armoury with representations of weapons, standards, armour, arrows, bows, quivers; utensils and furniture of various kinds; sacred fields with ploughing, sowing, reaping going on—the king sails by on a canal." What an alluring description! But each room had one bare bulb, about 25-watt, and all but two of them had burned out!

Deir-el-Bahari, Hatshepsut's lovely temple, probably designed by her consort Senenmut, has, I believe, the most beautiful setting in Egypt. So many temples stand only on the level desert. Here a great cliff, called "Lover of Silence," rises sheer at the end of a valley and makes a magnificent curving backdrop to which the design of the temple is beautifully adapted. Here are no overpowering colossal columns, but an inviting composition of broad terraces rising gently to a spacious, low building. An avenue of sphinxes, graced by the myrrh trees brought from Punt, approached the temple. Central ramps sloped gently from one terrace to another. At the sides porticos were built back against the face of the rock, their walls decorated with painted bas reliefs depicting the queen's divine birth, the expedition to Punt, and the transport of the great obelisks. Much of the bright painting is still clear after 3500 years open to the weather and blowing sand. The whole design is serene and lovely. The greenery of the delicate myrrh trees must

Deir-el-Bahari, Queen Hatshepsut's beautiful temple at Thebes, reaches out from the towering cliff, Lover of Silence. (*Zacher*)

have softened the sterile desert surroundings. It is possible to see a large model of this temple in the Metropolitan Museum in New York.

The Punt story attracted us particularly, because that expedition seemed quite like our Brigantine *Yankee's* cruises among the primitive islands of the Pacific. It was all so plain to me—the ships, the trade goods they took, the houses on stilts, the native king, his wife with the pendulous breasts (just the shape of the ladies of the New Hebrides), the exchange of presents, the strange things brought back, the fishes they saw, the trees they potted (like Bligh's breadfruit), the new animals, and the huge heap of spices which the queen herself is measuring.

At the Ramesseum, the great mortuary temple built by Ramses II, lies his fallen but still impressive colossus. It had stood 57 feet high, all beautifully chiseled and polished Aswan granite. The weight is calculated at 1000 tons, transported in one piece 200 miles down the Nile.

Since Ancient Egypt's monuments have survived so many centuries, through earthquakes, battles, defacing by zealous Christians, Moslems, and tourists, plus outright destruction for supplying their stone to new buildings, one is apt to think they will last "forever." But destructive forces are constantly at work. Blowing sand eats at granite. The drastic temperature changes from the daytime heat of the desert to its nighttime cold are hard on stone. And in some cases a saltiness from the soil rises and gnaws through tomb and temple walls. Present-day archaeologists can point out serious deterioration that their own eyes have witnessed.

The temple of Medinet Habu is the most southerly building of Thebes West, another place for Baedeker and the satisfaction of recognizing scenes he describes. I liked best those on one outer wall showing Ramses II hunting goats, wild donkeys, and wild bulls in a marshy setting with birds on the wing, plants, and waterfall, wonderfully true to nature. By this time I had seen so much glorification of Ramses II by his own order that I began to wonder if he had ever hunted a wild bull or if he was just boasting to posterity and the gods.

One morning when we were fresh and energetic we visited some of the tombs of the nobles set in a more open part of the desert than the dramatic Valley of the Kings. The village of Qurna mingles with the tombs. Various attempts have been made to move the inhabitants so that the whole area can be systematically dug and studied. But even building a new village with cinema did not avail to dislodge the people of Qurna. Not only were they home-loving, but they regarded themselves as heirs to the workmen of

Donna Grosvenor is dwarfed by these medium-sized statues in the court at Edfu Temple. (*Zacher*)

the Theban necropolis who lived here more than 3000 years ago, and even as rightful heirs to the nobles who were buried here. From the time a tomb was first closed to the present day, the valuable contents have filtered out bit by bit, to the profit, great or small, of the inhabitants of Qurna. Sometimes the appearance of a genuine antiquity would be recognized by an archaeologist or the sudden unexplained prosperity of one who had long been poor would rouse official suspicions and lead to investigations. But for one culprit who was caught, innumerable others more cautious have continued mining antiquities under their houses.

The Qurna scene is quite irrational. Mud huts, cubes of houses, and nobles' tombs are all mixed together. Entrances to the latter are labeled "Ramose, No. 55," "Amenemheb, No. 85," "Nakht, No. 52," or "Amen-wehsu, No. 111," and often have a concrete approach. Some are open to the public, others are excavated and locked up, but still labeled with their "street numbers." All around them village life goes on: goats, kids, creaking sakias, tethered camels, black-shrouded women carrying water jugs on their heads, children scrambling up and down the sand hills and trailing tourists with the persistent cry of "baksheesh."

The tourists themselves complete the extraordinary picture. In droves according to language they follow guides who speak French, English, German, or Italian, guides who may be reliable and well-informed, guides who may be university students with one course in archaeology to their credit, experienced *galabia*-clad dragomans with a sheaf of dog-eared calling cards and letters of recommendation, or dragomans who know a minimum of foreign words to go with a minimum of information. The tourists are just as assorted: a well-dressed Middle Eastern diplomatic couple, a string of Danes listening to English explanations, an Italian blonde in skin-tight velvet slacks, the English and Americans with cameras. About the only kind of tourist missing is a child. They are not often brought to Egypt. The faces show all states of mind, ranging from keen interest to obvious boredom, from fresh ambition to weariness of heat, sore feet, hunger, and dust, from bewilderment to enjoyment of Baedeker playing. And yet all this population does not make for crowding as there is lots of open space, with plenty of tombs and temples for all. We never had the sensation of others treading on our heels.

The days went by too fast. Mildred and Victor left on the *Delta;* Ted arrived. The friendly mayor came down with another bouquet. I had never seen one like it and decided it was a pharaonic style. The roses were arranged all in one plane on a truncated triangular framework, narrowest at the bottom. I thought it would suit an ancient funeral procession very well, and was charmed by its unusual style. As we sat in the after cabin chatting, the mayor told us in guarded tones that there was a real archaeological find almost ready to be revealed. By the time we came back downstream. . . . This is Luxor's perennial state of mind, almost the mentality of a gambler.

chapter XI

≈

Luxor
to Aswan

≈

I came out from my pharaonic spell once the *Yankee* was out in the river again in the world of green fields, mud villages, feluccas, and our own navigational uncertainties as we continually sought the deepwater channel. We soon reached the Esna dam, 2865 feet long, completed in 1909, and entered the lock alongside in company with two or three feluccas. On leaving the lock, we took in tow the one alongside us till it could catch the breeze. It was bound from Baliana to Aswan with a squarish load of straw piled so high that the crew could set only half the sail above it. However, with a fair wind the load itself acted like a sail. There were five men aboard, one a rather handsome Douglas Fairbanks type. The resemblance was borne out by his agility in the unreliable rigging. However, in this respect there are many Douglas Fairbankses young and old on the Nile. Way aloft, a clinging figure

Felucca sailors clamber aloft using any slight hold for hand or foot.

will be seen furling and securing the sail, moving gradually down with the job, his horny feet grasping the worn spar in familiar places where some slight knottiness of a circling line affords the very slightest support. It was a continual marvel to us. Some of the boats on the river had seen us several times, for we each advanced at different rates and stopped for different intervals. Ahmed had heard that the felucca men had a name for *Yankee*. They called her *aroosa*, which means bride or doll. We thought this was a lovely compliment.

That night we tied up alongside a phosphate-loading barge at Bassalia. Ahmed came back from his usual reconnoiter ashore to say that we had all been invited to the Club. The situation reminded us of evenings in the South Seas where we would join the small local group at the Mess. Three married couples, three bachelors, company houses, no one but each other for company, their children playing in the compound, the meal served by a bare-footed—no, not an islander this time, but a young man just back from the war in Yemen. The manager had one office, the geologist another. The women tried to grow flowers. The dust settled. For the evening we were a welcome diversion.

The next day we went to see the phosphate mine. A company car drove us away from the river, through a village on the edge of the cultivation, out into the desert to the mine. In a broad, open excavation, hundreds of men were forcing brown phosphate lumps out of the earth damp with river seepage. Except for such a modern tool as the iron pickaxe, the spectacle might have been pharaonic. We stood at the edge of the excavation and watched the hundreds of thin figures digging, bending, prying, lifting, carrying. The work was too muddy for *galabias* and the men wore full calf-length pants belted at the waist, brown with phosphate and almost continually wet. They worked in twos and threes levering and dislodging the brown ore, loading the wet lumps, most of them the size of big cabbages, into crude baskets (just like those shown on the temple walls), then hoisted the load to their shoulders and carried it up the slippery path to the desert level. There the phosphate was transferred onto camels which took it to the river bank. There another labor force hammered it into smaller pieces; still another loaded it into the shoulder-size baskets and carried it in endless file across a long, narrow plank for a gangway to dump it into the 200-ton hold of the waiting barge. This was not slave labor. These men were not abused. The work was not killing. But it was hard, muddy, and painfully primitive and it paid 46 cents a day. There was not one bit of mechanization in the whole mine. Hands, feet, and backs did the job.

The phosphate here runs to 60 or 70%, and Egypt is sixth among the phosphate-producing countries of the world.

Back at the ship, we invited the little Company group aboard, knowing they were curious to see how we lived. When we were ready to leave, they sent us off with a big bouquet of poinsettias and chrysanthemums. I went below to arrange them while the *Yankee* continued upstream. I found I had to wash all the leaves, because they were coated with the brown phosphate dust. I remembered Rauf Shadi's remarking how nicely rain could clean everything—trees, grass, even the air. I had never appreciated rain as a bathing agent before. In Upper Egypt they even have to explain to children in school what it is. One downpour would probably wash away half a village. This beautiful weather was marvelous for cruising and photography, but I am afraid I would find it an additional discouragement at Bassalia to watch phosphate dust settle on the flowers.

It was almost night when a bad looking section of river appeared ahead. "Let's pack it up for the night," Irving said as he backed her down a hundred yards and found a spot where Ahmed could place our anchor in someone's bean patch till morning. We couldn't figure out why the farmer watched that anchor all night, but in the morning he was satisfied that no damage had been done.

When three powered barges appeared, coming downriver in single file, sounding every few yards, we started up toward them. *Yankee* drew a few inches more water, but we figured they should know where it was deepest. Just before we met, the loaded lead barge did a spectacular 180-degree turn when his bow struck and stopped dead while the stern kept going. Our turn for a spectacular maneuver was suddenly upon us. Wide open, the diesel and propeller growled at this treatment in shallow water. Steering became wild and unpredictable as we squeezed between the grounded barge and the two that followed close behind. Somehow we missed them all. Then for half an hour we slowly bumped across this shoal area and were very glad when, past the locks at the next dam, navigation improved.

Thirty miles south of Esna, approaching the district capital of Edfu, we were surprised to see considerable new construction on the west bank: lines of new houses, small covered docks with power boats, and some form of industry behind.

In mythology Horus fought a great fight here with Seth, in their Abel-Cain relationship. We wanted to tie up to the west bank to see the Temple of Horus, but deep water seemed to be to port near a railroad station. Ahmed made some inquiries and came back with a "pilot" who said he could get us to an anchorage across the river. Without great confidence we set out under his direction. Just beyond midstream we went aground. The bottom was sand, of course, and we could easily have backed off, as we usually did, but the pilot kept motioning us ahead. Perhaps we had only to climb a small hump on the river bottom. But the farther we pushed the *Yankee*, the more the sands shoaled until we were stuck hard in about four feet of water. At that the pilot gave up. In fact I have no further recollection of him at all because numerous other problems occupied us.

Now the motor alone could not get us off, so Irving lowered the dinghy and he and Ted sounded all around the ship to find the nearest deeper water. Just as they got back, ready to start kedging operations, a large felucca came drifting at us from shore, bearing a welcoming delegation of important personages grouped amidship and anxious to reach the *Yankee*.

With night coming on, Irving did not want to see any officials just then. He did not want their weight aboard and he didn't want that felucca alongside pushing us harder into the sand. Figuring there was no time for Ahmed's Arabic courtesies, he discouraged them emphatically in English. The words didn't matter; the idea got across and just before they collided with the *Yankee* their helmsman finally put the tiller over and they drifted away. Maybe we had insulted the mayor, but darkness was coming and the river was dropping all the time.

But right now our whole aim was to get the *Yankee* afloat. Irving and Ted rowed out the 30-pound Danforth anchor and the four men heaved and hauled, aided by the electric winch. At the wheel I ran the motor full speed, put the wheel hard over one way, then hard over the other, trying to work a trench in the sand. Nothing availed, and now it was dark. But we could not give up as she would be stuck even harder by morning. Irving got out the five-part dacron tackle, which has helped at many a hard job, and carried out another anchor. We resumed the heaving, hauling, accelerating, and turning, and at last our efforts moved her. Struggling through very gradually deepening water, the *Yankee* came afloat. Now what could have happened to that pilot, I wondered?

Next day it turned out fortunately that the mayor was away and the officials had been smaller fry; Ahmed of course soothed them and we were then presented with the key to the city. A public relations man showed us the big new sugar company plant we had noticed from the river the day before. We passed the new company housing, a General Director's house, a school, and tennis courts, and were given morning tea at a shiny new Clubhouse. Its style was a compound of American motel and Louis XVI.

We had heard that there were about 35 Japanese and 12 Americans working here and asked to visit the latter. Under the Development Loan Fund, the New York firm, Parsons Whittenmore Overseas Co., was setting up a sugar cane pulp plant for making paper. The men were real overseas construction types, accustomed to doing a job and living with few amenities in far corners of the world. They had been here two years and expected to stay one more, then turn over the operation to the Egyptians. A couple of the Americans came aboard later and talked more about the project. We heard not the usual complaints about workmen, but about management. The man who will run the paper mill after their departure has had no paper experience. There are no plans for transporting or distributing the product. It must be shipped by barge, but barges are scarce even now. It sometimes seemed to them as though the whole purpose was simply to set up a big new operation just to look at.

We felt on surer ground at the Temple of Horus. It is a temple of the Greek period begun in 237 B.C. But it is better to call it Ptolemaic than Greek, because nothing of that period in Egypt suggests anything the word Greek brings to mind. Although Egypt was ruled by foreigners, they proclaimed themselves descendants of the pharaohs of old and accepted the culture of the land. So the temples of this period seemed as Egyptian as ever to us. The Temple of Horus at Edfu is the best preserved of all Egyptian temples and would be in even better condition if early Christians had not cut out the faces of gods and kings with determined zeal. A magnificent structure, its superhuman dimensions are surpassed only by Karnak: 450 feet long and 261 feet wide, the majestic pylons 118 feet high. Moreover, stairs inside these pylons make it possible for us to stand on their summits, and look down into the large courtyard surrounded by its colonnades and backed by the great columns of the hypostyle hall, still roofed with its original stone. Before the entrance to the hall stands a colossal, but beautifully simple, granite statue of the Horus falcon wearing the crowns of Upper and Lower Egypt. A matching one lies fallen at the other side of the entrance.

The walls here are full of information: lists of provinces, cities, princes, temples, lands, feasts, genealogies, offerings—a mine of details. And Edfu was literally mined by the great French archaeologist, Mariette. Amelia Edwards in 1874 writes: Once . . . "nothing was visible of the great Temple of Edfu save the tops of these pylons. The rest of the building was as much lost to sight as if the earth had opened and swallowed it. Its courtyards were choked with foul debris. Its sculptured chambers were buried under forty feet of soil. Its terraced roof was a maze of closely packed huts, swarm-

The authors have been filming in Edfu Temple under the glare of a colossal granite Horus falcon wearing the double crown of Upper and Lower Egypt.
(Zacher)

ing with human beings, poultry, dogs, kine, asses, and vermin. Thanks to the indefatigable energy of Mariette, these Augean stables were cleansed some thirty years ago. Writing himself of this tremendous task, he says: 'I caused to be demolished the sixty-four houses which encumbered the roof, as well as twenty-eight more which approached too near the outer wall of the temple.' " The actual labor of digging out this enormous temple was hard to grasp even as we stood in the basin of its excavation with higher buildings all around. Edfu, which took only 180 years to build, is a more perfect unit than Karnak, which grew through seventeen centuries.

Close to the temple we experienced an Egyptian-style supermarket. Helter-skelter in an open lot, little stalls were set up where everything necessary to live here could be bought—camels, donkeys, food, grain, primitive hardware, clothes, and such services as hair cutting, donkey trimming, and soldering a handle on a tin can to make a cup. Horse and carriage took us back to the boat and we sailed some distance before the towering pylons disappeared from the skyline.

Next day on the river we sighted the straw-carrying felucca. We had passed them once before and thrown some cigarettes aboard, so now felt well acquainted. With no wind at all to take them south they were anchored in midstream and waving at us frantically. We hoped they weren't going to ask for a tow all the way to Aswan, but when we came close and Ahmed had exchanged the proper greetings, it turned out they wished only to be towed up to another felucca anchored a short distance ahead. It was easy to oblige and they seem inordinately pleased. In fact the usual gestures of thanks just wouldn't do and Douglas Fairbanks broke into a joyous jig on top of the cargo of straw. We could only speculate on why they wanted so much to join the other felucca. For sociability? For protection? Perhaps for food, as they said they had already been becalmed for two days.

In another day we reached the narrowest part of the Nile, only 1640 feet, at Silsila, the site of great sandstone quarries of ancient times on either bank. On the starboard hand, a strange rock formation looked like a jagged natural column surmounted by a table top. And beyond that, quite close to the river's edge, nestled among brush and low overhanging cliff appeared what we later thought of as "our temple."

It was of reasonable size for humans, nicely proportioned, a wall between two embedded columns covered with familiar looking inscriptions and surmounted by a little cavetto cornice. It wasn't really a temple at all, probably simply the wall of a noble's bomb. There was no entrance to anything, but it was charming. Just a little to one side was an inviting spot for

On the *Yankee* we considered this "our temple." Tied to a bush between a curious rock formation and this charming little building, we felt accepted compared to our awestruck reaction at Egypt's huge temples.

the *Yankee* to poke her bow, and we all clambered ashore. We could make up our own story about our "discovery." There was no information in our guidebooks. All the better. But I felt the need of some token of recognition, something we should say or do. Then I knew. To the left of the central wall was a rectangular recess about two feet high and eight inches deep. It needed an offering. The Bassalia poinsettias and chrysanthemums were still fresh. I put them in a large glass coffee jar and found the proportions all right. The niche was a difficult place to reach, even with Irving boosting me, and I felt rather like a felucca sailor aloft with nothing good to hang on to. But the offering was placed and looked bright and appropriate and satisfying as we sailed away.

Kom Ombo was the last free standing Egyptian temple we would see and had the loveliest location for a river traveler. It stood high above us right at the river bank, bright blue sky showing between its columns. The elaborate capitals give it a romantic rather than an overpowering air. There were no stupendous pylons. Like Edfu, it belongs to the Ptolemaic period and is unusual in being dedicated to two gods: Horus the Falcon and Sobek the Crocodile.

The present, however, held greater interest for us than the past here at Kom Ombo. In the morning we were to meet General Anwar Bahaa El-Dines who was in charge of the tremendous resettlement program here for 70,000 Nubians whose villages, upstream from Aswan, will be drowned by the waters held back by the Aswan High Dam. The desert east of Kom Ombo town is to be irrigated for the Nubians to farm and they will live in government-built villages nearby. General El-Dines impressed us as a very capable administrator for this big job, and we liked him personally too. He was big and unpretentious, friendly and direct. We wished there were such a man to run each of Egypt's new enterprises.

Mr. Mahmoud Gawish, the local director of the Kom Ombo Company, would take us to visit the new villages. This company originally irrigated and planted sugar cane, made molasses for the Kom Ombo Sugar Company, and supplied stalks for Canex. We went through the sweet Turkish coffee ritual in his office before getting into the two cars.

The village we inspected was Debod, named for the old village in Nubia The first evacuees had come here in November, and now in late December the population was 1395, made up of 487 family units. Our hearts sank at the sight of New Debod. Everything was laid out in straight lines. "Looks like a bowling alley," said Win.

The uniform houses and courtyard walls were of dark gray stone, all

The impersonal straight lines of the government-built village where the Nubians will be settled contrasts rigidly with the picturesque homes they have had to leave as the waters rise behind the new Aswan Dam. (*Zacher*)

attached to each other in the size of small city blocks. There was no vestige of shade except from the walls of the houses, and here the people crouched on the hot sand. Only children ran about.

This couldn't be as bad as my first impressions and I looked farther. Trees had been planted, just little dry sticks with protective fencing around them, but shade would come in time. At one end of the village stood one entirely different structure, the white mosque. The doors of the houses were not uniform. They were the precious wood doors brought from their old homes. We entered a small courtyard and a guide explained the plan. Each family has one or two bedrooms, a kitchen, a divided courtyard with separate entrances for animals and people, and a faucet with running water.

The interiors were a real surprise, nothing like the cave-like mud huts of poor Egyptian villages. There was a high iron bedstead with brightly embroidered gay valance and bedspread. Colorful woven mats were hung on the walls, photographs and bright magazine pictures often had some ornamental framing if only of colored paper. Best dresses hung on pegs.

The kitchen was equally marvelous. Utensils were few and often made of tin cans with handles soldered on, but they hung in perfect rows. Shelves were edged with scalloped or pointed newspaper. A homemade wire scouring pad holder was nailed over the principal shelf on which stood a Primus stove, the chief cooking agent of Egypt. Cleanliness and decoration were apparently necessary conditions to the Nubians. It was explained to us that in their desert country, with only a few cultivable yards by the river's edge, the men could not make a living. So for generations they have gone north, some to go to sea, but most to work as domestics in prosperous Egyptian homes. Which came first I cannot say: natural cleanliness and honesty (for which they are also noted) or training in good households. They would send a large share of their wages back to their families and visit them every two years.

A bashful bride was squeezed into a corner of the kitchen watching us with great curiosity. She was still wearing a profusion of thin gold jewelry in necklaces, bracelets, and forehead ornament. Her *mylaya* partially covered a dress of red and yellow print as bright as all the interior decoration. This was a real change from the drab fellahin and we were eager to learn more about the Nubians.

Mr. Gawish drove us on to see other parts of the resettlement project: a small hospital, a big central bakery for each sizable village, the tractors leveling the desert for irrigation. Three hundred tractors of different nationalities are doing the job. What a problem in spare parts! A total of 33 villages are being moved, and the total of 70,000 people includes 55,000 from Nubia plus 15,000 who work away from home. The last of them were to be here by June first. We went to the huge pumping station which will raise the Nile water beyond the ability of thousands of shadufs, so that 50,000 new acres can be farmed. The Nubians have never been real farmers, but change must come.

chapter XII

Aswan

At Aswan the Nile breaks through a granite barrier and tumbles through the First Cataract. This is not a waterfall or fast enough to be called white water, but the amount of current and the great jumble of rocks have always been a serious obstacle to navigation. Not an insurmountable obstacle, however, even in ancient times, for there were so many desirable things to the south: land to be conquered, slaves, all the strange products of tropical Africa. So Breasted tells us of a pharaoh about 2500 B.C., "The enterprising young Mernere then commissioned Uni to establish unbroken connection by water with the granite quarries by opening a succession of five canals through the intervening granite barriers of the cataract; and the faithful noble completed this difficult task, besides the building of seven boats, launched and laden with great blocks of granite for the royal pyramid in only one year."

149

These canals or channels must have been dug at low water, and though it seems an extremely difficult order to carry out, it is quite in line with the engineering accomplishments of the pyramid builders. In later years these channels choked up at times, but were always cleared again, for the ancient kingdom often extended to the Second Cataract 200 miles farther and the lines of communication had to be kept open. The famous granite island of Elephantine rose near the lower end of the First Cataract, and here the Lord of the Elephantine had a natural stronghold and control point for halting all passing traffic.

The word Assuan originally meant market, and it was obvious that this rapid and constricted part of the river had an important destiny, especially important again today.

The *Yankee* became engaged in the first of the fast water and found an ideal berth out of the current just below the Cataract Hotel. A few feluccas, painted and cushioned, tied up here for the short winter season's business of taking hotel guests for a sail in the Cataract. Our lines made fast to small trees on the port hand, the *Yankee* lay gently against a steep rock, her bowsprit over the bank serving as our gangplank..

The Cataract Hotel is unique. I would say it was Victorian in Moorish style. Dark woodwork and columns, high ceilings, much of that wooden filigree in cabinets and "harem screens" stylish in American and British drawing rooms of the period, and pointed horseshoe arches outlined in striped tiles altogether composed a decor that made me at least dream. of Arabian nights. Down the long corridors, the white painted woodwork and doors to bedrooms relieved the darkness. How many layers of paint had they accumulated through the years? Nothing so modern as plastic or plywood spoiled this old-fashioned hotel.

I hurried into the New Cataract Hotel, an annex in Hilton style, only long enough to get my hair done and never deserted the Old Cataract again. Its broad tiled verandah commanded a splendid view of the fast water, and there at all times of day guests gathered around little tables for drinks or tea or Turkish coffee. I spent every spare moment there myself, fascinated by the assortment of people in this wonderful setting. Americans and British were fewer than in Cairo and Luxor, but many other European nations were represented and I believe every country of the Middle East and many from Africa. One day I encountered in the corridor a delegation from Nigeria whose flowing robes made *galabias* look like sheaths. They were accompanied by Egyptian Army officers wearing many decorations. Our admired friend General El-Dines was among them and he later brought a friend

Yankee ties up below the Old Cataract Hotel at Aswan. Colorful Arab hangings with geometric appliquee shade the old-fashioned verandah. (*Zacher*)

aboard. Irving and I were below and had not heard anyone on deck when suddenly our diesel engine started. Irving dashed up to find General El-Dines proudly showing off our Morse control just as Irving had demonstrated it to him a few days before.

The Cataract Hotel verandah had another delight for me—the beautiful appliqueed Moorish hangings from the eaves to keep the sun from guests' eyes. These must have been common in Egypt fifty years ago, for we had seen them, worn and faded, shading stalls in the Cairo bazaar, but these at Aswan were fine specimens. Each was the size of a double bed sheet covered with one huge, intricate, rather geometric design. I think they were originally used for the fine Arab tents. I loved to sit here, with the varnished top of the *Yankee's* mainmast glinting through the trees, and listen to the variety of languages and speculate about those around me: archaeologists, Russian engineers for the High Dam, Syrians, Lebanese and Turks, tourists, a missionary or two, European families from Cairo who had come for Christmas, and the Egyptians themselves, all being served by waiters in the long red-sashed oftanes, which are wraparound garments as opposed to the pullover *galabias*.

Every morning Irving and I sat up in bed and watched through our stern windows for the moment when the sun would strike the rocks of Elephantine, as it picked up different shades of pinks, browns, and grays. Aswan granite is beautiful stone on which cutting and polishing brings out more hidden quality. We saw many evidences of the ancient quarrying methods where lines of holes had been drilled into which tightly fitting wooden wedges were driven, which swelled when wet and cracked the rock apart. Not far from town we visited the Unfinished Obelisk. Weighing over 1000 tons, it would have been the largest of them all, but was never completed, probably because of a crack which appeared on its surface. Still lying in the quarry, it mutely told us of work abruptly interrupted. The long surrounding trenches had been cut down to about ten feet by thousands of man hours of handwork. The "cutting" was done by the fantastically long process of rubbing the granite with another hand-held rock, to wear it into dust which could be thrown out. Then more rubbing and more dust, on and on and on! In following orders for granite obelisks and colossi, the weight was reduced as much as possible by quarrying in the rough form desired rather than in big blocks to be shaped later. The boats were loaded in a bed of sand at a time of low water and then raised by the flood, but that arrangement seems but a small part of the process of how these 1000-ton loads were moved from quarry to boat, adjusted, supported, and the estimates for their

Near Aswan the tremendous Unfinished Obelisk of granite shows how these thousand-ton pieces were cut from their rock beds by workmen rubbing with hand-held stones. As the powdered granite was thrown out, the workmen's trench deepened. (*Zacher*)

flotation successfully made.

Irving watched all traffic that passed through the Cataract, but there was not a great deal. The feluccas unloaded below the fast water. Of course we could expect no chart of the channel, but he noticed the course the occasional barges took. We had a sail in one of our neighbor feluccas, not just for the delightful sensation of skimming back and forth across the uneasy swelling water in a picturesque craft, but also to pick up any additional clues about judging safe areas. In the shallow draft felucca, we tacked around black rocks and over behind Elephantine near Kitchmer's Island. Ahmed pointed out a mansion where he had been a house-party guest in the old days. There were just a few such houses built in what we thought was one of the most desirable locations in Egypt. How I wished I could know the stories of them all. We identified the low green-roofed white plaster house of the late Aga Khan, and on a desert hill behind it his splendid domed tomb. Though I had no idea of it then, that was one story I would step into.

As usual, everyday concerns were all mixed in with the marvels. But one day could hardly be called an everyday matter: Christmas. Though we had heard no carols or ads and were enjoying perfect summer weather, December 25th was approaching. Of course, this setting was truer to the first Christmas than our snow, holly, and evergreen picture. Ahmed and I went to market not by horse and carriage this time, but by felucca, tacking against the wind down toward the town. We first walked up to a man who was selling chickens and small birds and asked about a turkey. Nothing simpler! He led us to his house and in the courtyard presented several turkeys to choose from. I didn't know what points to look for in a live turkey, but put on a sagacious air and made my selection. He wanted to kill it in front of me so that I would know I was getting the right one, but I turned my back and let Ahmed do the witnessing. Then we went off to do other errands while the seller plucked and cleaned it.

For a Moslem market town, the rush and crowding certainly gave a Christmas feeling. Most of the crowd was clad in *galabias* and *mylayes*. The donkey carts were so thick that I seemed to be menaced half the time by the animal and the rest of the time by the high, muddy wheels. Russian families were out shopping for toys as well as food. One shopping bag said "People's Republic of China." Now why did it say that in English? I am sure those Russian wives of hefty build were as pleased as I was at the variety of fresh things: eggs, peas, beans, big glowing tomatoes, oranges by the hundreds, the especially good Egyptian cucumbers, potatoes, onions, and

A Russian bulldozer works in the powdery desert sand hills for the Aswan
High Dam. (*Zacher*)

garlic. This was probably a better assortment than they could find back home and perhaps they would be sorry to leave Egypt. We had seen the blocks of apartments where they lived in segregation as usual, making no friends locally.

It was hard to watch everything and not step into a puddle on the unpaved streets. That was another hazard. Since there was no rain I could only conclude that the puddles came from slops thrown out of windows. Outdoor tailors were bent over their sewing machines. Rows of tiny shops displayed bolts of yard goods partially unfolded to hang on the breeze, stationers' stacks of dusty notebooks, baskets of all shapes and sizes, and one big window suggesting a department store. An occasional horse cab parted the throng, but no automobile tackled these streets.

Ahmed found the Cooperative. A long line of determined Russian women at the meat counter were bent on getting meat that didn't look worth the struggle to me. I was very happy, however, to find flour and cheese both of which had been unobtainable in Luxor. One cheese was labeled "Gouda" but came from Poland. Another labeled "Edam" came from anywhere but Holland. The supply was limited, but Ahmed turned his most persuasive talents on the boyish manager, explaining that we were about to spend three weeks in Nubia where we could expect *no* provisions and we needed more than a day's ration.

This young man spoke some English and informed us that he was leaving in a few months for the University of California to get his PhD. in sociology! I couldn't imagine how he was going to follow a lecture at graduate level with so little English at his command. He was surrounded by a great living sociological laboratory, but perhaps it would take a PhD. from California to make something of it. We returned to two little boys Ahmed had set to guard our purchases. One was having a cigarette and shoeshine, perhaps in anticipation of his earnings. I was glad I did not have to figure what was fair payment. There was no protest at what Ahmed gave them so I asked how much it was—twelve cents each. We picked up laundry we had left on arrival. Such services were always available in the towns if one had Ahmed to locate them! Then a fair wind took us back to the *Yankee*.

In the late afternoon the men departed for some night photography at the floodlighted works of the High Dam, so I was able to carry on with my best efforts for a Christmas Eve supper and the next day's dinner. When I heard them returning, I quickly plugged in the little glittering gold tree on top of the hatch which a friend had given me the year before for our Nile Christmas. Food, presents, and poems helped the festivities, but Ted and Win produced the real masterpieces. Win, whose wide newspaper experience had included cartooning, had been working for weeks, unknown to Irving, on a hilarious book of drawings entitled "Irving and Exy Sail the Nile," over which we laughed to the point of tears. Ted had made a surprise Christmas tree for the table. Some evergreen from the bank set in a brick was festooned with colorful cutouts in the shape of Hathor, Horus, camels, and feluccas. Popcorn from the Aswan market made a pile of snow around it, and if one looked closely, one could see that the red wrapping of the brick said "Finer filter for finer flavor." It was the first all-adult Christmas Irving and I had ever spent, but perhaps the five-year-old Yankee made things seem young and gay.

I turned in for a peaceful end to a Christmas Day, I thought, but I was wrong. Irving had noticed the river dropping and had twice slacked out our lines. Our felucca neighbors thought it wouldn't drop any more, but it did. When Irving got up at 2:30 to slack off some more, the *Yankee* heeled sharply to starboard. This time she was aground on solid rock. He took a long ¾-inch nylon line from our starboard quarter far along the riverbank, but no amount of pulling moved her. Ahmed was up, and a felucca neighbor who slept on his boat was giving a hand. How could Ted and Win possibly sleep through all this, I wondered, but we were all too busy to go below to wake them. Then they appeared over the bowsprit! They had been to the opening of the New Cataract Hotel night club.

"What's happening?" I heard Win ask as he took in the scene of activity and the canted ship.

Ted's reply was to the point. "Skipper's got the big salvage tackle out and you know what that means!"

Of course it meant more heaving and hauling, but by four o'clock the *Yankee* had not budged. Irving concluded she was impaled on a point of hard granite which stuck up the centerboard slot. None of us slept very well at a steep angle the rest of the night.

What had happened to the river? We learned that the level had been purposely raised for the passage of a peculiar boat, which we would meet later. Now the Aswan Dam sluices were mostly closed to keep the river low for the next six months!

The situation needed Ahmed's words rather than our heaving and hauling. Unfailing as usual, he came back from the telephone to say that the river was being raised again for the *Yankee*. Even the pharaohs couldn't have done that! We later heard that the engineer at the dam thought Ahmed was Nasser's secretary. Irving figured a half day would do it, but it was night before she floated clear, as the flood had to back up from the dam down-stream some 200 miles. While we waited, some of us went off in a taxi about thirty miles downstream in search of a camel market we had heard about. It didn't materialize, but the dusty drive, mostly out of sight of the river and behind a dull bank, made me realize how marvelous it was to see Egypt from the river. Since the life of the people had always been insepa-rable from its life-giving water, it afforded the perfect view of the country. Driving through the valley would be monotonous, dreary, and terribly dusty.

Of course, we saw the Aswan Dam works, escorted by the public re-lations officer after proper inquiries by Ahmed. Size is the greatest feature of the dam, for it is neither experimental nor extraordinary in construction. It's basically a giant geographical blockage of the river. 43,000,000 cubic meters of earth and rock will be moved. It will be nearly a kilometer, six tenths of a mile, in thickness, and the lake above it will be the second largest man-made lake in the world, 311 miles long.

The Russian engineers were not very conspicuous, as the Egyptian labor population is so large in the employ of the Osman Ahmed Osman Company, a big Egyptian engineering firm. We were told that no job had ever equalled the continuous manhours here, as operation goes on 24 hours a day, for an expected period of eight years with no Sundays or holidays off. In several places we noticed the number 144 in large figures. It was then 144 days to the May 14th deadline when the first major part of construction was to be completed—and it was! By that date the channel would be ready to divert the Nile from its age-old course so that in the dry river bed the foundations of the dam itself could be laid.

We were readily allowed to go down for a close-up view of the work in this channel, with no hard hats or safety measures. It is not simply a matter of diverting the Nile into a large canal. To generate power the water must flow through great tunnels for electric turbines. Eight huge tunnels were being dug through the granite, and we could stand right in them, with 160 feet of the granite wall over our heads. Another 200 feet will be built on top of that for the total dam height of 370 feet.

The tons of rock which had been removed were hauled away in 25- and 30-ton trucks, of Russian and English make respectively. Their great loads were then dumped into barges of 250-ton capacity and carried out into the stream, to be dumped in the right places for an upstream and down-stream wall which would be high enough by May 14th to shut off the water from the dam foundation area. We were invited aboard the pusher

For the Aswan High Dam, tunnels 55 feet in diameter must be cut through granite to divert the flow of the Nile for irrigation and flood control, and for hydroelectric power. (*Zacher*)

boat which shoves these heavy barges into midstream and told to stand in the bow. At a given signal the whole bottom of the barge opened longitudinally, the rocks went thundering down, a big wave seemed to swallow it, and, released of its load, the barge practically shot into the air. There was a cunning attachment which allowed it to jump up suddenly without breaking loose from the tug.

This was the most dramatic aspect of the Aswan High Dam construction that we could possibly have witnessed and actually taken part in, and we were more than satisfied. However, I wish I might have been there looking over the shoulders of Khrushchev and Nasser on May 14th when the Nile first flowed through the great tunnels. We felt Egypt deserved great credit for meeting this deadline. There were bad moments the following September when the peak of the Nile flood reached an extremely high level and nearly crashed over the preliminary walls protecting the dry river bed. By the time Lake Nasser has reached its full height, provision will have been made for a runoff basin for extraordinary flood heights, but 1964 was not the year the Egyptians wanted the Nile to break records.

After our privileged visit to the tunnels, we viewed the whole enormous layout from a high vantage point available to the public. Then the men wanted to clamber along an edge of the huge excavation for one more camera angle. As I was waiting, a great commotion arose in that direction and I ran with hundreds of workmen, fearful that that particular edge had given way. But the cause of excitement was a fire in some high scaffolding. *Galabia*-clad figures. clambered around just as they do on the lofty felucca spars. Hoses which wouldn't reach were uselessly brought to the scene. No CO_2 fire extinguishers appeared, but the blaze was put out somehow. Egypt's ways are seldom the most modern or efficient, but numbers and manpower do many jobs.

The Aswan High Dam is to control water so that 1,000,000 new acres of land may be irrigated and become productive. 700,000 acres now under cultivation will be able to produce three crops a year instead of one. Artificial fertilizer, to be manufactured right near the dam, is to do what Nile silt has done for the land for past centuries. There is some question what will happen when the silt the river carries clogs the sluices of the dam, but that is not expected to occur for another 500 years, so doubtless a solution will be worked out before that time. The first explosion which started work on the dam was touched off by Nasser in January 1961. The final completion date is expected to be about 1970.

If this High Dam would only do for Egypt all that is sometimes

Yankee, the last foreign seagoing vessel to pass Aswan into Nubia, points her bowsprit at the white lines that mark the site of the High Dam, which should be completed by 1970. (*Zacher*)

claimed for it! However, Egypt's population is increasing at a rate that literally swallows up all progress in irrigation. By the time the dam project has added the million new acres for cultivation, there will be more people per acre than there are now. Even more than the High Dam, Egypt needs to bring a halt to the rapidly rising birthrate. That is a project far more difficult than dam building.

Back aboard *Yankee*, where she was now carefully moored away from that sharp rock that had impaled her, we prepared to force our way up through the Cataract. Today this is not the exhausting struggle, requiring hundreds of men pulling on long ropes, that it was before 1902 when the original Aswan Dam was built by the British. The height of this dam was increased in 1912 and again in 1923. Now the Nile is backed up till the water level is over a hundred feet above normal. Just five miles south of this dam the new one is being built another two hundred feet higher.

After May 14th no ships will be able to pass from the lower Nile to the southward into Lake Nasser and the land of Nubia, for there will be no locks around the High Dam. The *Yankee* had come here with not much time to spare, but at the end of 1963, it was still possible to rise beyond the Cataract by a series of five locks and then continue on over the waters, were we had just assisted at the dumping of 250 tons of rocks.

Our passage of the Cataract was plenty exciting, but not desperate. Large whirlpools and swirling muddy waters in strange, crooked, rocky channels all add up to fun in a craft built like *Yankee*. Still, it was with a certain relief that we negotiated the locks, where our mast cleared an overhead bridge by just four inches. Here we entered Nubia. Off to starboard, on the high, rocky bank we could see the broad white painted stripe where the high dam would be. We motored past the vast construction site, rounded the broad pipes spewing out black dredge mud, waved to a motorboat or two moving by us on business, and from one got the surprising friendly response of "Hi, Yank!"

chapter XIII

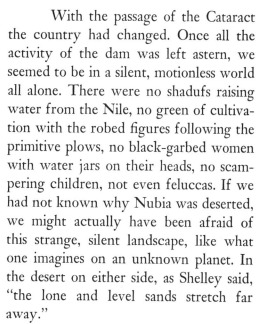

Nubia

With the passage of the Cataract the country had changed. Once all the activity of the dam was left astern, we seemed to be in a silent, motionless world all alone. There were no shadufs raising water from the Nile, no green of cultivation with the robed figures following the primitive plows, no black-garbed women with water jars on their heads, no scampering children, not even feluccas. If we had not known why Nubia was deserted, we might actually have been afraid of this strange, silent landscape, like what one imagines on an unknown planet. In the desert on either side, as Shelley said, "the lone and level sands stretch far away."

Into this impersonal setting the deserted village of Beshir intruded a sense of human sadness. Off to port we saw its cluster of now uninhabited mudbrick houses, their black doorways gaping at us like a stare. The precious wooden doors had gone with the people. We put the *Yankee's* bow to the shore and climbed off the bowsprit. Everything was as the villagers had left it, but in time the water would rise to the lowest doorsteps and inexorably invade the rooms, mounting slowly but relentlessly to drown the whole scene before us and cover the village with the impounded water of the Nile.

Beshir was built on a rocky shore and everything was irregular—the angles of the houses, the paths that had to wind around a big rock instead of going straight, the levels of the different buildings, the natural steps worn among the rocks where people had gone up and down, the contours of the rocks, the light they caught, the color they revealed. It was the irregularity of human beings, the adjustments of their living to the natural setting. What could be more different from the resettlement villages we had seen near Kom Ombo, where everything was laid out in impersonal straight lines, right angles, and uniform repetition.

The people of Beshir hadn't left much behind—not the great discard pile that Americans would leave if a whole community moved. There were pots of various sizes, a pair of shoes mostly soles, a mudbrick grill, some mud ovens that couldn't be moved. A hanging loop of woven strap swayed like a ghostly noose in one doorway. One house had been whitewashed and decorated with some childish paintings of flowers. Could it have been a school?

As we climbed to the highest part of the village, our feet followed the contours that theirs had. There were no gardens, no fields here, only a couple of very short palms by the water's edge. Off to one side lay the graveyard, for the living had had to leave their dead behind. But looking the other way I realized what all the people would surely miss most—the river. Here it was wide, almost like a lake, and little bays indented their shore with the sound of lapping water. The water had always been there to rest their eyes upon, to watch in its changefulness. There was an island offshore. Sails would go by. The river had always been part of their lives.

We did not induce this mood of sadness. It was there, intensified for us by our impressions of New Beshir. Down below, the *Yankee's* familiarity broke up our depression as reason wouldn't, though we told ourselves that progress in the form of the dam had to have its victims, that there were worse things in the world than moving, that millions would benefit from the suffering of comparatively few. But all these reasons didn't completely suppress our imaginations as we looked out before going to bed at the moon shining down the deserted byways of Beshir and sparkling in beauty on the black waters of the Nile. Surely they too had often found it beautiful.

As the *Yankee* fared southward through Nubia, we met other scenes of

A Nubian village looks over the Nile. Its people have recently been removed because it will be drowned by the huge lake rising behind the new Aswan Dam. (*Zacher*)

abandonment and departure, but nothing later ever hit us with the pathetic impact of Beshir. The Nubians, we noticed, had an eye for decoration. Over doorways or on a white front wall, an openwork pattern of mudbrick ornamented many houses attractively. Others had designs painted in white almost like a lacy border. Then there were whitewashed houses with whole scenes telling how the owner had made the *hadjiz*, the journey to Mecca which each good Moslem longs to accomplish once in his life. The means of transportation was the subject for the artist, and rather childish lively representations of automobiles, steamers, and airplanes recalled memories of the wonderful pilgrimage.

We put the bow in near one village whose only remaining inhabitants were three or four shepherds and a last flock of black sheep and goats. A felucca was there and would soon load them aboard. Two cows were already standing in the hold, but the shepherds lingered. Ahmed, accepting a drink of tea, sat under the trees talking with them. The beautiful contours of the sand dunes and hills had drawn the *Yankee* to this particular place. Here the desert looked exactly the way one dreams of it, but seldom sees it. There were no rocks at all, just flowing curves and drifts of pale golden sand. It seemd too bad to mar the purity by our tracks as we climbed the smooth hill. But what fun to run down its warm, soft surface, the way one plays in snow or jumps in a haymow. After the shepherds had made their midday prayers, they loaded the last little black lamb aboard and the felucca moved off down stream. *Yankee*, heading in the opposite direction, laid moving shadows of her masts and rigging on the smooth, towering surface of sand. We were actually sailing through the desert.

At some villages, boxes and chests were piled near shore waiting for the baggage boat, the waterborne equivalent of a moving van. In another place the Government steamer, with a barge larger than itself on either side, already well filled with humans and cattle, was loading as many more people as possible. I saw a slender, black-draped woman come out of her house in the doorway to rest her eyes one last time on the home she was leaving. Remembering my own feeling when I closed my own front door behind me for eighteen months, I felt a wave of sympathy imagining her feelings as she turned away forever.

But another day we came on a scene of quite different mood. A large crowd was gathered in front of a small mosque and they seemed to be jumping up and down. The men's *galabias* were clean and their turbans snowy white. The women were all wearing their brightest reds, oranges, and pinks. Here they do not all cover up with *mylayas*, and when dresses are colored,

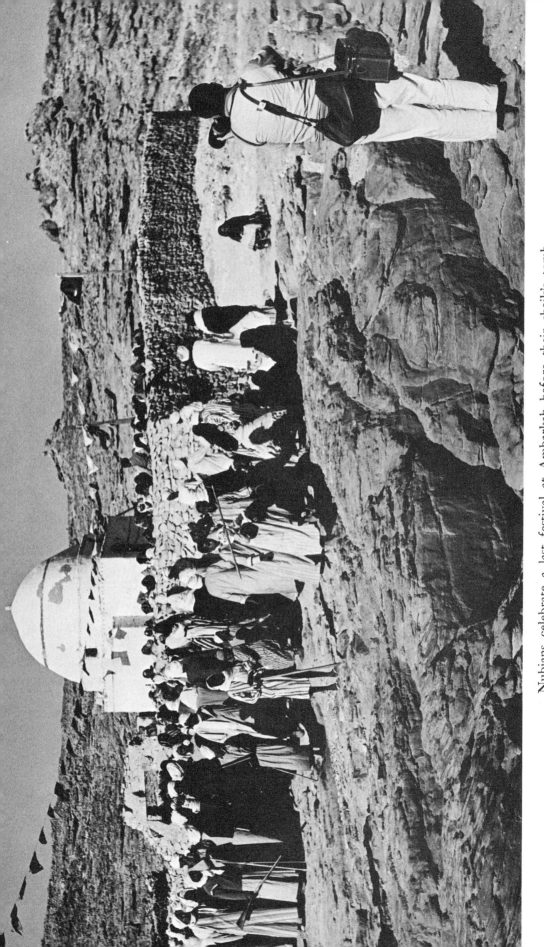

Nubians celebrate a last festival at Ambarkab before their sheik's tomb.
(*Zacher*)

they are always in some shade of red, never blue, green, or yellow. A last festival was in progress for a certain sheik, that is, a local saint. Perhaps he was a jolly saint and required joyous celebration. Everybody was having a fine time and of course we wanted to join the fun. Ahmed was told that later in the day they were all going to a settlement a bit farther upstream where this most important sheik was buried. They would celebrate all night and next day carry out some final ceremonies at the tomb.

We went along till we spotted the white domed tomb on the hillside, and tied up to wait, not very sure just what we were waiting for. For a couple of hours nothing happened, but then four or five small feluccas appeared off the point racing toward us with a fresh breeze. They put in alongside the *Yankee*, and their crowded male passengers hurried ashore over the long, wobbly planks they hastily laid down. Delighted with all this lively activity, and watching closely to see if anyone was going to fall off those insecure planks, we were about to follow the last of them, when to our amazement the deck opened up and out from the hold emerged a whole cargo of brightly clad ladies! Though they must have been stowed down there like sheep or bags of cotton, they were in a holiday mood and tripped ashore in the wake of the gentlemen.

We counted eleven feluccas here for the celebration, nearly 500 people we estimated. On one 25-foot boat we had counted 59 passengers.

By the time we got up near the tomb a dance was going on, getting faster and more exciting all the time. A couple of men were beating drums, others were dancing singly or in groups of three or four, while their friends stood around them clapping, singing, cheering, and for good measure firing a gun now and then. There were quite a lot of shotguns in the crowd, casually slung over the shoulder, to be used, it seemed, just to express exuberance. When a man just couldn't sing or clap or dance enough to express his excitement, he would shoot into the air, the water or the ground. In spite of all these waving guns we felt no alarm. There was absolutely no sense of violence, hostility, or potential rioting such as we had sensed at Nag Hamadi and in some other crowds. There was no liquor to cause trouble, and everyone was just having a great old time.

The women stood at some distance from the men's dance, watching it from higher ground, giggling behind their hands, looking us over with restrained curiosity, but most of all looking over each other's display of jewelry. They were wearing all they had, a big display in thin twenty-carat gold of necklaces, bracelets, pendants, earrings, nose pieces, some as big as a silver dollar, forehead pieces, and rings. For the first time we heard the *zagharett*, the shrill, tremulous cry of the women, an expression of wonder.

Win was doing his best to get pictures of the whole lively scene and close-ups of the interesting faces. Nubians are a handsome people, with gentle, regular features. Though they are darker than most Egyptians to the north, their facial characteristics are not Negroid. It is rather a mystery where this attractive people came from, with their open, pleasant ways, clean, honest, and never beggars. The best way to photograph the men seemed to be to join the dance, so Win jigged around and leapt up and down with them, snapping away when he could. They thought he was such an addition to the dance that they didn't want him to stop for changing film, so rather than interrupt the flow of good fellowship, Win, we saw, was maneuvering one film out of and another into his camera while jumping about with the best of them. Of course the usual thirty-pound bag of lenses and spare cameras was hanging from his shoulder all the time. He claims he could not walk straight without it.

The one serious matter that day was the ban on taking pictures of the women. If any of us approached with cameras raised, the group would draw back, turn around, pull a veil from somewhere and make perfectly clear that women were not to be photographed. Even Win might not have been so popular if they had realized what those long lenses of his were doing at times.

Ahmed had joined some of the village elders who were not leaping about and had a long talk. I often wondered what all his long conversations were about. He had a way of getting on good terms with every sort of person—officials, generals, the raw new men in power, felucca skippers, children, village mayors, ladies of any age or type, servants, and of course the people like himself who had been the privileged ones, educated in the West as well as in their own country. These people were the victims of Egypt's Revolution just as the Nubians were victims of the High Dam. Ahmed's old friends had lost not only money and land and possessions, but they could feel no certainty in the future or plan for their children. What they still had in businesses or land, mines, or crops might be taken away from them any day with no warning and no appeal. These decisions came by absolute decree, not by due process of law. None of them wanted the days of Farouk back. They realized that land reform and redistribution were necessary. If a mill or factory or mine was nationalized, they were willing to continue to run it without owning it. But the new regime did not want to use such men, because their experience and savoir faire had been learned under the old regime and reflected foreign influence. The new men, who had often come up through the Army, did not want the others telling them how to do things, even if the results would be better that way.

We understood that this was the nature of revolutions and Egypt was showing it to us first hand. We groaned over all the mismanagement we saw, the projects that looked good but weren't thought through, the waste of money the people needed in their own country thrown into the war with Yemen, the building of rockets, and loans to the Congo. If we despaired, how much more did they! At least Egypt's revolution had been practically bloodless. In other revolutions, men like Ahmed might be dead. Occasionally we heard talk of prison camp and wondered how many men were sent there without trial. We met one, but naturally he did not want to talk of the experience. There were many things people didn't want to talk about. It was even best not to have much noticeable contact with foreigners or much mail from abroad. Of course in Cairo there had to be foreign contacts, but in Upper Egypt the people and the little officials had heard a lot of indiscriminate ranting on the radio against foreigners, so all outsiders were The Enemy in many minds.

Tourists were the exception. They seemed to be accepted in their limited orbit as a special phenomenon. The *galabia*-clad figures who observed them from afar probably did not think of them for what they primarily mean to Egypt: a source of hard currency. To those who had anything to do with them, they meant possible baksheesh. Annoying as that constant cry coud be, it was a natural approach by the very poor to those strange transients who seemed to live so affluently. If the Government had been wise enough in the tourist business to suppress all the baksheesh-beggars, it would probably have been wise enough to put good light in the temples, and to set cetain standards for approved guides as Greece does. We wished most of all that the Government could run a good postal service. Mail was simply unreliable. In our own experience some letters and cables never got out of Egypt; others never reached us. The post offices certainly inspired no confidence. People swarmed around the windows with no suggestion of lining up. In Assiut it took even Ahmed an hour to mail our letters. When I left a letter, I felt as though I had dropped it into a dustbin. In Luxor's big hotel I tried to buy the necessary stamps at the desk, but though the clerk accepted everybody's letters, I found he had no definite idea of how much to charge by weight to Europe, to the United States, or to South America. When I desperately put more stamps than I thought it could possibly need on one important letter and asked him if he thought that would do, he assured me it would and then added, "I hope." In another tourist hotel, all incoming mail was piled on the counter and any guest could look it through and help himself. In fact, in one post office I was motioned behind the counters to look for any letter around there I thought might be for us. If we were unhappy about personal mail, how discouraged were the complaints of businessmen! As a matter of fact we lost some but not much mail, but the whole uncertainty was extremely unpleasant. Of course, as someone pointed out, the postage on a heavy airmail letter to the States was more than some men earned in a week.

Ahmed came back from his conversation with the Nubian elders and reported some interesting bits. "This celebration will go on all night and next day they'll wash the green cloth cover of the sheik's tomb. They'd like it, Skipper, if the *Yankee* would tow them to the place for washing. When they're all resettled south of the Dam, they'll build another tomb. In a few nights now the sheik's servant (a middle-aged man) will have a dream as to where the new tomb is to be located."

Ahmed answered questions about the *Yankee* and all of us. He had apparently got as far as telling about our world cruises in the Brigantine *Yankee*. "He has sailed around the world seven times," one old man exclaimed, "and we are afraid to go to Kom Ombo!"

This same old man also questioned Ahmed about some of the deserted villages we had visited. Were there dogs and cats left behind? We had seen a few and he shook his head at the thought of the poor animals left in the desert. Sometimes the thoughts of such a different people seem unfathomable, but how easy it was to understand this man's kind concern for the animals.

That evening Irving made a very successful contribution to the festivities. Taking our Very pistol with a parachute flare ashore, he made sure he had everyone's attention aroused, and those nearby were wide-eyed at the size of the huge barrel. Then, when the moment had been properly built up, he fired the extraordinary weapon into the sky and the rockets burst in glorious color and descended gently, still flashing, till the awed silence changed to gasps and shouts of marvel and admiration. They had to be satisfied with one performance as we didn't have shells to spare. But I think a whole night of rocket firing would not have been too much for this audience. They loved it.

The night was really cold, and bundled into our woolens, we wondered how the Nubians could make out in their cotton clothing. Those who danced got exercise to keep warm, and as the celebration went on all night, perhaps everyone exercised into warmth. We weren't up to all that revelry, however, and returned to the *Yankee* enjoying the joyous sounds at a distance. Before we went below we saw the *Delta* pass in the moonlight and felt sorry for those who had to miss some of Egypt by traveling at night, and who had no idea of the fun of finding Ambarkab and taking part in a Nubian celebration.

chapter XIV

≈

Digs

≈

"Then as we were Niling along, off to starboard we noticed some temple columns and a houseboat with a sign in English and Arabic, Registration of Documentation! We pulled up alongside and met the archaeologist, Lotfy El-Tanbouli." That is how my diary started the account of our first encounter with an archaeological dig in Nubia.

The imminent disappearance underwater of so much of Nubia rang alarms in the back rooms of museums all over the world. Scholars and scientists persuaded universities, museums, and governments to finance the last possible expeditions to gather evidence of what life had once been in Nubia. Many countries with credits in Egypt allocated piastres for this purpose. So now Egyptians, French, British, Dutch, Poles, Americans, Yugoslavs, Germans, Japanese and Spaniards (to name only those we heard of) were working against time in Nubia. They had so many questions. What was this country like before it became desert? What people and animals lived here, when and why did they leave? What can we add to our knowledge of Greece and Rome from the remains of forts, inscriptions, even the scrawlings of the passing soldiers on the ancient Egyptian temples? These defacing initials, dates and comments are now dignified as "graffiti" and interest archaeologists. What was the early Christian history here with Coptic churches, their mural art, forts, and burial grounds? Against whom were they defending themselves: Romans, Egyptians, or later Moslems? Some of these questions may seem very academic to most of us and yet there may be clues in Nubia to revelations of great scope about our past. Our own experience of Egypt had made us realize that our own roots were here, just a little deeper than they are in Greece and Rome.

Lotfy El-Tanbouli was a delightful person. Joining us for tea in the after cabin, he told us that he was working alone at this small temple of Gerf Hussein. We thought the solitude must be rather dreary, but our expression of sympathy on that score led him to give a hilarious account of his trials when working in a famous place, like Abu Simbel, that attracted tourists. He would be up on his scaffolding puzzling over a partially obliterated inscription when some tourists would call up to him, "Come and show us the temple!" Or, if he was working down low, passers-by would pick up his reference books, look through them, lose his place, or even walk off with them. The archaeologist to them was just part of the antiquities to which their tickets gave them access. Laughing at his stories put us on common ground with this Egyptian stranger, as the old Nubian's concern for the abandoned dogs and cats had. It is such a pleasure to feel this meeting of minds, no matter how trivial the bond. If one could only hit upon them, there were undoubtedly hundreds of such bonds between us and the Egyptians of every sort all around us, though we looked so different to each other.

Lotfy El-Tanbouli certainly treated our interruption of his work most graciously. He was "recording" the whole temple before its drowning, and with his explanations and the limited scale of a small temple we could understand how an archaeologist worked. He was filling notebooks with beautiful little drawings of every remaining figure, inscription, hieroglyph, and even every line on the walls of this temple. Day after day the workmen would move the scaffolding or place the ladders so that he could systematically record every square foot and locate it according to a numbered diagram of the temple. Photography was also used but could not begin to do his job, for little shadows made by the inscriptions themselves would obscure what his eyes and pen could reveal.

Gerf Hussein was carved out of the bedrock by local workmen in the reign of Ramses II at the orders of Setaw, a noble of high degree, and dedicated to the god Ptah. It seemed to us Ptah showed up a great deal less than Ramses who, as usual, was represented in a number of colossal statues. This comparatively small, country temple followed the plans of the great ones, with pylons, colonnaded court, central hall 45 feet square, anteroom, and innermost sanctuary. Of the eight statues of Ramses in the hall, only one will be preserved, and the archaeologist placed us in the spot where we could best appreciate its fine carving and the expressiveness of the features. Then in the sanctuary he showed us two finds which had rewarded his devotedly careful study. Each of us had to climb his ladder to see for ourselves the bit of gold, about 3/4 inch square, still on the forehead of the statue, and behind the ear of another a little piece of linen covered with gold—after 3200 years! To what color and richness of the past these tiny bits bore witness! Lotfy El-Tanbouli's pride and delight in his precious finds told us something else—all the indefatigable study, dedication, and love that make an archaeologist half artist, half scientist.

"Niling along" again, we tied up for lunch by a houseboat made into a hospital ship and were pleased to be invited aboard. Our impressions were far from pleasing, however. Everything was dirty, especially the galley. The equipment was so meager it seemed practically useless—just a few basins, chipped enamel pitchers, dried-up pieces of rubber tubing, a rusty laboratory stool, and rows of stained bottles, a few lying on their sides on the floor, and flies everywhere. I have seen much medical equipment in the South Seas and small Oriental and African ports that does not meet American standards, but I had never seen anything referred to as a hospital that offered as little as this. The young doctor said he traveled around this district, but what he could accomplish we could not imagine. His assistant looked as slovenly as the hospital.

They were both so friendly and cordial that we wanted to think better of them. When they offered a cup of tea we felt we would be horrid to refuse, but we envied Irving who had stayed back on the *Yankee* and we drank the tea only by steely determination. It did us no harm, however. I felt sorry for any patient who sought help here. It is a good thing no crystal ball told me we would desperately need the services of a Nubian hospital before long.

This was New Year's Day, and though we had no expectation of a celebration, we sailed into a memorable experience. The wide river was quiet and empty of other craft that afternoon. The desert shores are particularly lovely here, rolling away in gentle curves of pale gold interrupted in places by low

Yankee visits an Austrian archaeological camp at Sayala in the Nubian Desert.
(*Zacher*)

rocky cliffs of soft, mellow shades. Then we noticed another interruption: the olive green of scattered canvas tents and one scarlet canopy, a bright curving flash against the desert. A felucca was moored against that western shore and we steered toward her. The red and white flag at her stern we could not identify. Then out upon the farthest rock stepped a jaunty figure. He swept off his broad-brimmed canvas hat, revealing a twinkling face with trim Vandyke. We were now close enough to hear him say, as he placed his hat over his heart and performed a courtly bow, "Velcome!"

This was the Austrian Mission for Safeguarding Nubian Monuments, sponsored by the Vienna Museum of Natural History and led by Dr. Karl Kromer of the University of Vienna. Our charming greeter was Dr. Johan Jungwirth, curator of the museum and specialist in Physical Anthropology and Prehistory. We were invited to tea under the scarlet canopy, and Viennese charm took over the deserts of Nubia. Four other members of the expedition were Austrian and, as at all digs, they had with them an Egyptian Inspector. But unlike all expeditions, they were on the friendliest terms with their Egyptian colleague and told us, of course within his hearing, how much they appreciated him. I am sure this was true, but I think Viennese grow up learning that it does no harm to pay compliments, smooth all relationships, and extend hospitality to strangers. The *Yankee's* company were willing victims of this charm.

We really did feel "velcome," and when they asked quite hopefully how long we could stay, Irving decided we would not go any farther that day. "Splendid," said Dr. Kromer. "Tonight our Kuftis will put on a Fantasia," (pronounced with all the a's long) "and tomorrow we will show you our work. You must have dinner with us tonight."

One of the most interesting things we learned at this dig was the role of the Kuftis in Egyptian archaeology. These are the workmen, 48 here at Sayala, recruited from the village of Kous about 25 miles north of Luxor. Sir Flinders Petrie, a venerated name in Egyptology, first trained workmen from that village a hundred years ago. From the beginning he set a high standard of workmanship and taught his men with great patience and understanding. Now the third generation is supplying labor for the digs and taking pride in their share in unearthing Egypt's past. The Kuftis start in their profession as basket carriers, removing the ten, twenty, thirty or more feet of dust that has buried the past. We watched them next day, a continuous line of carriers marching in threes or fours from the site to the river bank, each man with a basket of dirt on his shoulder, singing as they marched while a leader kept time and set the tunes. The chanteyman was most important to

The Kufti workmen have been trained to remove sand carefully so that no shard or bead is lost which might add to knowledge of ancient times. (*Zacher*)

the spirit of the dig. It seemed as though a basket did not hold very much, but each man makes three to four hundred trips a day and gradually tons of earth are moved.

Even the carriers are trained to load their baskets very carefully, watching for any tiny bead or fragment of pottery. The next step up is to work on laying out skeletons, brushing away dust without harming dry, brittle bones. Eventually a worker may become a real assistant. One old man was pointed out to us—"He worked for Petrie," as we had heard someone say in Greece, "His father worked for Schliemann."

The Kuftis had brought with them all their food for two and a half months: a very hard bread which they dunk in the Nile, some dried chopped-up greens, onions, and *foul*, the mainstay of the Egyptian fellah. They also undertake to store the archaeologists' gear from one season to the next. The Viennese were here for their fourth year now.

But we saw another side of the Kuftis that evening at the Fantasia. It was a very cold night on the desert and the moon was full. Between the Austrians' tents and the Kuftis' camp we sat in a row of deck chairs. All the workmen were in a semicircle in front of us already singing when we took our places. Their leader stood in front of them and directed with a long palm stick. The tunes were monotonous, but not the spirit. They were having a fine time, faces animated, lots of life in their singing, eyes intent on the leader. Then a couple of men began to dance, everyone clapping in rhythm. Our Austrian friends translated the words of the songs. There were lines of greeting to the professors, lines of welcome to us with much repetition. Then the leader would call out a new verse and all would join in, "Now the breeze is coming and the afternoon is getting cooler," or "We will marry a maiden from barbarian Hamat" followed by the thought, "We will marry a maiden from barbarian Austria"! After all, it's all in the point of view. One verse which particularly intrigued me was "Honey on the macaroni!"

A clowning dancer jumped into the center of the ring and his friends got all kinds of laughs out of humor that escaped us in meaning but not in quality. Then a dancer appeared with another man on his shoulders, but all in one costume, cavorting with lively steps and gestures, managing his double height with the greatest skill and comic attitudes. We were already intrigued by this expression of the life of the camp, its fun, its leaders, its jokes among the initiate. But then came an actor we could scarcely imagine coming from what seemed a downtrodden class of society. The young man leapt from the outer darkness into the center of the "stage," startling in a short white dress of sequins, a bright scarf over his head, falsies of some sort making him into a cabaret girl. He wiggled and jerked and sprang about to the uproarious delight of his friends. They loved the act and we did too. But where in the world had the white sequin dress come from? Well, the Austrians said, the Kuftis had brought it along just for this kind of fun. They would put on a Fantasia every night if encouraged. We had never dreamed that Egyptians had all this fun in them. Maybe people really had a good time in those mudbrick villages. Maybe the men did, I decided. I couldn't believe there was much fun in a woman's life in this country. But how rare it is to get a peek into lives so different from our own.

The camp stirred early in the cold next morning. When I looked out on deck at 6:30 three men were in sight: one crouched on a nearby rock brushing his teeth in Nile water with his forefinger, another folded up in prayer, and a third praying standing, very tall and dignified in his long *galabia*, facing east. The sun was just showing over the east bank, lighting up the sands on our side, but not yet spreading any warmth.

Across the broad still water, very blue this morning, smooth untouched sand stretched away around dark, rosy rocks and distant pyramidal peaks. I had never realized that a landscape with no trees could be so beautiful. The Austrians had one of the loveliest settings in all Nubia, and I am sure they will always remember how it looked on those happy mornings, so far from their own country but close to the homeland of their minds. For six fortunate men here, how many hundreds worked on the same subject thousands of miles away, within four walls by hissing radiators, extracting the truth second-hand from papers, not from the desert sand.

We walked over to the Coptic cemetery to see some skeletons still in their opened rock-sided graves. Though these bodies were not mummified in any way, the dry air had preserved them amazingly. Hair and even the rounded flesh of breasts remain after nearly 2000 years. In the "potsherd garden" hundreds of pieces are laid out as they were found, a giant jigsaw puzzle where one man was carefully drawing the record of each piece. From a height we looked down on the large-scale excavation of a Coptic fortress and church slowly emerging from the sand as the singing Kuftis carried off its ten feet of cover.

Back near camp Dr. Jungwirth was explaining about his skulls and bones, all neatly cleaned and labeled in plastic bags.

"About five in a hundred of these people are naturally blond. From the flesh we will be able to identify blood groups—blood grouping is my specialty. Apart from archaeology we are learning to establish paternity. I am a most feared man in Vienna!"

A hilltop excavation frames the tent village of the diggers close to the Nile.
(*Zacher*)

The Nubians are definitely not Negroid, but there were Negroes among them, slaves. "We even found slaves' chains in some of the deserted villages," Dr. Kromer told us.

"What shall I do with this?" Ahmed's voice came over my shoulder. He was holding a large, whiskered fish. Jerking my mind away from skulls and dried flesh, I set it to the immediate problem.

"Do you think you can get someone to clean it?" I asked. Ahmed thought he could, though as it turned out something went awry and I did it later, finding the most clinging interior layer of skin that ever stuck to me. I baked it that night and it wasn't bad. Irving was as complimentary as he could manage to be: "Good for a river fish," he said consolingly.

The young prehistory man, Reinhold Engelmayer, thought we ought to see his "rock carvings." He had found over a thousand. So we all took off in the *Yankee* for a picnic lunch, towing the expedition's felucca astern. The oldest drawings are pre-dynastic, of perhaps 7500 years ago, not so very old compared to some in Europe, but still informative of a totally different life in Nubia. Traced in white paint, they show elephants, rhinoceri, giraffes, lions, and ostriches, and also little boats with many oars. When we read that experts could see the same influences here and in Spain we were dumbfounded. No wonder people want to find all the clues Nubia has to offer! It is said that regarding the ages when there was life in most of the Sahara desert, archaeology has hardly begun.

As we passed a small deserted village, we noticed a flock of sheep near the river and two or three people. These were the desert dwellers, Dr. Kromer told us. They seemed to come from nowhere to investigate the empty villages. Some of them lived by raiding, and the doctor felt uneasy about the camp protected today by only two Austrians.

"But there are the Kufti," I said.

"Yes, but they are not in the camp. They are over the hill digging," he replied anxiously.

"Are these people armed?" I asked.

"They don't have guns, but neither do we, not one in the camp. But they have swords and daggers. I like it best that they have the sheep with them, so they cannot move so fast. I would not like them to come with just camels. One day two tall, handsome youths appeared from the desert—just to have a look, I hope."

What a jumble of different and fascinating elements in Nubia: archaeologists, Bedouin raiders, slaves' chains, bodies with round flesh, Christian paintings, cloth of gold from 3200 years ago, and at the same time the hydro-

Bodies buried for two thousand years in the hot, dry sands of Nubia are better preserved than mummies. (*Zacher*)

foil that sped past every day taking tourists from Aswan to Abu Simbel, not to mention the little Dutch-built *Yankee*, the familiar home for five of us.

Our Austrian friends were such perfect hosts that in their goodbyes they urged us to bring the *Yankee* to Vienna some day. How we would love to. If a certain canal from the Main to the Danube is completed and if political considerations allow, maybe the *Yankee* will get there. The second *if* is the greater. But here in the freedom of the Nubian desert, there were no national boundaries for the archaeologists from all over the world. Their search for knowledge made them one.

chapter XV

≈

Abu Simbel

≈

It was as if we hadn't known what we would find at the end of the next day's run: sailing along through the desert and suddenly beholding a sight so overpowering that it seemed beyond the means of men: the great temple of Abu Simbel. Indeed it is only partly man-made, for it has not been built there, but entirely hewn out of the great rock cliff. Seeing it for the first time was almost like discovery anyway, for words and pictures cannot fully prepare anyone for the experience.

Ramses II ordered this temple for the sun god Re-Harakhti 3200 years ago, and master craftsmen produced statues, reliefs, and paintings that far outclass those of other Nubian temples, mostly of a provincial order. Who was the genius who chose the site for this temple, who visualized its creation out of the sand-stone cliff, whose eye determined the marvelous proportions? It is too bad we can't place his name alongside Ramses' here. The conception was sublime and the execution was on a monumental scale. The architect was carving out nature, not just making pieces.

Many pictures of Abu Simbel do not do it justice because they are taken as close up as its size will permit. I believe it should be seen from a distance that puts it in harmony with the landscape. We should see it with the desert rolling away on all sides and the river winding into the southern distance. Then the 65-foot sitting colossi measure properly against hill and sky, and legs and knees almost as thick as the *Yankee* do not look grotesque or rough. Obviously they should not be finely finished. The smaller figures, though they are colossal too, contribute properly to the grandeur. The great falcons at the corners are suitable birds for gods. The cornice of praying baboons makes a delicate upper border.

For days we looked at Abu Simbel from many angles and distances, and I concluded that the spot from which one is meant to look at it is from the height to the north. I believe the master planner stood there.

The temple changes with the hours of the day, and since it is a sun temple, it is not surprising that the sunrise hour is its most glorious. The cold, dull sandstone comes to life in a warm coppery glow as the sun bathes it. Then through the day the changes follow as the spotlight moves and shadows fall, short or long. In the cold desert moonlight Abu Simbel loses its vitality. Here, late in Egypt's long history, comes out loud and clear the full echo of the earliest faith in the sun, giver of life, manifestation of god to man, glory of the heavens. With its daily departure comes the clear sense of its journey through the underworld, the kingdom of the dead, the cold darkness, the rule of Osiris in his eternity, from which the sun alone returns.

There is an ultimate greatness to Abu Simbel which the world does not want to lose under the waters of Lake Nasser, and so for more than ten years the discussion has been going on about how to save it. The final decision has been to cut the temple into blocks of about 30 tons and reconstruct it on the heights above. The week we left, this work began, and that whole operation will make a great story. No one knows how successful the moving will be, whether the temple can be safely transplanted, what impression a different background will give, or, most important of all, whether Abu Simbel can possibly preserve its original stupendous effect.

Though my real enthusiasm is for that total effect, we of course found a closer study extremely interesting. Whereas the great legs, feet, and hands of the four colossi sitting outside the temple are rough and heavy, the

The authors are about as high as Ramses II's ankle at the front of the temple of Abu Simbel. At the side of the throne in relief are two Nile gods, below them a line of fettered prisoners. (*Zacher*)

faces of Ramses are fine. (The head and shoulders of one now lie broken on the ground.) The handsome, powerful king wearing the great double crown looks out across the river with an expression that still makes us feel the strength of his personality. His queen Nefertari and some of his favorite children (he had over a hundred) are the "small" figures by his knees. Actually the queen is about twenty feet tall and the children twelve or fifteen.

Before going through the door into the great hall, I stopped to look at the carving of the Nile god Hapi, on the side of Ramses' throne. I had been surprised that the Nile god had not figured more prominently in all Egyptian art, so was glad to see him/her here. Obviously he/she was both masculine and feminine.

The whole temple reaches 184 feet into the mountain and this huge hall is 54 feet broad and 58 feet deep, its ceiling supported by eight square pillars adorned with fine statues of the king. Far, far inside, the sanctuary with its four gods is hard to see until eyes become accustomed to the dimness. On one day of the year, the rising sun shoots its first beams directly into this deepest holy of holies, where the rock pedestal for the sacred boat stands before the gods.

I found that the famous north wall of the great hall was a good place to be alone with Baedeker, to follow his explanation of the huge painted relief carving of the Battle of Kadesh on the Orontes in Syria. This was Ramses' own victory, his prime claim to military prowess, and a day of dramatic personal heroism which he never wanted the world to forget— and it hasn't. Personally I felt his one big victory was overrated in comparison with those great campaigns year after year of my old hero Thutmose III, who had planted his banners on the Euphrates 250 years before. But just the same it was fascinating to follow Baedeker's description of the Kadesh battle scene: the mighty Ramses with his battle axe raised high, the march of the army, infantry and chariots, the horses being fed, the soldiers at rest, the king's tent, the council of war, the questioning of spies, the river-girt fortress, the prisoners, the surgeon treating a wound. Like some modern art, this great mural is not constrained by a need to put physical objects in their literal perspective in time or place or relative size. The artist had a big story to tell and he set it forth on one wall so that anyone can understand it.

It is hard to realize that Abu Simbel was completely lost to the world for centuries. Some time after the Roman period the sands began to drift in and cover it. Then it was "discovered" by the indomitable Swiss explorer Burckhardt in 1812. Five years later the Italian archaeologist Belzoni partially cleared it, but that work was not completed till 1910.

A hundred yards to the north stands the Temple of Hathor, which Ramses II built to honor his wife Nefertari. Alongside to the south is a small rock temple which was quite dramatically discovered by the party of Amelia Edwards in 1874. It was the greatest day of her Nile voyage when one of the party, taking a desert walk, discovered with his cane that something interesting lay beneath the sand. All the others rushed to the spot and dug for the rest of the day, eventually gaining access by a hole they could squeeze through to a chamber with untouched paintings in fresh colors. In another day they had recruited a hundred natives from a nearby village and excavated a large part of this little temple. I was glad that Amelia had the thrill of a real archaeological find, for no one had ever enjoyed and appreciated more the wonders of Egypt and the interest of a voyage on the Nile. The great pleasure and satisfaction of the trip stands out on every page of her account, full of careful observation, personal delight, and the gift of expression in both words and drawings. In founding the Chair of Egyptology at University College, London, to which Sir Flinders Petrie was appointed, she made her permanent contribution to Egyptian archaeology.

There is a strange little footnote to history in a small courtyard at the south end of Abu Simbel. There stands a tomb about two and a half feet high, of black polished granite, with the inscription:

Sacred
to the memory of
Major Benjamin Ingham Tidswell, Royal Dragoons
Born 11th May 1850
Died 18th June 1885 while serving in the Heavy Camel Regiment
with the Nile Expedition

What a strange intruder in Ramses' temple!

All our experiences at Abu Simbel were not exalted, however. Some were quite comic. We had arrived late in the afternoon and tied up to the houseboat of a Dutch archaeological expedition. The scientist sitting on the afterdeck barely answered our greeting, rather to our surprise. After we learned what kind of sightseers he had observed, however, we realized why he had developed a certain coldness to all of them. He thawed later. Our own observations of sightseers started unexpectedly about ten that evening with the arrival of a strange vessel, the *Dolfin*. We had seen her once before, towing up the Nile, and thought she must be broken down, but no. Her deep propellers were unprotected, so they had been removed and she was being towed to Aswan; even so she drew seven feet. This was the vessel after whose passage of the Aswan locks the water was lowered, stranding the *Yankee* Christmas night. Designed in Italy and built in Alexandria she was not at all shiplike. Enormous slanting windows came within a few inches of the water and her passengers sat four deep in airplane chairs on either side of a center aisle. Today she had picked up eighty Austrians in Wadi Halfa. They had been supposed to arrive there by plane at 9 A.M., but had not appeared till 4 P.M. They were therefore making a nighttime visit to Abu Simbel.

The charming, and very tired, young wife of the captain led them into the temple, which was lighted for their benefit. The captain was much nicer than his boat and we enjoyed talking with him in the streamlined bar until his tourists returned. After an hour's stay they all sped off into the darkness, back to Wadi Halfa.

On subsequent days we were to watch such one-hour visits at all times of day or night. The hydrofoil brought tourists from Aswan almost daily. The river boats which made the same trip in two days were nothing for a sailor to admire, but they managed to keep their paddlewheels or propellers turning. Some offered a fair degree of comfort and charm, but a few were definitely undesirable, with short uncomfortable bunks and little privacy. Then there was the Sudan Railways boat which had some cabins, but also took deck passengers and cattle.

On these assorted vessels came travelers from all corners of the world, drawn to the magnet of Abu Simbel especially now that it was threatened. At their arrival the temple lights would be turned on and we would take advantage of the illumination to get better acquainted with the great building ourselves. But the light was so poor—just some bulbs strung around here and there. What poor repayment Egypt was making for the interest that had brought these travelers so far!

The quality of the guides was as uneven as that of the boats. Sometimes I could have told the visitors more myself. There was one excellent young woman, however, whom it was a real pleasure to watch and listen to. She not only knew her subject, but could explain it in French, English, and Italian. Moreover she had a real talent for handling her flock— firm, tactful, and flexible. The day I followed along, she had just finished her Italian version in the inner sanctuary of Hathor's temple and was about to switch to French when there was a great commotion near the temple entrance in Arabic. Another group with the local archaeologist was about to come in and they wanted the light. In this smaller temple, a movable light was carried around. She got halfway through her French discourse when the light was yanked away and her tourists were left in darkness and partial ignorance.

Such short visits they all had! There was no time to climb the hill for the view with the full effect of Abu Simbel in its total setting. There was no chance either to learn more facts or simply to let the feeling of the extraordinary place take over. We met four young people who had rebelled against this state of affairs, a Canadian couple, another Canadian girl, and an American man, all of them still close to the student age. They had arrived as deck passengers and refused to leave in an hour; they would stay four days till the Sudan Railways boat returned. We admired their spirit. There was no such thing as a rest house, but they had sleeping bags. There was no restaurant, but surprisingly enough there were a couple of little palm frond houses out of sight down the beach, where they had found they could get tea, rice, and something resembling a meal once a day. We found there were two or three other foreign "inhabitants" here, nearly living on air, it seemed to us. The young people had tried sleeping in the temple, but there were interruptions like the *Dolfin*'s visit all night long. So now they had found some ledges up the hill where they could camp.

"Come up to my cave," one of the girls invited Win.

Two of them called one evening, and although at first we had labeled them beatniks, we found they were well-mannered, nice kids for whom seeing the world required a good deal of fortitude and determination in the place of easy financing. As they left our comfortable cabin I realized how very cold the desert night was and offered some spare blankets. I knew from their eloquent thanks that I had hit the right spot, so I followed up with an invitation to breakfast. The orange juice, coffee, eggs, and bacon made a real hit, but the blankets had been even more appreciated, I gathered.

We made various short trips in the vicinity, once returning under sail with a light breeze that inspired Irving to sail the *Yankee* right up onto the beach as nearly into Hathor's temple as I think any ship ever came. Abu Simbel made an incongruous backdrop for our bright red and white Genoa jib. Ahmed ran to tie the bowline around Queen Nefertari's leg, surely the strangest mooring the *Yankee* will ever have.

There had been no marketing in Nubia, but we had left Aswan well stocked with fresh food including 150 eggs. Fresh bread had given out, and I was making biscuits, muffins, and cornbread. We had also what I might call the Egyptian equivalent of hardtack—the usual round, flat bread,

The *Yankee* appears to have tried to sail into Queen Nefertari's temple which Ramses II built close to his own tremendous Abu Simbel.

toasted and dried so that it kept indefinitely. The Commodore of the Cairo Yacht Club had sent us off with a supply of this and for reasons of space I had almost thrown it away, but now was very glad to have it, as we really liked it. There was a small village, Ballana, not far across the river and Ahmed reconnoitered there and came back with bread and tomatoes. I think the food that our young friends were getting in the palm frond shacks must have come from there, though it was not apparent where anything grew.

At the Dutch dig we had seen how the desert could bloom. A big clay pot of amphora shape had been set in the sand to keep drinking water. The small amount of moisture that seeped through its porous sides had created a tiny encircling garden, and the Kuftis had even planted some greens around it.

We visited the comfortable houseboat of the Oriental Institute of the University of Chicago and were shown some of their most precious pottery finds. It seemed to us they lived the best of any of the digs, and they even had a power launch and a Swiss Air hostess! But a dig we particularly enjoyed was young Nick Millet's for the American Research Center with the support of the National Geographic Society. They were living on the *Osiris*, the last dahabia built by Thomas Cook in the 1930's. (The Nile was where Cook's got its first start into big tourist business.) The old-fashioned cabins, the spacious high afterdeck, and a lovely double curving staircase helped us to imagine the elegance of the last of the Nile houseboat era.

Though this expedition at Gebel Adda was American, it included a couple of Germans, a Swiss artist, and a Frenchman. It also included three young women. Everyone worked hard, starting the day very early, bundled and muffled against the cold. Everyone in Nubia was working against time. They were uncovering a period at the very end of Ancient Egypt and in the first centuries of Christianity. We looked at foundations they had unearthed of stone and mudbrick pyramids: the last, small, distant echo of the great royal Old Kingdom structures. These too had underground burial chambers. The late "Ethiopian" pharaohs, so impressed with the mighty past of the people they had conquered, had copied farther south by the Fourth Cataract the greatest monument of the pharaonic age. There the remains, of unmistakable shape, still stand. These at Gebel Adda Mr. Millet called later "provincial pyramids."

Then he showed us the graves of the early Christian era. In the dryness of the desert sand, bodies had been as well, if not better, preserved than by mummification. Some of them were macabre sights, with flesh still slightly rounded. But the graves yielded many small, valuable pieces of evidence from which scholars fill in the picture of the past. In addition to beads, tools, weapons, and textiles, the American Research Center archaeologists prized a well-preserved jewelry box with carved inlay and an interesting thick cut-glass cup. They located churches with lamps and a censer, and also found evidence of the Moslem transformations. We wanted to know more about the first years of the Christian era. How sharp was the conflict here with the old gods and their conservative worshippers? Judging by Christian destruction we had seen of temple inscriptions and reliefs, the Egyptian followers of Christ felt as strongly about their beliefs as those who turned against paganism in Rome. Only the archaeologists can throw light into these obscure, but interesting years. Perhaps there is evidence here in Nubia of criticial events and decisions, turning points in the first centuries of a new religion that made Christianity what we know today.

Someone at this dig told Ted an amusing story. As the excavation followed a wall, it approached a tall telegraph pole which supported the main wires to Aswan from Wadi Halfa, perhaps all the way from Khartoum. The Egyptian Inspector with the exepedition kindly inquired if the archaeologists wanted to dig right there. As they did, he was quite willing to move the pole, but first he sent a man up to cut the wires! It was several hours before he had them connected again.

Back in Aswan we had complied with various frontier requirements for leaving Egypt and entering the Sudan, as the officials did not stay at the border. We watched for some little outpost where we should report, but when we finally found a policeman, he didn't seem at all concerned about us. And so we crossed into the Sudan and approached the Second Cataract of the Nile, the head of navigation, a spot to which Irving had dreamed of bringing his ship. We tied up in Wadi Halfa. Having come from so far at an average speed of about five miles per hour, was more incredible than if we had been deposited by plane in a matter of hours out of New York.

A Swiss archaeologist with the American Research Center in Egypt records findings at Gebel Adda. (*Zacher*)

chapter XVI

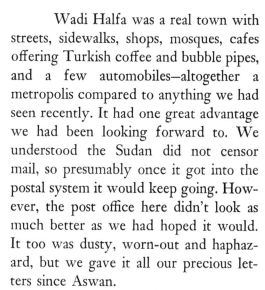

Wadi Halfa

Wadi Halfa was a real town with streets, sidewalks, shops, mosques, cafes offering Turkish coffee and bubble pipes, and a few automobiles—altogether a metropolis compared to anything we had seen recently. It had one great advantage we had been looking forward to. We understood the Sudan did not censor mail, so presumably once it got into the postal system it would keep going. However, the post office here didn't look as much better as we had hoped it would. It too was dusty, worn-out and haphazard, but we gave it all our precious letters since Aswan.

We had got used to the idea of Nubian villages drowning, but couldn't imagine a whole town like this disappearing under water. The lake would not rise to this height for two years, so Wadi Halfa was continuing about its business. Everything was going to be moved off all the shelves in store after store.

Wandering alone in a deserted Nubian village, I was tempted to bring back just one more pot.

Though there wasn't the inventory here that would compare with those back home, still it added up to a real investment in merchandise. What a pitiful refugee picture the evacuation would make.

We wanted to look just a little farther south to see the Second Cataract and its guardian forts, so we hired a rather old Chevrolet sedan for the forty-mile desert drive to Kumma. This was not the beautiful desert we had seen around the Austrian dig. Here hills of harsh black rock jutted out of the sand.

We stopped at the Rock of Abusir, the height from which to view the Cataract, the Gorge of Batn el-Hagar, meaning Belly of Stones. This great jumble of rocks and islands resists the strength of the river which fights its way through in rapids and drops and whirlpools, crashing and cascading, wearing and winning its way toward the sea. An impassable barrier to navigation, the Second Cataract is where Ancient Egypt stops and Africa begins, though there were periods when the pharaoh's control extended farther. But here is the natural division. Above the Cataract certain stretches of the river are navigable, but it is no longer the highway of Egypt.

At Abusir there is a lovely view of greenery and trees by the bank, the tumble of bright water and shining wet rocks, and beyond on the west shore the stretch of desert sands. A white-sailed felucca moved across the northern end of the Cataract as we watched.

But when we got back into the car we left all loveliness behind. The car bounced, jounced, jiggled, bumped, and rattled with every noise its metal could make. Sand poured in through the closed windows, floorboards, door cracks, and got into our clothes, skin, hair, teeth, and cameras. I don't think I would have minded the sand if the country had appealed to me. But it seemed positively hostile, with its jagged hills of black rock which no river had ever smoothed. There was no place for the eyes to rest. This was not fit for human beings. I certainly hoped the car wouldn't break down. Forty miles here would be like a thousand in reasonable country.

When we reached the old fort of Kumma at the southern end of the Cataract and came out on a height over the river, things were good to look at again. Only 300 feet across the rushing water stood the larger companion fort of Semna. It was in the Middle Kingdom, about 1900 B.C., that Sesostris I became the first pharaoh to lead his troops south of the Elephantine and beyond the Second Cataract into Kush. At about this time Abraham was tending his flocks in the Land of Canaan, with a people who had not yet settled down to agriculture. About a hundred years later Amenemhet III of the same Dynasty would erect the great engineering works in the Faiyum.

But before that Sesostris III had his engineers cut a channel 260 feet long, 34 feet wide, and 26 feet deep through the rock of the First Cataract where the Old Kingdom Canal had been neglected. Then, leading his war galleys into Nubia, he found a natural location for twin forts at Kumma and Semna at the fast waters of the Second Cataract. One of his boundary markers there still bears the inscription: "Southern boundary made under the majesty of the king of Upper and Lower Egypt, Sesostris III, who is given life for ever and ever: in order to prevent that any negro should cross it by water or by land, with a ship, or any herds of the negroes, except a negro who shall cross it to do trading . . . or with a commission. All kind treatment shall be accorded them, but without allowing a ship of the negroes to pass by Semna going down stream, forever." Even the caravan trails came close to the river here, so the forts could guard and control all passage by land and by water.

Through the centuries Egyptian power surged back and forth past this natural and man-made barrier. About 1430 B.C., under the empire, the southern boundary was pushed hundreds of miles farther south to Napata by the Fourth Cataract, and Kush, the country beyond this Second Cataract, became the responsibility of the viceroy, known as the Royal Son of Kush. After Egypt's imperial glory passed, the direction of power reversed and what the great pharaohs could never have imagined happened. Their Egypt came under the rule of the Kings of Napata for a century, from about 750 to 650 B.C., the so-called Ethiopian Period.

But these African rulers had no chance of holding their lands to the north against the growing Assyrian power. After a few generations of pharaohs, who opened to their southernmost subjects some of the wonder of Egyptian civilization, they withdrew even south of Napata, making their capital at Meroe. With the protection of five cataracts between themselves and the Asiatics, they lost all contact with the north.

These were the pharaohs who again built pyramids. What greater expression of majesty and power could possibly occur to a king who had seen Giza? Piankhi, a great warrior and the first Nubian pharaoh, had his pyramid erected near Napata. His successors followed this example and later queens and nobles had their pyramids too. Many of these surprising ruins can still be seen all the way to Meroe.

My thoughts went back to the days when Sesostris III built his mighty pair of forts. A good garrison could defend these narrows against any enemy, and could control, inspect, and tax all passing goods. The fortifications had been strong and deep. The best lookout spot in the ruins today is the little temple built at the orders of Hatshepsut and Thutmose III. At a window in that temple, I was standing as far south as I would come on the Nile. Alone for a few moments, I watched the river rush seaward below me, trying to reconstruct in my mind ever so faintly the personalities of those ancient rulers and the greatness of their Egypt.

Nearer Wadi Halfa we visited Buhen, another fort of the five that Egypt found necessary to build in this narrow strategic part of the Nile. Buhen owes a debt to Amelia Edwards, for the Egypt Exploration Society has kept Professor Walter Emery excavating fruitfully there for several years.

He has uncovered a layout that sounded to me more like a medieval fortress town than Nubia. The strongest and best designed of the Nubian forts, Buhen included town and temples. The dry moat was kept whitewashed so night attackers could be seen and shot from special loopholes above. Walls were sixteen feet thick and thirty feet high. Parapets, scarp and counterscarp, inner and outer defenses, double doors and drawbridge all made the stronghold practically impregnable to attack from without. It did fall and was burned, but I think there must have been something rotten within.

chapter XVII

≈

Ibrim

≈

Wadi Halfa had an airport and one plane a week from Khartoum. And on this one plane arrived Donna and Gil Grosvenor from the *National Geographic*. Gil at sixteen had sailed across the Atlantic with us in the Brigantine *Yankee* seventeen years before. We had not previously met his charming young wife, but Donna did not seem like a stranger for more than two minutes. With them aboard we were seven, which I consider crowded on the *Yankee*. But Donna and Gil insisted they had plenty of space and privacy and, though that really wasn't so, the statement proved what good sports and adaptable shipmates they were. It was with them aboard that we made the most of several more days with *Yankee*'s bow on the sand of Abu Simbel. At last we sailed down the curving Nile out of sight of the great temple. Much as we hated to leave our most dramatic mooring it was

The authors under *Yankee's* bowsprit at Abu Simbel. (*Zacher*)

high time as engineers were about to start the 36 million dollar cutting and moving operation. No one aboard *Yankee* wanted to witness that.

We were bound downstream. The current helped us along, but the old friendly fair wind from the north was now blowing at our bow, so that we often wore slacks and woolens, except in the middle of the day, especially if the sky were overcast. Of course the change from solid blue sky to occasional overcast did not mean rain; it just meant that January was advancing.

One day as usual we had no set destination, but toward the end of the afternoon some splendid ruins of an old fort high on the starboard hand decided the question for us. We must have all been gazing upward on that side of the ship at the interesting stronghold, strategically placed on the dominating headland, because we never saw something on the river which we later wished we had.

The fort, Kasr Ibrim, dates back to Roman times, the most southerly Roman holding in the province. But there were both older and later structures here too. In some chambers cut into the steep rocky shore are shrines which tell us of the deeds of viceroys of the great pharaohs. A century ago, we are told, there was good color in these shrines, but since the first Aswan Dam the high Nile has flooded them and considerably damaged inscriptions and paintings.

Long after the Roman garrisons had been stationed here, a Christian church arose, "a large and beautiful church, finely planned, and named after Our Lady, the Pure Virgin Mary. Above it there is a high dome, upon which rises a large cross." It sounds like one of the finest monuments of Egypt's early Christian period, but it would take a lot of archaeological knowledge plus imagination to picture it now from the remaining pillars and arches. Ibrim was attacked by the brother of the great Saladin, the Crusaders' enemy. The Christian town was destroyed and the people taken prisoner. The cross was burnt and the muezzin climbed to its place on the dome and chanted the call to prayer. Like many other churches of that era, Ibrim's became a mosque.

We did not know Ibrim's history as we turned in toward shore there and found a sandy spot to ground the *Yankee*. In fact I never saw the pillars and arches or the ancient shrines, though some of the others did and I learned their story. But remote Ibrim, of which I had never heard before that day, assumed unforgettable importance in my life and Irving's.

There was some archaeological digging going on here. The workmen's camp was just off our bow, but the British scientists lived on a houseboat tied up across the river at the little village of Aniba. We put off our own explorations till next day.

Before breakfast the excavating party landed near us and offered only a minimum greeting, but we attributed that to the morning cold and the early hour. After breakfast we started up the hill, all except Ahmed. The view of the river and surrounding country was lovely, and as we looked about the walls of the fortification, five photographers were considering the best angle for their pictures. For Irving this usually means getting the ship into the picture, so he suggested that I sit on a low wall and he would climb a higher one behind which he could compose me, the ship, the winding river, and the distant desert.

I was posed as directed and waiting when I heard falling rocks. The wall had given way under Irving. I saw him throw his arms over the crumbling wall in an attempt to spread his weight, and I dashed forward to try to break his fall. But his move only served to pull out a big V of rocks and when I reached him he was lying face down, blood streaming down the side of his face, jagged rocks on top of him, dust all over him and even a big stone in his ear. I yelled "Help!" and lifted a rock off his back, then asked him if he could speak. He groaned.

He had been knocked out, but very briefly. The others came running, and still not feeling the full effect of his injuries, Irving sat up and expressed his disgust with that old drylaid wall and himself for climbing it. But we soon had him lying quiet and Gil ran down to the ship for water and medicine. Tearing up a T-shirt, I at least had something to clean him off with when the water bottle arrived. Then we could see the awful cuts. A big three-cornered one above the temple gaped right down to the bone. His nose was cut up and there were other gashes on all sides of his head, a very big one at the back, which we didn't discover then as we didn't want to move him much.

I managed to read the directions with our medical supplies and put plenty of furacin ointment on the wounds as gently as I could. Irving could talk and move his arms and legs, all good signs with a head injury. His skull was not fractured, though taking a quick, unwilling look at the rocks, I realized that was just because the sharpest, heaviest rocks had not hit the most vital places. But he was going to have to have stitches and we needed a doctor.

Where was there a doctor? I tried to think. Then I remembered the visiting Peace Corps M.D. back at Gebel Adda. But how to get him? That was more than half a day's run in the *Yankee*. I thought of the hydrofoil.

It was now 9:15 and she would be coming by before long. If we could stop her, she could get the doctor for us, or perhaps take Irving to the doctor.

"Gil, shout down to the *Yankee* and tell Ted and Ahmed to take her out in midstream and stop the hydrofoil," I said.

Gil went to some spot where he could make himself heard below, and after a shouted conversation came back with the amazing news, "Ahmed has been talking to the workmen and they say there's a hospital across the river at Aniba." We could hardly believe it.

Ted, Gil, and Ahmed would go across with the *Yankee*. Win, Donna, and I began our wait; Irving stayed quiet with his head in my lap. It seemed there was nothing more we could do. I thought of that terrible floating hospital we had visited and felt extremely pessimistic. Putting Irving into such hands was worse than doing nothing, I thought. But I couldn't imagine myself sewing up his scalp. We waited. I suppose men have been injured around old forts like this ever since they were built. I wondered if Irving's chances in this remote spot were much better than a Crusader's attacking a wall and meeting a hail of rocks.

Then we remembered the British archaeologists, too far away to have heard the commotion. They hadn't seemed very friendly, but possibly one of them was a doctor or at least a first aid expert. Win set off to find them.

"They're probably all doctors, but not one an M.D." he said.

The first person he met was a young New Zealander. After the first greeting the young man said, "You know our chief isn't very pleased with you people."

"Why not?" asked Win in surprise.

"Well, you really should have given some help to our Egyptian inspector yesterday when he was drifting in the river."

It seemed their inspector with a couple of workmen had started across the river in the afternoon and his outboard motor had failed. Having neither oars nor sail, he was drifting helplessly when the *Yankee* came along. He had waved to us frantically and it seemed to him we coolly ignored him. As one of the most enthusiastic towers and rescuers afloat, Irving could not possibly pass up an appeal for help. We must have all been gazing at Ibrim's high fort when the inspector was trying to signal us. Certainly none of us had seen him. So that explained the archaeologists' curtness this morning. Win went on to find their "chief," at least armed with the knowledge of what sort of reception he would get.

In time he returned to Donna, Irving, and me with (according to his card) "The Reverend Professor J. Martin Plumley, M.A., M. Litt., Herbert

Thompson Professor of Egyptology, University of Cambridge, Selwyn College," a large, tweedy man. He at least knew some questions to ask which we hadn't. "Did he bleed from the ears? Did he vomit?" We were glad we could say no to both.

Professor Plumley had brought along a couple of Kufti and the makings of stretcher, but we all agreed to wait for the doctor. He was able to tell us, however, that the doctor was good. Of course, I didn't know how good that was, but felt slightly encouraged. Then we heard a few words about courtesy of the river, which we did not think we deserved, but nothing was to be gained by continuing that subject and Professor Plumley then seemed ready to bury the hatchet.

Even now it was an hour's wait—a long hour—before the *Yankee* got back and Dr. Samir Shalek Farag arrived with the hospital stretcher and bearers. As soon as we saw him we felt better. He was not the hospital boat type, but a confident, capable-seeming, stocky, clean young man. He took a good look at the wounds, pulling back the flesh as I don't think I could have, and knew what needed to be done. His men got the stretcher under Irving and we all left the scene of Roman wall, fallen rocks, blood, and dust. I decided now that Irving was much better off than the battered Crusader I had imagined.

Irving himself directed his getting aboard to the clear space on the foredeck. Handing the heavy stretcher across the jagged, wobbly stones of the shore and over the water was not a good moment, but they made it successfully and Ted got the *Yankee* underway. On the other side we tied up to a barge and there was more awkward clambering to get ashore. Somehow I had a moment to notice what a lot of brigands those stretcher-bearers looked like, half of them barefoot, the rest in clodhoppers, and one with a rifle over his shoulder, their long *galabias* flapping about. By this time two or three uniformed policemen had appeared and asked "Who pushed him? Did she?" I left that to Ahmed.

The little, low hospital building, which would be evacuated in another month, was beseiged with men, women, children, and babies. But which were patients, which nurses, and which spectators I had no idea. Irving was carried into a room with three beds. A patient was shooed out of one as we arrived. The bearers found it difficult to get the stretcher in place on the corner bed, so one of them clumped up on the bed with his big, dirty bare feet and solved the problem that way. The lumpy mattress sagged beneath its brownish sheet. But Dr. Farag gave a shot of tetramycin and tetanus. To me the hospital seemed just terrible, but the doctor and the antibiotics were fine.

Sterilizing was done on a Primus cookstove on the porch, which appeared to be the Out-Patient Department. The sterilizing pan was clean inside, but solid black with soot on the outside. It was carried past me many times as I paced the hall outside the "Operating Room," and two pictures of Nasser with his gleaming smile leered down at me from opposite walls. Inside were Dr. Farag, a dentist to assist, and faithful Ahmed who had got past hospital defenses if there were any. Through a gap in the curtain on the glass part of the door I could see just a little—not Irving, but moving figures, and I thought I could gauge whether they were getting frantic. The "orderly" kept going by with his sooty pan. It didn't seem to me a needle actually got boiled here in Aniba.

The hospital imprinted itself on my memory. I decided it had never seen soap. I conceded that beds and sheets had known rinsing, but I couldn't see that anything had ever been scrubbed with soap. Without those plentiful antibiotics, even the doctor's skill and Irving's constitution might not have sufficed. It seemed to be a long job. The anesthetic was local and I guess we should have been glad there was any at all, but it didn't quite offset the effect of the iodine that was poured into those wounds.

Irving had fallen at nine o'clock. It was 2:30 when he came out of the "Operating Room," his head in a turban of bandages with sixteen stitches, and a variety of lesser bandages on various punctures the rocks had made all over him. We had *Yankee* sheets and blanket on top of the hospital's now, but there was scant comfort in that sagging bed. Dr. Farag very kindly offered his quarters, but we were happy when he made no objection to our taking Irving back aboard by evening.

Sometime in the midst of all this trouble and strain, the inevitable had happened. A friend of Ahmed's had shown up. This time it was not a cotton dealer or an important relative or an Old School Tie friend. It was a kind-faced old Nubian on the barge alongside. He had recognized Ahmed because he had once worked for his brother, and approached him bowing and bringing a gift of dates, all his two hands could hold. It was not only his recognition of Ahmed, but his own expression of sympathy for our troubles and we were touched.

After dark the stretcher-bearers again took up their load, one of them still swinging his rifle. At last Irving was back in his own bunk. He felt better at that and we all did. I boiled water for the orderly, the doctor gave the day's final shot, and left us pills to be taken during the night. Perhaps it was only the extreme discomfort of all his punctures, stitches, and a head

The steady northerly breeze in her sails holds *Yankee* quietly but firmly on desert sands. (*Zacher*)

that hurt in every position that kept Irving awake. But what kept me from sleeping was the realization of all the things that might have happened to us if those rocks had landed differently. We might have a fractured skull case, an unconscious skipper, or even worse. These thoughts could hardly lull me to sleep.

Dr. Farag was on hand in the morning. Ahmed gave the police a statement that seemed to satisfy them and wisely phoned Aswan and Cairo to forestall rumors. The doctor thought we should stay in Aniba under observation for ten days, but Irving thought we should leave early next morning. Again Ahmed had to be the mediator even though translation was not necessary. Irving said we could get to Aswan in a day and there were doctors there. He signed a statement saying we were leaving against the doctor's advice. We took the supply of pills. That evening Irving felt worse and ran a little fever. This was the time when the soldier of the Crusades would probably have started to lose ground, but in another few hours the fever dropped and Irving perceptibly turned a corner toward recovery. We sailed at daybreak.

Ted and Gil were experienced yachtsmen, but it was still a good thing for Irving's peace of mind that there were no piloting problems between Aniba and Aswan. The water backed up by the dam is deep all the way. But by late afternoon Irving was sticking his turbaned head on deck, not from anxiety but from a renewed interest in the cruise. We didn't push on to the Aswan locks till the next day, but everything was going well with our patient and we moored one last time off a deserted village.

So it was the fourth day after the accident that Irving went into the German Mission hospital in Aswan. The white tile, white basins, and a nurse's clean uniform looked like the Mayo Clinic to us then. The doctor took off the turban, soaking the dried blood as well as he could to ease the process, and I had a look at what seemed like big, black, lumpy sailmaker's stitches, a novice sailmaker at that. But Dr. Farag had done a first rate job. We now have to look closely to see the scars.

chapter XVIII

≈ The
Begum
Aga Kahn

≈

For our visit to the Mission hospital, we had left the *Yankee* above the old Aswan Dam and locks. Now, after some minor delays over Customs and Immigration, we started along after lunch. Ahmed's friend Osman Ghaleb, the owner of the tourist ship *Delta*, came along for the ride. Locking through was quite simple, though I am sure Irving wished us back into the last century before the dam was built when the feluccas and the old dahabias had to shoot the rapids of the Cataract. I, however, was satisfied with Amelia Edwards' exciting description: "We slid down—thanks to our old friend the Sheykh of the Cataract—in one short, sensational half hour. He came—flat-faced, fishy-eyed, fatuous as ever—with his head tied up in the same old yellow handkerchief and with the same chibouque in his mouth. He brought with him a following of fifty stalwart Shellalees; and under his arm he carried a tattered red flag. This flag, on which were embroidered the crescent and star, he hoisted with much solemnity at the prow.

"Consigned thus to the protection of the Prophet; windows and tambooshy (saloon skylight) shuttered up; doors closed; breakables removed to a place of safety and everything made snug, as if for a storm at sea, we put off from Mahatta at 7 A.M., on a lovely morning in the middle of March. The Philae, instead of threading her way back through the old channels, strikes across to the Libyan side, making straight for the Big Bab—that formidable rapid which as yet we have not seen. All last night we heard its voice in the distance; now, at every stroke of the oars, that rushing sound draws nearer.

"The Sheykh of the Cataract is our captain, and his men are our sailors today; Reis Hassan and the crew having only to sit still and look on. The Shellalees, meanwhile, row swiftly and steadily. Already the river seems to be running faster than usual; already the current feels stronger under our keel. And now, suddenly, there is sparkle and foam on the surface yonder—there are rocks ahead; rocks to right and left; eddies everywhere. The Sheykh lays down his pipe, kicks off his shoes, and goes himself to the prow. His second in command is stationed at the top of the stairs leading to the upper deck. Six men take the tiller. The rowers are reinforced and sit two to each oar.

"In the midst of these preparations, when everybody looks grave, and even the Arabs are silent, we all at once find ourselves at the mouth of a long and narrow strait—a kind of ravine between two walls of rock—through which, at a steep incline, there rushes a roaring mass of waters. The whole Nile, in fact, seems to be thundering in wild waves down that terrible channel.

"It seems, at first sight, impossible that any dahabeeyah should venture that way and not be dashed to pieces. Neither does there seem room for boat and oars to pass. The Sheykh, however, gives the word—his second echoes it—the men at the helm obey. They put the dahabeeyah straight at that monster mill-race. For one breathless second we seem to tremble on the edge of the fall. Then the Philae plunges in headlong!

"We see the whole boat slope down bodily under our feet. We feel the leap—the dead fall—the staggering rush forward. Instantly the waves are foaming and boiling up on all sides, flooding the lower deck and covering the upper deck with spray. The men ship their oars, leaving all to helm and current; and, despite the hoarse tumult, we distinctly hear those oars scrape the rocks on either side.

"Now the Sheykh, looking for the moment quite majestic, stands motionless with uplifted arm; for at the end of the pass there is a sharp turn to the right—as sharp as a street corner in a narrow London thoroughfare. Can the Philae, measuring 100 feet from stem to stern, ever round that angle in safety? Suddenly, the uplifted arm waves—the Sheykh thunders "Daffet!" (helm)—the men, steady and prompt, put the helm about—the boat answering splendidly to the word of command, begins to turn before we are out of the rocks; then, shooting round the corner at exactly the right moment, comes out safe and sound, with only an oar broken!

"All dahabeeyahs, however, are not so lucky. Of 34 that shot the fall this season, several had been slightly damaged, and one was so disabled that she had to lie up at Assuan for a fortnight to be mended. Of actual shipwreck, or injury to life and limb, I do not suppose there is any real danger. The Shellalees are wonderfully cool and skilful, and have abundant practice."

We were about ready to tie up to our former pleasant berth below the Cataract Hotel when I heard Osman ask something about the Aga Khan. "Would you like to visit his widow, the Begum? She is a friend of mine!" This sounded marvelous. Of course Cataract rocks were strewn between us and her doorstep, but Osman's suggestion merely gave Irving an excuse to explore in that direction. We had sailed over that way in a felucca one afternoon, but that vessel drew only one foot to our four and a half. In the Nile there is no looking through clear water for obstructions below the surface, so we could only guess at our course and proceed slowly. Still floating, we crept past one smooth black rock after another, rounded corners, and resisted swirls of current, very strong in unpredictable places. To my surprise the *Yankee* arrived safely below the Begum's large white house. Three ladies appeared on the terrace above and Osman called out, "Your Highness, may we come and pay our respects?"

The tallest of the three figures replied cordially. No doubt the Begum's curiosity was aroused at the unexpected sight of our shiny "aroosa" flying the American yacht ensign in front of her house. We put the bowsprit in to shore, tied a line around a tree and clambered off. From then on things happened as in a dream.

The Begum was charming and beautiful; she had had the title of Miss France before her present title. She was a large woman, now middle-aged, but age will not change the structure of her perfect features. She carried herself like a queen, had a smile to compare with Ingrid Bergman's, was dressed in a lovely two-piece wool from Paris, spoke excellent English,

The tomb of the Aga Khan tops a desert hillside at the First Cataract. Below it the Begum's house and gardens are her home for the winter months of beautiful weather on the Nile. (*Zacher*)

and also spoke eloquently with her expressive dark brown eyes. Her graciousness made us feel really welcome and we were soon telling her about the *Yankee* and our cruise and enjoying her delicious tea. The two other ladies we had seen on the terrace were her young secretaries: one French, the other Arabic-speaking for the Begum's Egyptian stay.

Here she and her husband built their winter home for the perfect weather of Upper Egypt. Many of us wrongly associate the late Aga Khan only with race horses (he won the Derby five times), the French Riviera, and the yearly rite always in news photographs of balancing his weight against a donation of gold or diamonds from his Ismaili followers. But we should also know that all that treasure was distributed to the needy of the Ismaili Sect and for schools and community projects. The Aga Khan had also played an important part in world affairs.

Born in India in 1877, he received an education which combined the European, the Oriental, and the religious. At the outbreak of World War I, his pro-British stand influenced his part of the world. As a Moslem he eased the peace terms for Turkey after the war and was active in reforms in British India. In 1932 he represented India at the Geneva Disarmament Conference and then at the League of Nations, of which he was President in 1937. At the time of the Second World War he had withdrawn from political activity.

We found that the Begum was interested in photography and we asked permission to take her picture there in her home. She assented pleasantly and continued to talk to Irving while Gil and Ted hopped around for different angles. I noticed, however, that every time the shutter snapped the Begum somehow was looking in the right direction and usually smiling her lovely smile, though she never seemed to interrupt her conversation or be even momentarily distracted from what Irving was saying. It was a most accomplished performance.

Time was nothing to us in these delightful circumstances until we suddenly realized it was dark.

"Do you mind if the *Yankee* stays where she is overnight?" Irving asked. "I don't believe we can take her through the Cataract now."

"Oh, but I can pilot you!" replied the Begum. "I know every rock in the Cataract!"

I never saw Irving so willing to take a pilot before. None of us hesitated. Taking a chance was nothing new to the sturdy *Yankee*, but being piloted by the Begum Aga Khan was definitely a novelty. We all trooped down to the ship, climbed aboard by the bowsprit, and let go the mooring line. Irving took the wheel and the Begum stood high on the deck behind him. Following her confident directions, we headed downstream. This was a different and longer way than we had come.

For three quarters of an hour Irving steered in response to slightly French-accented instructions: "A little to the right. Now straight. A little more to the right." None of the rest of us spoke, and the *Yankee* floated on through the night. The Begum never hesitated or changed her mind. We slid behind the dark shade of Elephantine, took channels we had no knowledge of, sometimes caught sight of a black granite shape close by, but gradually all began to feel quite safe in the hands of this extraordinary pilot. She brought us in to our old berth below the hotel, and we said our goodbyes on the dark deck. But her goodbye included an invitation to return in the morning for a sail in her private felucca.

"It is the only one on the Nile with an orange sail," she told us. "I had it made by a sailmaker in Cannes. I had to draw the shape for him. But you will see, it fits!" We weren't in the least surprised. Everything this remarkable woman did would turn out well. She was not one to blunder.

The next day, before the hour appointed for our sail, we went to the tourist landing not far from her house where Ismaili pilgrims and ordinary tourists go ashore to visit the tomb of the Aga Khan, a lovely domed building topping a desert hill, a Moslem silhouette against the sky. The Aga Khan and his wife chose the site and planned the tomb, but it was she who carried out the plan, with the same sureness we had seen in her character the night before. The best of builders needs to be watched anywhere, but in Egypt it is especially hard to achieve excellence. Only first quality materials were to be used; construction must be careful at every move. (It was far from easy to get such results.) Outside, the pink and yellow sandstone blend into the desert colors. Inside, pink granite pillars are carefully matched and beautiful white Carrara marble is cut in decorative Koranic inscriptions and arabesques. The marble sarcophagus, intricately carved, is like a delicate ivory jewel case. Here the Begum too will be buried.

Only a dozen people may enter at a time, so the tranquility of the mausoleum is not disturbed. At the side of the entrance we paused to read an inscription about the great man buried here and the building of the tomb. Then we followed a red carpet to the sarcophagus and noticed the fresh red rosebud placed there every day by his widow. At the side a reader intoned the Koran in the best Moslem style. A beautiful voice and reading technique are accomplishments that the faithful admire.

Feeling very privileged, we took the private walk down to the house.

Borders of petunias and kosmos made a pretty garden. We passed the screened enclosure where the Begum keeps five or six delicate gazelles, and then she came to meet us with a welcoming smile. Half of the *Yankee* crew went back to sail our ship for pictures of the other half in the fairy tale felucca. The floating boathouse itself looked like an Indian pavilion, with its curtains of green and white stripes.

In the Begum's felucca there is no sitting on wooden thwarts. Everyone reclines. The whole craft is cushioned in green. The captain's *galabia* was white and of course spotless. *Yankee* and felucca seemed to be doing a sort of dance together as they tacked and dodged each other in the light breeze.

After we had all, except Irving, had a turn in the felucca, we went up to the house again. Donna and I, combing our hair in front of the Begum's mirror, were impressed with the simplicity of her room. It was comfortable but not lavish. There was nothing of Hollywood here.

In parting, we asked the Begum if she would like to have dinner with us at the hotel. As she hesitated, Ahmed threw in, "Or on the *Yankee?*"

"Oh, no!" I gasped—inaudibly, I hoped—while everyone else was chorusing "Oh, yes!"

There was no hesitation in the acceptance now, and as the hostess problem was just beginning to take shape in my head, the Begum was saying in a most friendly way, "What can I bring?" as though this were some kind of neighborhood party.

Feeling quite hopeless I was mumbling, "Oh, nothing, nothing," when she answered herself. "I'll bring the ice cream!" What an inspiration!

While the others went off to see Kalabsha Temple I considered my problem. The best food Aswan had provided had been our Christmas turkey, but there was no time now to buy, kill, pluck, stuff, and roast a turkey. I would have to depend on the *Yankee*'s lockers, and the best thing in them was S. S. Pierce's lobster. But a fresh vegetable would be nice, so without Ahmed I tackled the market and brought back some fresh peas. Alas, they were not as good as some we had had before; I served the Begum Aga Khan rather tough peas. But the lobster Newburg and rice were all right and the ice cream, "praliné," was superb. The secretaries came too and we had just enough knives and forks for nine.

Either the Begum had a good time or we were thoroughly deceived. She told us stories of a forced landing in Africa when she was just a bride, of visiting archaeological digs of all kinds, of her own attempt to cruise the river. We found a really adventurous spirit added to all the charm and looks. In fact, after knowing this remarkable woman, I felt that her intelligence and character were even more remarkable than her beauty. When someone told me she was one of the wealthiest women in the world, I could only reply, "I am sure that if all that wealth disappeared, the Begum would be all right."

Next day we had to come down to earth, but only as much down to earth as we ever were in Egypt. With Ahmed's help, our path was always smoothed and anything seemed possible. Remembering our trials of all sorts on the Alexandria to Cairo passage, we appreciated all the more the charmed life we had led since. The weather, so important on a boat, was always favoring. None of us had been sick, though that had been predicted for Egypt. Provisioning had been much easier than I expected and Ahmed took half the job off my shoulders. We had fresh fruits and vegetables almost all the way. Even meat wasn't as impossible as I had feared. Turkeys were best, but chickens were often obtainable. Legs of lamb were recognizable. Beef never appeared above Cairo, but veal did, though I can't possibly describe the cuts and never could match them up to illustrations in the cookbook. Anyway, most of our canned food was still in the lockers.

We got away from Aswan one afternoon with a good supply of fresh provisions. The wind was ahead now and the river a little lower every day. Going aground would be a more serious matter on our way downstream, as the current would push us on harder every time we struck. We touched a few times that afternoon, but managed to keep moving until about four. Then we really got stuck.

The job of getting the *Yankee* afloat was now quite familiar. Irving and Ted would get the dinghy over. One would row and the other would sound all around to find where deeper water lay. When the bottom was plain in Irving's mind, he would come back for our thirty-pound Danforth on a very long nylon line. Then all hands would heave and haul, helped by the electric anchor winch, backed up by hand power on the jib sheet winch. Then with one or sometimes two anchor lines bar taut, and the diesel pushing wide open, Irving would put the wheel hard over one way, then hard over the other, working the *Yankee* to make herself a way through the sand. This went on for a long time that afternoon and it didn't look as though we'd succeed. But this situation has looked that way before and there's always one more try that may do the trick. If we had to stay there all night, we'd be on even harder in the morning and would have to get a barge or tug to pull us off. We kept trying and just before dark she came off. We moved far enough to make sure we'd float all night and yet not be in the channel. How good the ship felt free and afloat again.

Irving was disgusted with himself next morning when a downstream barge got by unnoticed while we had breakfast. "I should have stayed on deck," he said. It would probably be wise to follow a barge for the next day or so where the river was most shallow. They might not be sure of the channel, but they could go aground first.

Then my diary goes on, "The popovers didn't pop. I made an aspic and it didn't harden." January 18th wasn't starting out very well. We went aground a few times gently and got off with the motor. Then again in the afternoon the bottom got a real hold on *Yankee*. Irving came back from sounding that time and said we'd have to pull her over a shoal. So we went into action as before. The diary tells it: "We heaved and hauled with engine and electric winch. We jumped on the bow and on the stern. We even tried to sally ship (running back and forth from side to side in unison as we used to do to good effect on the Brigantine *Yankee*). Irving worked her from side to side. She bumped and bounced and struggled. I really didn't think we'd make it. A tug went by. Irving didn't hail them as he still believed we would get ourselves off, but they turned and were just coming back to help when we got free. Good old *Yankee*.

"After Edfu it blew harder and harder. We put the bow into the bank for the night. Bumped quite a bit at first, but during the night the wind went down.

"Turkey was good." So the day ended better than it began.

chapter XIX

≈

Aswan
to Assiut

≈

It was no hardship, we felt, to return the way we had come. We would keep on learning about the country, ancient, Arabic, and modern, as long as we stayed. At Luxor, I again took Baedeker to temples and tombs, hoping to cram into my head all I possibly could of the great sights and little details so that I might keep Egypt alive in my memory for the rest of my life. Much as we loved this country, we did not plan to return. And three factors that made this cruise so wonderful could not be repeated: the prestige of the *National Geographic*, the presence of Ahmed, and the fact that the High Dam had not yet closed the passage into Nubia. What we learned about Egypt in the future would have to come from books and museums, and we realized our interest would be lifelong. But we would never come back, with or without the *Yankee*.

At Luxor, Donna, Gil, and Ted

left us and their places were taken by one old and one new friend from California: Gould Eddy, who had sailed his own yacht in many Honolulu and Acapulco Races, and Allen O'Brien, who had also done some ocean voyaging. In our last six weeks on the Nile I especially wanted to learn more about present-day life in this country. Except for a few meetings with outstanding people, we did not have access to the planners in Egypt as a well-accredited journalist does. We were not anthropologists and could not study village life. On that subject, it was hard even to find much reading matter. The latest anthropological study I read was written in 1926, but as things change very slowly in Egypt, I still found it quite informative. I got an even better insight into village life from Taha Hussein's *My Egyptian Childhood*, a beautiful, even poetic account. This distinguished man started life as a blind country boy whose early education consisted of learning the Koran along with other village boys. Then followed some bewildering, lonely years in Cairo at the Azhar University, but in time his genius asserted itself and he became Egypt's most outstanding man of letters and for a period was Rector of Cairo University and then Minister of Education. Egypt at present does not encourage anthropologists, probably because they do not want publicity about the lot of the fellahin.

But though we were not experts, we did have some advantages over most tourists. We could stay a great deal longer and we could move our home anywhere on the river by which almost the entire population lived. If some of the officials had realized the places this freedom of movement and our own curiosity would lead us into, they would probably have wanted to put some curbs on our investigations. I suppose they assumed we would visit only the showplaces, ancient and modern.

I thought that one of the lowest rungs on the Egyptian social scale was surely occupied by a skinny, ragged man who used to come to the river near our mooring and fill four or five black goatskins with water, then trudge away with those bloated, heavy, repulsive-looking containers on his shoulder pole. The Nile water we thought was best for floating upon, but we saw it used for irrigation, drinking, cooking, refuse, sewage, and also for washing greens. It is the source of all life in Egypt, but it is also the source of death, not only because of unsanitary conditions, but because of the bilharzia parasite. To quote from Jean and Simone Lacouture's *Egypt in Transition*, "The water in the ditches and canals and even in the Nile shallows is infested with a death-giving parasite, the bilharzia. This is a tiny mollusc, the larvae of which enter the body through the skin. This parasite undermines the whole organism, attacking the bladder and the kidneys, causing ulcers and fistulas, completely upsetting the intestines. Contaminated faeces are returned to the canal and the cycle of disease is complete. The frightful, endemic disease has affected 80% of the population, including about 95% of the fellahs, the parasite being less common in the towns. People with this sickness do not feel any acute pain, but waste away slowly so that a boy of fifteen easily looks stronger than his father."

So far apparently, attempts to reduce bilharzia have been ineffective, as the farmer, entirely dependent on irrigation, is in and out of water day after day. Science is seeking a predator for the parasite and such a discovery would do wonders for Egypt. Of course, like many achievements of modern medicine, this would also increase the population. But in this case better health in adults might lessen their urgency to have children to work for them. One reason for large families would not be so strong.

As we traveled through this crowded valley where 27,000,000 people live in an area not much larger than Maryland, we felt more and more strongly about the population problem. Egypt is well aware of it and beginning to take definite steps to hold the line. But their efforts are small and slow in the face of the enormity of the threat. All the additional third of arable land that irrigation from the new High Dam will create will be overtaken by a greater increase in population before that land begins to produce. The longer we stayed in Egypt the more we wished the Government would put all its efforts into pressing domestic problems instead of foreign relations. We could understand that after centuries of subjection and oppression it was necessary for the new Egypt to hold up its head in the world, to command attention, to show that it would not be ignored or delegated to political oblivion. But we did not like the ways they chose to assert their importance. Raising Egypt's own standard of living would seem the best way to rise in the esteem of the world and at the same time help themselves.

Some of our early impressions of villages had been thoroughly discouraging: dirt, mud floors, flies, animals and people living together, blindness so very common.

We talked to Om Seti, the remarkable Englishwoman who lived in the country near Abydos, about village life. "There are all degrees of life in the villages," she told us. "The women you see carrying pots of water from the river are the poorest. It is the first step up to have someone carry water for you. The women who live better you don't see outdoors. They don't carry water or work in the fields. They stay inside. Some of the families are very well off." We found that hard to imagine in the beginning,

225

Two desperate situations: the need of the man doing the sounding who is for a new suit of sails and the position apparently beyond the point of no return.

but began looking for differences in village life. Apparently it did not all operate at the lowest level.

We were able to visit Om Seti's "adopted family." As we walked into their courtyard, we saw a girl washing dishes in a basin *with soap*. Hardly conscious of mudbrick construction, we climbed a flight of stairs to a well-swept porch and sat on a wooden bench with cushions covered in cotton print, and drank tea. The young wife was a stunning Arab type with a strong nose and big almond eyes set off with dark kohl. She wore a bright yellow and pink dress and some gold jewelry, quite a striking lady. We saw where straw and dung fuel were stored on the roof and bread set to rise in the sun. A Primus stove and a mud oven did the cooking. This was certainly not one of the poorest families. Perhaps others were even more prosperous.

Om Seti pointed out the new medical clinic and told us of improvements she had seen. The radio brought instruction in housekeeping and child care. In another town we visited a "combined center"—school, clinic, and agricultural experiment station. But at the present rate of progress in education and population control, Egypt will not achieve much for the millions. The radio which instructs also blares out endless, repetitive propaganda against Israel, all foreigners, and any given object of official hate. Education means teaching what the rulers want taught.

One day we set out to see the camel market at Farshoot, a small town several miles in from the river. Six of us were squeezed into a small Citroen, and having taken a wrong turn, we found ourselves on dirt roads driving past acres and acres of sugar cane, with much interesting camel traffic. A bridge took us across a dry canal in which hundreds of workers were digging to enlarge its capacity for the increase of water after the completion of the High Dam. Their only tool was the pickaxe, with which they loosened the soil and shoved it into the little pharaonic, palm-frond baskets. A digger would hoist the basket onto the shoulders of a carrier, who would clamber up the high bank and dump it. Donkey carts were carrying the piles away in five- or six-hundred-pound loads to dump elsewhere. Base pay in Egypt is supposed to be about sixty cents a day, but in reality is more often about forty cents. Labor is more than plentiful so there is not much point in modernizing.

As we bumped along beside this canal, we did not expect any automobile traffic, but we did meet a bus and just managed to squeeze past. Then there came toward us a tall camel with a great beamy load of stiff, dry sugar cane stalks. Unwisely, his driver chose to get by us on the side away from the canal, where the embankment continued on up. We squeezed over toward the canal as far as we dared, but that simply did not leave room enough, and his load caught on the luggage carrier on our roof. This brought the camel to a forced halt. The animal got scared, the driver tugged on his lead, the canal workers heaved on the load. All the helpers were yelling, and the camel made horrible noises that expressed the same sentiments as his ugly, panicked features. We jumped out of the car, fearing it might turn over. Something had to give and it turned out to be the luggage rack. Allah works out such senseless, unnecessary difficulties.

The next camel that came along passed us easily on the other side. Then a relatively fine Chevrolet sedan appeared behind us and the owner invited us to ride with him until we got onto a paved road again. Who was he and where did he fit into the Egyptian picture? I wondered. He was an English-speaking Esso salesman, a pleasantly bourgeois rescuer. We asked him about the recent rumors of a sudden shortage of kerosene and bottled gas. The shortage was real enough, and we heard various explanations. Without kerosene for all the Primus stoves, the people would be in serious trouble. Before we left Egypt supplies began coming again to the little stores, but such sudden threats to their essentials must be a worry to the people.

Though Farshoot's camel market did not afford good photographic opportunities, it was an interesting experience, recorded on memory rather than film. I am tempted to say that no tourist ever came to Farshoot. At least I can say there was no evidence of such. We left the car at a corner of the fenced-in acre full of goats, sheep, cattle, donkeys and camels. But animals were few compared to the thousands of people. Irving and I were immediately surrounded by so thick a crowd of children and young men that we could hardly see where we were going. Dust rose all over the field and settled upon us and into our lungs. The camels were at the far end of the enclosure, so with our pressing entourage we moved in that direction. But there was not a chance of a picture of a camel in this crowd. We couldn't get that much open space. We tried, and then needed to change film. The natural thing was to look about for a corner where we might possibly sit or at least prop some of the items used in this operation. One corner was fairly free, but a man was defecating there. I looked farther along: another man, same occupation. So we stood in our own dusty cluster and juggled film, boxes, and reels with sand billowing around.

If we could only have got to a height, perhaps onto some rooftops adjacent to the field, we might have succeeded with pictures. But the difficulty of approaching a Farshoot home-owner and putting across that idea seemed insurmountable. This crowd was not begging for baksheesh and it was not hostile. But neither was it friendly. It was thick, persistent and unpleasant. Where Gould and Allen might be, we had no idea, but Irving and I felt we definitely wanted to leave. Heading back for the car we carried our adherents with us. Determined to stay close to Irving and not acquire a separate cluster of my own, I gave up some of the breathing space and heedlessly walked much closer behind various kinds of hind hoofs than I ordinarily chose to. Progress was difficult, but at least it continued and we finally reached the car.

Seldom have I felt more uncomfortable than in that Farshoot market. A crowd like that was explosive. How easily it could be touched off. One good harangue by loudspeaker could make a riot. When next I read about a riot in the Middle East, I will have some idea of its potential.

We did not meet many officials on our way downstream, as it was now Ramadan, the holy month of Islam when the devout may not eat or drink between sunrise and sunset. Most of Egypt follows this custom and Ahmed was quite doubtful that it would be abandoned, even with official permission, by the workers at the High Dam. For strict observance, not even water may pass the lips during daylight hours, and some go so far as to spit out their saliva rather than swallow it. But even the less strict were fasting these days, and Ahmed did not try to make contact with people he knew would be tired, listless, headachy, and thinking only of that sundown meal. From early afternoon we would see people of all degrees sitting staring out over the river, waiting for the sunset. Then with the first meal tiredness would seem to disappear and the evening would be lively and sociable. In the late hours it often seemed best not to go to sleep, but to have another good meal about two or three A.M. to fortify oneself for the day of fasting ahead. The result from our point of view was a partial paralysis of the country and little spiritual benefit. But Islam's ways are hard for a Westerner to understand and should not be dismissed with prejudice.

We did not mind missing official greetings, and were particularly willing to pass Nag Hamadi unfeted by "the boys." Although hundreds of Nile sailors had been waiting hours or days, the bridge opened promptly for us because of our Government connections. We powered through, followed quickly by a few dozen feluccas. Then we met many more bearing down on the bridge with a strong fair wind. After the first scramble of smaller craft came the "straw fleet," several big feluccas piled high and wide (about five feet of overhang on each side) with dried sugar cane and fuel for the kilns of Kena and El Ballas. Their high cargo provided as much

Yankee moors alongside one felucca while another sails past and a third waits with its smoothly built cargo of golden yellow straw.

windage as the sails as they swept toward the bridge opening. Two passed through, but the next two, with loads bumping, seemed about to tie for the entrance. The men yelling and shaking their fists at each other from the top of the straw stacks must have been the skippers, for the man at the tiller behind that huge cargo was certainly in no position to make decisions or give orders. He could see nothing but a wall of straw and must have steered by someone else's directions. For a while we thought there might be a boarding and battling on top of one of the straw stacks, but then one vessel got a bit of advantage, and pulled ahead and away from the other.

At that moment we noticed that the bridge was beginning to close. Impossible! How could a bridge tender close as two wind-driven vessels were bearing down on him? No! No! It must be a mistake. Surely he would stop his machine. But the moving bridge kept narrowing the gap and the feluccas kept coming. Maybe the first one could get through, its load below the bridge and its mast through the remaining aperture. But the opening got smaller and smaller. No hope. As it clanged shut, the first felucca, helpless with its fair wind, crashed into the structure A sickening sound of breakage reached us. The bowsprit and bow wrecked against the pier, the felucca lay plastered against its enemy, the bridge.

Little figures ran around overhead. Which were responsible for this unfeeling deed so horrible to a sailor? Obviously no one was going to right the wrong, but at least we could help the sailors out of its consequences. We turned toward them and threw a line. The skipper scrambled down from the straw stack and made fast the line on his quarter. But it wasn't a good fastening and let go at the first pull. We tried again and slowly succeeded in pulling the craft away from the bridge, not an easy job for *Yankee* since we were towing the windy thing by the stern and could hardly steer with such a drag. However, we got her over to the shore, where a week's work would repair the damage.

The fourth felucca had not crashed into the bridge, but was blown against a downstream extension of one of the piers. So we turned to this next victim of the Age of Sail. We were able to get our towline to their bow and had less trouble maneuvering them to the bank. How we wished we could listen in on all the post mortems of that episode, but the thinking of Nile skippers had to be conjecture with us.

At Assiut we saw old friends again. There is a large Coptic population here, and these Christians of course were not observing Ramadan. We heard that a troupe of Bulgarian folk singers and dancers was in town and Allen and I decided to go. Various folklore groups from east European countries had toured Egypt this winter, and having heard of them here and there, we thought it would be interesting not only to see their performance, but also to see their Egyptian audience. Ahmed, hunting up tickets for us, got bitten by the mayor's dog (just one more proof of his constant helpfulness), but finally found that our old friend, the Director of Youth and Recreation, was the best source. In fact the latter offered to accompany us and help us get in. As it turned out we were very glad to have him and his football halfback frame.

The show was to start at nine, but we were advised to come early. As our car approached the "auditorium," we got into a huge crowd, filling the streets and pressing against the solid wooden fence around the great tent where the show would be given. Mounted police were trying to control the mob. Our friend leaned out the front window and kept telling policemen something about "Captain Irving Johnson." Anyway the car kept moving almost to the fence. We got out, and forming a wedge behind our friend, forced our way to a closed door in the fence. He could open closed doors, however, and did. We literally shot through, because our little wedge was picked up and propelled by as much of the crowd as could surge through before the door closed again. For a short space of time we had no more control over our movements than a piece of driftwood in a whirlpool. It was not a happy sensation and I was grateful that it didn't last long.

The tent was a fine sight and accommodated 3500 people, probably more that night. It was made entirely, top and sides, of those sheet-sized Moorish curtains in intricate, symmetrical designs that I had admired shading the verandah of the Cataract Hotel. Our football hero put up seats for us in front of the front row. This seemed rude on our part, but before long others had set up seats in front of us.

The show was first-rate, with fine costumes, good music, dancing and singing, lots of life. We and about 4000 others loved it, and watched and applauded happily till 11:30.

This crowd was quite different from the one in Farshoot's market. Everyone was in Western dress. I had to remember not to think of Egypt entirely in terms of villages. But in our short visit I would have no better chance of understanding these people than the fellahin. Perhaps the hope of the future was here. How large and how influential was this middle class? We certainly had common ground in our enjoyment of the Bulgarian troupe. Upper Egypt must be hungry for entertainment if so many would almost fight to get into the "auditorium." I saw cultural exchange in a brighter light.

Our lovely hostess at tea next day was Miss Laura Alexan. We drank out of fragile cups and munched on cakes so delicious that it was hard not to be greedy, in a palace of the past beautifully located on the banks of the Nile. Her father had built this mansion in 1910, of materials and decoration of such quality that with good care everything still looked elegant. The heavy satin brocade draperies of Nile green were like new. The great entrance hall with its marble pillars and the imposing staircase was suited to magnificent occasions. A billiard room, correctly hung with hunting prints, might have been ordered from Abercrombie and Fitch. Italian workmen had been imported to do the woodwork.

But this palace told a different sort of story from Farouk's. I tried to read its past in the surroundings and in the family pictures. Laura Alexan, now in her sixties, was one of eight children. They were shown in one picture in their teens, all lined up in correct, dark school clothes. I admired their father, not only for his imposing style, but for the humorous eyes in that dignified Victorian-father face. There must have been lots of lively fun in this great house.

"We girls had to learn how to bake cakes and sew," Laura Alexan was saying. "In Cairo you could order anything from the shops, but not here in Assiut." Her description reminded me of antebellum life in our South, with privilege and responsibility mixed in a great plantation home.

That afternoon Miss Alexan drove us to Miss Lilian's Orphanage, which she had been concerned with for many years. Lilian Trasher had come here as a young missionary in 1910. She took in her first orphan baby then, and when she died in 1962, her orphanage sheltered 1200 children. About 10,000 have passed through it. The care of these children was the great life work of one exceptional, devoted woman. Many times in the early years she didn't know where the next day's food was coming from. A great deal of support, far more than simply food, came through the years from families like the Alexans. Without them Lilian Trasher's work could not have succeeded, but without her spirit and inspiration the wealthy Coptic families of Assiut would not have had this great and useful outlet for their philantrophy.

The orphanage has been criticized for being less than gleaming white and well dressed, but to me one of its values was that the children came first, rather than the outward appearances. Mama Lilian was never able to refuse one child who was brought to her. The only limitation was that she could take only Christian children. There were hundreds of children, from babies to sixteen-year-olds, the day we visited. They were all clean, well fed, healthy and smiling—a tremendous achievement. Scrubbing (with soap) was going on all the time. It is true that paint was peeling off well-worn cribs and tables and that small sheets were often made of flour sacks. Clothes were not ragged, but neither were they uniform or particularly attractive, and there was no lovely lawn. But as it is, it is not too far removed from Egyptian life, so the young people can go back to their villages without much dislocation.

Since Mama Lilian's death her assistants have carried on, aided by such workers as Miss Alexan. A young couple who were to take over the supervision had just arrived. They spoke no Arabic and they would have everything to learn about Egypt, but if they had some of Lilian Trasher's spirit, they too could accomplish miracles.

From the orphanage we drove to the nearby village of Beni Mor, where Gamel Abdul Nasser was born in 1918. We called at the mayor's office; he was away, but his deputy, a relative of Nasser's, greeted us in the big courtyard, with a handsome tree in the center, where Nasser receives on his rare visits. This was not a really poor village, but a lively one with the usual quota of donkeys, goats, and hubbub.

Driving with us that afternoon was another charming lady, Mrs. Huzayyin, whose husband is Rector of Assiut University. Only seven years old, the university is bursting with growth in all directions. Engineering students everywhere in Egypt far outnumber those in the next category, Science. Arts students are comparatively few in this counttry with so much need for modernization. Assiut can accomplish more than just teaching, for its importance will also lie in serving the people of Upper Egypt as an important center other than Cairo. Students here should not have to go through the ordeal of dislocation in a big city, as previous generations did. President Huzayyin seems quite equal to a tremendous task.

Mrs. Huzayyin, like faculty wives elsewhere, was trying to help the community as well as the college. She showed us the beginning of crafts which are being encouraged in villages like Beni Mor. I was so pleased with even this small showing of creative work by women that I bought more hand-painted cards, beads, and table linen than I probably should have. But I am not sorry to have contributed to that cause or to have a colorful, nicely embroidered tablecloth with village scenes from Beni Mor. But like many things in Egypt that tablecloth makes me wonder: who was the woman who designed those little figures? What was her part in Egyptian life? Would we be congenial if we only knew each other?

chapter XX

≈

New Valley

≈ One watery place where the *Yankee* certainly could not take us was Kharga Oasis, 150 miles into the western desert from Assiut. This was the Great Oasis, the largest of several in the valley where once flowered a prehistoric river parallel to the Nile. These oases are now nourished by underground streams, and at Kharga the bed of a prehistoric lake provides soil that can be cultivated. The oasis is in a big depression about 100 miles long, not much more than ten miles wide, and six feet below sea level.

During the Old Kingdom Kharga had its own governor, and a population of about 50,000, and was known for its vineyards and vines. But living conditions worsened and the vineyards gave way to date palms. The ancient people had their wells, but the Romans built subterranean aqueducts in the sandstone. Caravans from the Sudan traveled this valley from oasis to oasis. Cambyses, the Persian conqueror, in 525 B.C. sent an army of between 10,000 and 20,000 men with 5,000 camels north along this route. They passed through Kharga, but never reached their destination, the Oasis of Siwa, and perished in the desert.

Today Kharga is the center and starting point of the New Valley project. In the 8,304,000 acres from south of Aswan to the Qattara Depression (which we used to read about in World War II), it is estimated that 3,633,000 acres can be cultivated if enough subterranean water can be found. In the first Five Year Plan (1960-5) 125,598 acres were to be brought into production to support a quarter of a million people. There were to be sixty villages, twelve administrative centers, and three main towns. The Valley was to produce large quantities of wheat, meat, poultry, and vegetables. Such was the Plan on paper.

Having read these figures we wanted to see what was actually happening. Besides a trip to a desert oasis was alluring.

We left Assiut in a hired Lincoln powered with a Fordson diesel on a hardtop road. The desert was neither as beautiful as the golden drifts of Nubia nor as harsh and hateful as the jagged rockiness south of Wadi Halfa. The color was softer, the rocks small. Limestone protruding through the sand was polished to a gray-white sheen, as though enamel paint had been spilled here and there. For about three hours our drive was smooth and pleasant, but we saw few signs of life. Once we passed an Army post and a prison camp. The oasis route has been a place for criminals and political prisoners since ancient times. After about three hours we started on a steep downgrade into the depression, but the town of Kharga was still an hour farther on. The road was poorer now, and we bounced and jolted. Then we got a flat tire. Walking about while the driver changed the tire, we came upon the bleached skeleton of a camel. What a world of difference there was in driving this 150 miles in Egypt's coolest season and making the trip by camel or donkey during the hottest season of the year.

We resumed our drive but soon had another flat. This time there was no spare for changing. Since we had only five miles to go, we considered walking, when something that looked remarkably like a motorcycle cop came along, the only such person we had ever seen in Egypt. We could not even credit Ahmed's helpfulness with this apparition, but Ahmed was ready to carry on from there, jumped onto the back of the motorcycle, and disappeared down the desert road.

The rest of us had about time to eat our lunch, brought from the *Yankee*, when a shiny, clean, light green Volkswagen bus drove up with Ahmed in it. This was a Government car which his persuasive ways had

High above the Nile a towering spar dangles a good luck charm from the very top. These stone-laden feluccas breast the current with light northerly wind.

acquired for our use. We drove into Kharga in comfort and through the gates to what is called "Farouk's Guest House," built I suppose during his reign. It had imitation French furniture, gilt in the salon, two telephones, two bedrooms, and a cook, and it was all ours.

A young public relations man arrived to take us on tour. New Kharga is as raw as a town of the Old West, but it is a creation not of hardy individuals but of Government. Apartment houses, a movie, two hotels and some private houses are being built. But since even a large town in Upper Egypt seems like exile to a Cairene or Alexandrian, Kharga will not be a very popular post.

The part we were most interested in was the village of Nasser outside this town. Here are seventy newly settled farmer families from Sohag, a town of 50,000 north of Assiut. Each family is provided with five acres of land, a house with two beds, a donkey and a cow. The houses, being separate, seemed less like cell blocks than the resettlement houses outside Kom Ombo, and there seemed to be a happier, neighborhood feeling in this new community. These people wore the old-fashioned *galabia* and *mylala*, but the young agricultural advisers were in Western clothes. We saw the precious water gushing up from the vast underground reservoir. But water must be properly spread over the land, and so here machines were leveling the desert for irrigation, as the flooding Nile so perfectly leveled its valley through the millenia. This is an enormous and expensive task, in fact so tremendous that it seemed to us the New Valley could not repay its reclamation cost. It could become a resettlement area and possibly support its own people, but with the nearest market 150 miles away, it did not look profitable.

Old Kharga, the original oasis town of 8500 people, had passed the point of being picturesque; in fact it was squalid. We explored its narrow crowded dirt streets, some of which turned into tunnels, as the warren of buildings closed in not only from the sides, but overhead, so that families seemed to be living in caves. We watched at a well as people crowded to fill the ugly black goatskins and stare at us. There was something oppressive, closed in, and strangling in this desert pocket that I had not felt in the poorest villages along the river.

We had seen a little and learned all we could from the public relations man, but that wasn't much. That evening, however, we found a real source of information. We had heard there were Americans here under the AID program. Since the Government man didn't seem able (or willing?) to lead us to them, we left our Early Hollywood lodgings and walked into

New Kharga on our own. Just one inquiry got us to the bachelor quarters of two American engineers, only one of them in Kharga at the time. He was a friendly, middle-aged, down-to-earth Kansan who rustled up some cups of tea and was quite willing to talk. He had worked in the Middle East for many years, spoke Arabic well, got along with the people, and believed in their helping "theirselves." As a specialist in drilling he was on loan to the State Department. He had been on this job three years, spending an average of four weeks here to two weeks in Cairo with his wife and children. A few years back, he told us, he had tried staying in the United States, but Indiana was not for him, and after punching a time clock for a while all he wanted was to get out of the Middle West and back to the Middle East.

Here they have dug a hundred wells from 1700 to 3000 feet deep. There seems to be plenty of good water and it is being replenished underground, from Ethiopia they believe. Tests as to its source are still under way. However, with so many holes the pressure is already going down, and the driller thinks that in five years pumping will become necessary, but only from 30 or 40 feet. At present each well supplies 1300 gallons a minute. It takes six days to drill a hole, three weeks and $17,000 to complete everything involved. This cost is about a quarter of what a hole was costing when the Egyptians started the job. Equipment is extremely expensive and hard to keep operating in this distant sandy waste. Trucks that cost $20,000 to $40,000 and heavy duty leveling machinery need real mechanics. It is all American equipment now, as the Russian trucks and tractors broke down too often to be worth repairing. In the morning our friend came over, Stetson hat in hand, to show Irving some of this machinery.

"They can grow things all right," he said. "They've raised thirteen cuttings of 'alfalfy' in a year. But paying for this whole investment and then making a profit is something else." He shook his head.

Driving out of Kharga, we stopped to visit the Roman temple of Hibis, dedicated to Amon. We were still rolling in the fine Volkswagen bus, but it too had a flat tire before long. Since we were near a tiny oasis outpost, Irving and Allen hiked in to see the little village among the date palms. It was wretchedly poor and we wondered how life was sustained at all at such a level. I doubt if the Romans liked being posted in Kharga, but with their usual energy they had built a temple and set their engineers at the water problem. Perhaps some day the New Valley again will be a better place to live.

chapter XXI

≈

Cairo

≈

I remember our last lovely day on the Nile. We were within reach of Cairo, and much as I looked forward to seeing more of that fascinating city, getting mail, seeing our friends at the Yacht Club, and having no more groundings to deal with, I was also very sorry to leave the beauty of Upper Egypt, the simplicity and pathos of the little villages, and the sense the river gave us of direct contact with all of Egypt's long history.

It was a beautiful day, and though we did go aground twice and had to kedge off, we had the final satisfaction of knowing that in all our Nile navigation we had managed by our own efforts and had not once had to ask for a more powerful pull. The wind was light and we set sail. Then we sighted the pyramids. It was almost as great a thrill as that first sighting over three months before when we had just emerged from the

Delta obstacle course. Then in the late afternoon, after lowering our masts, as we approached the Abbas II Bridge, a camel corps coming in from the desert rode across it, perfectly silhouetted for us: the long-legged, ungainly beasts with their serpentine necks and small heads, their strange gait producing the riders' queer but accustomed motion, the high-perched outlines of the men crowned with turban folds.

As the pyramids had announced Ancient Egypt to us, so this camel patrol seemed to signal another great culture of Egyptian history, the Arabic. I did not want to leave Cairo for a second time without exploring that side. It was only about a year before that I had been asking, "What all happened in Egypt between ancient times and Napoleon?" Historians and Islamic scholars answer that question in volumes and volumes. But at least now the period was not a total blank to me. After Napoleon's few years of French occupation, a great soldier, consummate plotter, dynamic leader, and cruel ruler, the obscure Albanian Mohammed Ali, seized power. He defeated the British in the Delta in 1817 and their fleet withdrew, then he treacherously massacred 480 Mameluke beys who had been his supporters and founded Egypt's last Dynasty. Two of his descendants' names are slightly familiar to us: Ismail, who presided at the theatrical opening of the Suez Canal; Tewfik, the grandfather of the unlamented Farouk. But from the time of Ismail, British "protection" was practically rule, and to this period belong the names of Sir Evelyn Baring (Lord Cromer); General Gordon, who was massacred at the downfall of Khartoum by the followers of the fanatical Mahdi; Kitchener, who came to avenge him and defeat the Mahdiists; and Winston Churchill, a young soldier on that expedition.

I could not expect to know Islamic Cairo any more thoroughly than I knew its history, but even a superficial acquaintance would be fascinating and I used all the time I could out of a week's stay in this quest. There were famous mosques to visit. The Mohammed Ali Mosque at the top of the old Citadel dominates the city, its high slender minarets piercing the sky. Known as the Alabaster Mosque, it has rich decoration under its great domes and around its spacious court. The Mosque of Amr is the oldest in Cairo, built in 642, but so much rebuilt that little of the original remains. The Saladin Mosque across the river from the Yacht Club was part of *Yankee's* habitual view of Cairo, particularly striking when floodlit at night. Al Azhar seemed to me the most meaningful, for it is the oldest Moslem university, where the first lecture was given in 975. (Bologna, the oldest university in Europe was founded in 1088.) Al Azhar also stands for tradition, Koranic law, and scholarship. It was a center of enlightenment and scientific discovery in the Middle Ages, although in recent generations it has been practically fossilized. At present it again feels new stirrings of life and progress.

The mosque I liked best was Ibn Toulun, the second oldest, built in 878 and renovated in 1296. Made of stucco-covered brick, its great outside walls suggest a fort more than a sanctuary. The huge courtyard is empty except for the central domed water basin. In the desert culture of Islam, water is closely connected with worship and ritual washing is most important. On four sides of the great expanse, arcades of pointed arches are surmounted by ornamental inscriptions from the Koran; calligraphy is beautifully decorative in Moslem countries. Legend claims that the frieze is made from wood that belonged to Noah's Ark, found by the Sultan Ibn Toulun on Mt. Ararat! There are beautiful patterns everywhere in this old structure: the lights and shadows of the hundreds of seried archs change with the progress of the sun or of the viewer. High on the walls, light and lightness come through the 128 windows of stone openwork, all different, like snowflakes in stone, or geometry turned to Arabic art. The curves and angles of the crenelations above the great walls border the massiveness with interesting style. Then to the side an old minaret, stubby in comparison to Mohammed Ali's, can be mounted by an outside circular staircase to where its muezzin used to call to prayer (this mosque is no longer consecrated). We looked over the great city, slightly hazy with dust, minarets pointing above it near and far, the narrow streets of Old Cairo just below us, the city growing progressively newer farther away, and the Nile cutting across the far side toward the Western Desert, the Mokattam Hills steep behind us to the East.

In the oldest part of the city I could still capture some of the romantic and mysterious sense of the old Middle East. I returned to the great Khan el Khalili Bazaar and again marveled at its exotic diversity: thin gold jewelry that the *mylaya*-clad women yearned over, tiny coffee shops, silks, rugs, brass, copper, silver; hammering of artisans, jingling of coins, yelling of camel and donkey drivers, duets of bargaining, the sonorous flap of *galabia*-clad figures; the faded geometrical appliqué on shades and awnings, all the wares old and new, valuable and trashy, buyers as serious as women at market or as idle as a bored tourist. I have never seen a place that could so stir the imagination with scraps and suggestions of caravans, slave traders, silks and spices, curved daggers, veiled women, fabulous riches, "ivory, apes, peacocks, sandalwood, cedarwood, and sweet white wine." There really seemed no bounds to one's imaginings. It was strange to contrast the wonder of all this to my mind with the opposite wonders back home: the infinite perfectly-packaged wares of a huge supermarket, the elegant, perfumed choices of a luxurious Fifth Avenue store. In this century they can coexist in one person's experience. I suppose it is the fascination of that coexistence that starts travelers on their journeys.

I found another spot in Cairo where the exotic would have a special appeal for a woman: in the design, decoration, and furnishing of a house of the eighteenth century. An English Army surgeon, Gayer Anderson, was so fascinated by that period that he furnished, preserved, and lived in such a house in Old Cairo. He is accused to having helped himself with some sort of immunity to treasures from museums, but now his house is a museum too. The angled entrance is traditional, for a passerby is not supposed to see within. The garden courtyard first received visitors. Then followed rooms with furniture of the period, ceramics, brass, copper, fine rugs, a painted ceiling brought from Persia, treasured objets d'art. The ground floor was for men, their visits, business, dining, coffee-making.

On the second floor were the harem quarters with divans, cushions and still other collections of beautiful objects. But what told me most of the life of these women of the past was the windows. These were not of glass for seeing, but of that carved and beaded wooden screening, called masharabia, and through these dark screens as through their veils the women saw the outside world. All over Old Cairo one still sees these wooden screens, sometimes set into a wall like a window, but usually built out, more like a large box than a balcony, and furnished inside with a cushioned window seat. I peered out through the tiny interstices. Below, the life and action, color and noise of a small market square looked so free; the masharabia barrier was so imprisoning. This conflict asked too much of coexistence. I could not imagine myself living behind the screens. I tried to think of the opposite to the eighteenth-century house of Cairo. I chose a New England colonist's in Old Deerfield and realized it was of the same period.

One day we visited the Coptic Museum in the northern part of town, where the seventh-century Arab conquerors founded the city of Fustat, which preceded Cairo by 200 years. Turning a few corners, we were surprised to discover that we were in a tiny ghetto. For in spite of the U.A.R.'s intransigent stand on Israel, there is still a small colony of Jews living in Cairo, and here was their synagogue. Next to it was a fifth-century Coptic church, which the black-hatted priest showed us. Then, taking us into its small, unornamented crypt, he told us that in this basement had stood the hostel where Mary, Joseph, and Jesus stayed. Could I believe this? Surely I would not have a year before. But since then I had seen so many monuments of two and three thousand years before Christ that, looking wondering around this little room, I thought perhaps it was true.

Near Cairo we were going to have one last chance to see something of the Old Kingdom. Its 5000-year distance in the past, its enduring pyramids, and the wonder of the emergence of our first well-known civilization combine to make this period the most marvelous for me in all Egyptian history. The first pharaoh we can name, Menes, united Upper and Lower Egypt and built a fortification known as the White Walls, on the spot known by its Greek name, Memphis, derived from the name of that first pharaoh.

Even after the center of Egyptian government moved to Thebes in empire times, Memphis continued to be an important city at the dividing point between Upper and Lower Egypt. Its buildings and temples survived the Greek and Roman eras and only succumbed finally to the depredations of the Arab builders of Cairo on the opposite bank of the Nile. Much of Cairo's stone was "quarried" from the ancient buildings of Memphis. Now almost nothing remains, except one colossal fallen Ramses II.

At nearby Sakkara we go back even earlier than the Great Pyramid to its predecessor, the Pharaoh Zoser's Step Pyramid. With its graduated sides, it shows the transition from the earliest mastabas (rectangular monuments) to the supreme engineering and geometric achievement of Cheops' tomb. Close by we descended the long broad subterranean corridors of the Serapium to many chambers, each with a tremendous granite sarcophagus of a sacred bull, the apis. This extraordinary worship dated back to the Middle Kingdom. And finally in the tomb of the Old Kingdom nobleman, Ti, we saw an archaeologist's treasure in painted scenes of daily life, still in color after 5000 years. At Sakkara, Memphis, and Giza my last impressions of Ancient Egypt seemed to open a view wider and longer than ever before.

Irving thought I would also enjoy a less visionary view, so he persuaded me to climb the Great Pyramid as a farewell gesture.

chapter XXII

≈

Cairo
to Rhodes

≈

It seemed as though we were on a different cruise when we left Cairo, for we had said goodbye to Ahmed and Win. Some unity in the *Yankee* was gone and a dream was over. Besides, we were saying goodbye to Ancient Egypt. In the reverse of reincarnation something of ourselves had seemed to go back three to five thousand years, something we would never retrieve. Nor did we want to. Let a bit of us stay in Egypt forever.

But Gould and Allen, Irving and I still had a few adventures ahead of us before we too separated. A new shipmate was added, however: Sherif Mazhar, the young man who had taken *Yankee's* lines in the dark that first night alongside the Yacht Club in Cairo. Sherif, an active, eager twenty-two, seemed like one of our old Brigantine crew.

We did not propose to retrace the "emotional route" through the Delta. We would leave the Nile just below

Cairo and take the Ismailia Canal to the eastward, to enter the Suez Canal at its midpoint at the town of Ismailia. But we might have known that there was no uneventful way through the Delta for *Yankee*.

In late afternoon, soon after entering the canal, *Yankee* tied up above a bridge which was to open at 1:30 A.M. There was a very strong current here running toward the bridge and no reasonable sort of dock to tie to. Irving found the best way was to turn around bow to current, put two lines ashore, both doubled back to the ship so that we could let them go from on board when the bridge opened. A low timber held the *Yankee* out from various shore obstacles. We should have had a peaceful wait there. But in addition to the usual onlookers and small boys, there was one a little older with big ideas. Irving first caught sight of him tugging at our mooring lines.

He had sized up our situation and concluded there was no way for us to get ashore. Therefore if he could cast us off in that current there ought to be some fun. He was right. *Yankee* would crash down through the bridge without benefit of its opening. And he was out of our reach. Irving gave him a powerful growl and he backed off. But he just assessed the situation anew and reached the same conclusion. So he returned to his little game. Irving watched through a porthole and knew that the remedy was called for which had never failed us yet. Very pistol in hand, he emerged on deck, the enormous one-and-a-half-inch barrel lifting shoreward.

But the enemy did not move. This was bad. Then Irving realized that the boy was immobilized with fright. Versed in the cowboy lore of comics and movies, he knew the deadliness of the American with the six-shooter. He figured his end had come. So Irving gave a short lunge toward him and the boy unfroze. He took off with his *galabia* riding high so far and so fast in the sight of all the lesser fry that all of them cleared out and never came near us again.

That left us only the problem of getting through the bridge in the dark. As it started to open at the appointed time, two of the men took in *Yankee*'s lines. This was a dangerous place to turn around and Irving had decided to back through the bridge, running the motor ahead to keep steerageway in the current. Backing through an Egyptian bridge in the dark sounded terrible to me. Then, to make matters worse, one of the biggest barges showed her bow on the far side, already advancing toward us. Sherif shouted to find out which vessel should go first. The barge! Coming up on us now she looked as big as a liner over the stern.

We must get our lines ashore again till she had passed. I just don't

The sight of tall, stately feluccas and distant minaret was duplicated time after time during our cruise.

know how that was done, but it was. Then we carried out the backing maneuver very nicely, turned around, and proceeded on our way. This was Delta navigation again, all right. But after three dark miles another bridge appeared and we had to tie up till its 9 A.M. opening.

Now, we thought, our final day of canalling would be easy, a big canal and a straight daylight run. Allen and I decided to make a dull day interesting by going back to Cairo for a last look, returning to *Yankee* that evening at Ismailia. But it is always dangerous on a ship to think that everything is in the bag. I'm still not sure whether to wish I hadn't missed the excitement. Irving will tell what happened.

~

The only sight of interest I expected that day would be a few slight hollows, where the ancient Nile-Red Sea Canal bed still showed. Extraordinary as this ancient engineering was, we had to use all our imagination to appreciate it.

About midafternoon our canal split into three. These were the "sweet water" supply for three cities: Suez, Ismailia, and Port Said. At this intersection our center canal narrowed and tall grass grew out in the water from both banks.

Just before we entered, a powered barge appeared ahead towing two more barges and three feluccas. Normally I would have gone on to squeeze past the half dozen craft with a canalman's inches to spare. But Exy's last instructions that very morning had been, "Now, Irving, be careful. Don't have any excitement while I'm away. We've been so lucky up to now."

Thinking of her warning, Gould said, "Irving, you could nose her into the bank in this wide spot till the tow gets by."

So like a good boy I did just that, trying to stick *Yankee*'s bow right on the point between the Suez branch and the middle one. The grass obscured the point just enough, however, so that we missed hitting it as planned. Our bow slid ten feet past the junction on the Ismailia side and then she stopped. It was too late to back up and correct this small error, but there was stacks of room left anyway.

Then it happened! The big tow barge charging up the middle of the canal never slowed down! Her speed accentuated the normal down current so drastically that even with diesel wide open I couldn't hold *Yankee* parallel with the canal another second. Her stern swung toward the tow barge till our lowered masts, projecting beyond our stern, overhung his deck by eight feet. Still nothing hit the loaded barge till his nice glass and wood afterdeck house came along. Then the noise started and didn't stop for some time.

When the masthead fittings caught the corner of his house, the hollow stainless steel tripod that held the masts at our stern crumpled up. Even though one end of the sticks was still in the steel tabernacle forward, their projecting ends were forced several feet to starboard, before a great crash of wood and glass drowned all other sounds. With the wrecking of his deckhouse now complete, our masts, no longer supported aft, dropped with a crash onto our starboard stern chock. On the way down they hit the bow of the fiberglass dinghy. It disappeared with appropriate noise.

In some mysterious way the mainmast had shoved itself directly under the mizzen, instead of being on top where it started. The main boom poked crazily skyward above the cockpit. But there was no time to figure out how the spars had got so mixed up. In seconds the next barge was upon us with no slackening of speed whatever. A *galabia* figure leaned over her bow to retrieve a shattered piece of deckhouse still stuck on our masthead fittings. Then the masts, now quite low, scraped along the length of the barge. Both Gould and Sherif were pushing as hard as they could with sounding poles, but the barge still closed in. Another shattering crash burst out as the stern of *Yankee*'s dinghy disappeared in combat with our adversary.

At that moment Sherif's pole slipped and he fell overboard, leaving the vibrating pole stuck straight down in the mud bottom of the canal. Now I had to stop the engine or the propeller might chew him to bits. Without power against the rudder, we ground closer to the barge till our tough steel rubrail on the port quarter dug a long crease in the barge's wooden side. With the extra strength born of desperation, Sherif had now pulled himself out of the water. When I saw his fingers come over our rail, I immediately gave the engine wide open again.

The third barge now approached, and to my horror I saw that one of her towlines had looped around the end of our mast. There was no time to shout to anyone. I dashed aft, leaped over our stern onto the bow of barge Number Three, and cast off that towline before it came tight on our masthead. Sherif appeared beside me, so we both pushed from the barge on *Yankee*'s tail feathers and clambered aboard at the last possible moment from the barge's stern. Arming myself with our strongest oak boathook, I proceeded to push on Number Four of the tow. I must have been desperately strong too, because this pole straight out suddenly broke in the middle and I nearly did a Sherif into the canal myself.

Number Five was smaller and quieter. Then a mere boy alone on Number Six simply put his tiller over and didn't hit us at all. Most of the others could have done the same. At that moment, as if to signal the end of the engagement, our flag, with part of the pole which had already broken off, disentangled itself from the rig and vanished into the muddy brown water of the canal.

I jumped back to the wheel, backed her off and we headed down the canal dead slow and feeling limp. To my utter astonishment Gould reported the dinghy to be generally in one piece. Every bit of gear was still inside it, although it was hanging down near the water, held finally by one hook forward and one hook aft. The other two hooks had broken. It was dangling low enough actually to scoop up a little water, but not enough to tear it loose entirely. So I gave Gould the wheel and hung down under the stern to retrieve the gear, lightening it enough so that we could gradually work it back up into a safe position. Then Sherif and I released the main boom from its precarious position sticking upward above the cockpit.

We tied up as soon as we could, alongside an empty barge, to see what else could be done. First the stainless steel tripod was extracted and Gould and Sherif walked across the barge to a dredge for tools to help straighten it out. In a short time it was completely serviceable. In the meantime I had been studying the mess of spars and loosening various wires to see if we could lift the mizzen back into the tripod. With help from the barge this was accomplished, and we found the mizzen was still in one piece with incredibly few scars to show for the brutal treatment.

Now came the mainmast. The forward end was still secure in its tabernacle, which was twisted sideways, but with no sign of failure, just twist. With even more hands from the barge and dredge and several from a felucca under the stern this mast was lined up and replaced in its normal position directly over the mizzen. No damage other than heavy scratches and some bent fittings! Never have I seen or heard so much crash of spars and boats with so little damage. Of course the tow barge, which never stopped or even slowed down, needed a new deckhouse, but we never saw or heard from him again. Gould summed it up. "I'm just as glad that wasn't my boat."

Sherif quietly wrung out his clothes.

Exy had the last word. "Next time don't be *that* careful!"

~

We rested up for a couple of days at the Ismailia Yacht Club. Irving went up to the Canal offices to see if their machine shop could straighten our twisted mast fittings. There he met the Director of the Suez Canal,

Mr. Younis, who seemed to him the most capable man we had met in Egypt. He had one of the most important jobs in the country too, and we have since learned that he has moved into an even higher position. Mr. Younis readily authorized the bit of work for the *Yankee* and it was done in a couple of hours. Carefully we hoisted our masts, watching for possible unseen damage. Miraculously all seemed in order.

The town of Isamailia had been built by the French canal company about a hundred years ago and laid out in a park-like plan. It reminded me of a French West Indies town. From the Yacht Club we watched the deepsea ships transiting the canal, even an ordinary freighter looking stately as she advanced at a measured eight knots against the desert background of the Asian shore. In another day we joined that traffic ourselves and before dark were tied up at Port Said's Yacht Club.

Port Said has changed since Egypt's revolution. No longer is it the enormous commissary for passing ships. Since it does not provide supplies imported from the Western world, ships do not stock up here any more, but lie at anchor only long enough to get their papers in order for the canal transit. Even small ship chandleries have been nationalized, as we realized when the Greek owner of such a business, which his father had started years before, came aboard *Yankee* and said he was hiding. His small firm had just been nationalized and the Government claimed his 1952 Chevrolet as part of the business. Wanting to keep it a few more days, he was evading the officials. He had no hope of earning a living now in Egypt and at fifty was going to make a new start elsewhere. He thought he'd try Nigeria.

Here Sherif left to return to his studies in Cairo. The look in his eyes told us how much he would have loved to stay with *Yankee*.

The Egyptian economy had seemed a pretty sad business to us, from our first discouraging impressions of Alexandria to this last example in Port Said. In our wonderful days on the river and among the ancient monuments, it had only occasionally been forced into our consciousness. We had said goodbye to all the best in Cairo. Now in Port Said we were glad to be leaving the worst. There was a patrol boat off the harbor mouth. As we headed into grey February Mediterranean seas that night, I felt as though the patrol boat might try to stop us, to entangle us in the authoritarian net that always threatens to drop onto the individual in Egypt. But the patrol boat was not concerned with us and beyond her I could almost feel the freedom in the air. To appreciate that sensation one must live for a time where freedom does not exist. Then never again can you take it for granted.

So, though I don't like getting right out into a head sea after a long stay inland, and though I couldn't eat the dinner I had managed to cook, I felt wonderful. And almost immediately my mind returned to all the wonder of the past four months.

It seemed another wonder in February that the sea smoothed out next day and the sun shone. That second night I had a beautiful two hours of moonlight alone at the wheel from midnight to two.

The distance to Rhodes was 400 miles. Irving had not been able to get a nautical almanac so we were going by dead reckoning. We hoped to get in in another day. Toward afternoon the breeze began to pick up—and from the right direction! We doused the motor and *Yankee* tripped along with a fair wind and everything set. The breeze strengthened and we ran. If this kept up, maybe we could make it during the night!

But then the wind gathered real strength. We took in the mule and changed from Genoa to regular jib. Soon even this was too much sail, and she was tearing along under main and mizzen both reefed. Sizable seas had built up and steering was a man's job. I was glad we had capable helmsmen beside Irving. Allen and ocean-racing Gould could relieve him so that the ship was always in good hands.

Irving was studying the chart of the Turkish coast. Nothing but years and years at sea, I thought, could enable anyone to identify the different peaks of the mountains of Turkey, seen for the first time in the gray distance. But for Irving they matched up with the chart and we set the course directly for Rhodes harbor.

By night, however, conditions of sea and wind had worsened to the point where it was not going to be an easy decision to choose between negotiating the narrow, rock-bordered harbor entrance and going around to the lee of the island to wait out the blow—in considerable discomfort and for an unknown length of time. Naturally we all longed for the safey of the harbor, but it was a bad entrance.

If Irving had not known the harbor from five previous visits, he could not have chosen to try it. The wind now blowing at 50 knots was increasing, seas crashing high over the outer breakwater and hurling themselves white on either side of the pass till they almost seemed to meet. *Yankee* headed for that awful spot. Irving started the engine and ran it in neutral so that if a big breaking sea suddenly slewed us about, he would have that extra control. He knew the right way was the way that looked wrong —to go closer to the rocks to port than anyone would judge, then make

Yankee leaves Abu Simbel never to return. Only the following week engineers started the cutting preparatory to moving the vast temple. Two months later the Nubian Nile was closed forever to navigation by the High Dam. (*Zacher*)

a sharp, last moment 90-degree turn. Gould saw the danger and let out a whistle. That stopped my breathing—if it hadn't stopped already. Now the ship was committed, big white-topped, black seas carrying her to the narrow entrance, where the Colossus of Rhodes once stood. No waiting now. Hard aport. In a smother Yankee shot between the breakwaters.

Inside we had protection, but the harbor was anything but quiet. Our mainsail slammed furiously till it was smothered and furled. The men put down two anchors while I stood by the wheel. The lines got fouled once, but this was a first-rate crew for any job. Then came the final order, "Finished with the engine" and we set the anchor light.

All next morning in oilskins we watched the show. We had got in about midnight. By two it was blowing 80 and we could not have attempted to enter. Now we could see the seas crashing over the breakwater and sometimes over the top of the big lighthouse. The entrance was a mass of rollers, breakers, spray, and rocks. Some boat was always in trouble with anchors or lines. Shore was only yards away and mail was waiting for us, but there was no question of launching a dinghy. Then in midafternoon the worst squall hit. Right in the harbor water was flying so that at times we couldn't see the breakwater. It passed and torrential rain poured down. Suddenly everything changed faster than I would have believed possible. The harbor smoothed out miraculously. All the local boats acted as though this were the end and I guess they knew. We could even go ashore.

And so ended the voyage on the Nile. Our inland *Yank* as back in her other element, the sea. We had been forcibly reminded of the difference in her two roles. But like us she had left a bit of herself back in Egypt, the memory of *aroosa*.

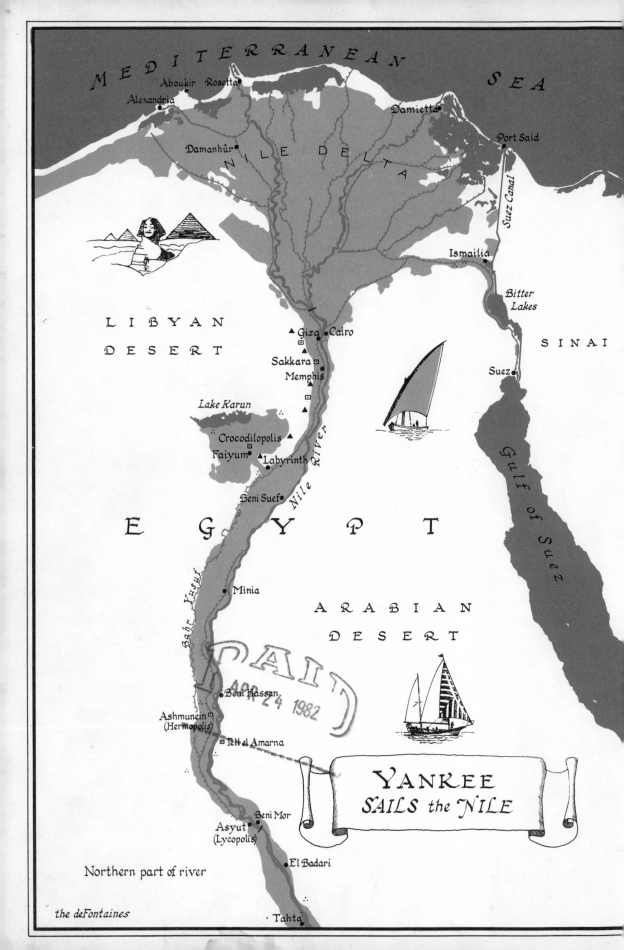